Architecture and Design versus Consumerism

Packed with examples and illustrations, this book sets an agenda for how architecture and design can help us transition from a system that prioritizes consumerism and economic growth to a system that addresses real wellbeing. The first chapters explore how economic growth and consumerism shape and are shaped by the professions of architecture, product, and landscape design and describe four central challenges of consumerism that designers are already addressing. The book investigates metrics designers can use to measure wellbeing, instead of simply measuring economic growth. The second half of the book explores how design activism works and its connection to growth and consumerist issues. These chapters examine financing of activist practices, highlight five specific methods that designers use in calling for social change, and investigate the power of these methods. The book closes with a speculative chapter about what design's role might be in a "post-growth" society.

Ann Thorpe thinks, writes and speaks on how architects and designers can be better change agents for the common good. Her experience includes work with nonprofit groups, government agencies, corporations, and academia. Most recently she taught at the Bartlett School of Architecture, University College London. She holds degrees from Stanford University, University of California Berkeley, and the Open University.

I0894786

ARCHITECTURE AND DESIGN VERSUS CONSUMERISM

How Design Activism Confronts Growth

Ann Thorpe

Routledge
Taylor & Francis Group
LONDON AND NEW YORK

To my mother, Lynn

First published 2012
by Earthscan
2 Park Square, Milton Park, Abingdon, Oxon OX14 4RN

Simultaneously published in the USA and Canada
by Earthscan
711 Third Avenue, New York, NY 10017

Earthscan is an imprint of the Taylor & Francis Group, an informa business

British Library Cataloguing in Publication Data
A catalogue record for this book is available from the British Library

Library of Congress Cataloging in Publication Data
A catalog record for this book has been requested

ISBN: 9781849713559 (hbk)
ISBN: 9781849713566 (pbk)
ISBN: 9780203119518 (ebk)

Typeset in Electra
by Saxon Graphics Ltd, Derby

Contents

Preface

"IKEA 'increasingly concerned' about Iran's nuclear program".

This headline gave me pause, until I realized that I had misread it. IAEA, the International Atomic Energy Agency is concerned, not IKEA.

Few people would disagree that we need massive political and economic changes to address challenges such as climate stability, inequality, or human health; but the incongruous IKEA headline conveys many of the real limitations of trying to solve these problems primarily in a business context. To what extent can any business, even if it were concerned, really bring about social or political change in the public interest?

Yet in terms of design, it feels as though we have been hesitant to explore the real political roots of activism and its context of social movements. Most designers are steeped in the marketplace. In addition, it's hard to link the systemic and sometimes abstract problems of consumerism and growth to daily activities. We're all so deep inside the system it's hard to see a way out. Meanwhile the rise of "social innovation" and "social enterprise" seems to offer designers the best of business and activism combined, without the hassle of politics. But there's no getting around the fact that confronting the economic system and engaging constructively in politics are central to design activism.

This book arises from a series of investigations over a number of years that started with sustainable design, progressed through design for sustainable consumption and arrived at the politics of design activism. My first book, *The Designer's Atlas of Sustainability*, includes a large section on the economic aspects of sustainable design, but it skirts overt politics. In an article for *Design Issues*, "Design's Role in Sustainable Consumption", I charted the environmental, psychological and sociological issues of consumption in terms of design.

As more of my architecture students wanted to take on the topic of sustainable consumption, I realized there was little material that dealt with the topic in terms of architecture and design. A common problem I found with the available sources was that they were either over-focused on technological solutions or promoted a simplistic transformational role for design without providing any real understanding of the systemic barriers within the economic system. The argument was for architects and designers to simply take on transformational roles because they should.

This argument is typically supported by design briefs, case studies and competition entries that all seem to say, "Come on, just do it!" Yet outside of the one studio or class that investigates "sustainability," students are often immersed in the business context for design. Students are groomed for conventional market expansion roles through standard portfolio development, final year shows and "design management" modules. Individual practitioners and researchers may meet at conferences to examine inspiring activist case studies and assemble systemic and necessary transdisciplinary approaches, only to return to institutions (private practice or universities) that reward siloed expertise, profitability and disciplinary purity.

The language of positive, easy opportunity ("10 simple ways to…") and moral exhortations ("just do it") are now sometimes concluded with the suggestion that, oh yes, architecture and design must also be "more political." But there is rarely any investigation of what this means in terms of design skills, training and practice.

Alongside this disciplinary situation, over the years I have observed the cultural and infrastructural variations in consumerism first hand. Although I hail from the US (a native of the Pacific Northwest), I have spent the past decade living in Europe (England). I am also connected to Scandinavia through blood relations (Sweden) and marriage (Denmark). I lived in India for nearly a year during graduate school.

Two examples, from urban travel and laundry, begin to suggest the complexity of the consumerism problem. In my suburban London neighborhood, most people have their washing machines under the counter in the kitchen and few people own driers. Smaller houses here are without the "utility rooms" that are found in many US homes; drying racks are moved around inside (by the radiator) or outside as the weather permits. If a household has a dryer, it is often a combined unit that both washes and dries. Moreover, here the norm is for front-loading horizontal axis washers (remember, they are under the counter), which are more efficient than the top-loading, vertical axis washers that are common in the US.

People tend to drive much smaller cars here, including "smart cars," than in the US, since fuel prices are very high and the roads and parking spaces are smaller. By contrast, my experience in the Pacific Northwest is that people try to travel more cleanly by driving a hybrid gasoline/electric car. According to hybridcars.com, the Seattle metropolitan area ranks ninth in the US for the highest hybrid sales, and on a vehicles/capita measure, neighboring Portland, Oregon ranks the highest in the nation for hybrid popularity.

In London, travel behavior is further influenced by policy "sticks and carrots." Sticks include London's "congestion charge" for driving in the central city during the week, and carrots, such as its recent "hire-bike" scheme. Yet people are wary of bike riding in London because drivers aren't used to cyclists and perhaps there isn't a culture to cultivate or pass on cycling skills and smarts.

Meanwhile in Scandinavian countries like Denmark, that arguably have much worse weather but are of similar flatness to England, bike riding is much more prolific. According to the city of Copenhagen's "Bicycle Account 2008," in Copenhagen 36 percent of commuters travel by bike compared to less than 5 percent of London commuters who cycle (the UK's Office of National Statistics, 2011). London has relatively little bicycle infrastructure, whereas Copenhagen has a great deal—parking, lanes, education, signals, and even special bicycles. Families ride together on one bike the way they might ride together on one bike in India.

If we look at these examples through the lens of architecture and design, we see clearly how the design of housing (spaces for laundry-related tasks), stations, streets, vehicles (bikes and cars), and services (hire schemes) influence patterns of consumption, and we could easily have added the design of clothing, bags and luggage (for commuter cycling) or the design of laundry machines and tools (such as drying racks).

Yet these examples also begin to suggest how politics, in the form of policy, and cultural patterns concerning everyday practices such as laundry and cycling, have an equally large influence on consumption. Transforming policies and cultural practices are political challenges, perhaps more so than technical ones. In certain ways we already have many of the technologies we need to transform our economy; we just don't have the political and social skills to apply them.

Sometime during my musings on consumerism and design, Tim Jackson and Peter Victor each published their accounts of a steady state economy. They argue that perpetual, consumerist economic growth is not the only basis for stability, and the economy doesn't have to either spiral upwards or downwards

— it could exist in a constructive steady state. Some people describe this as a post-growth economy. After undertaking a large study of design activism, I started to see how these pieces were fitting together—design, activism, and the problems of consumerism and economic growth.

For some, social movement activism may connote the past, 1960s-era protest, but over the past decade activism has been on the rise in a whole range of areas such as alter globalization, peace, poverty and climate. During the course of writing this book an amazing string of events unfolded across the world, putting a brighter spotlight on social movement activism. For example, the "Arab Spring" saw collective action bring down governments in Tunisia, Egypt and Libya, with ongoing uprisings in Syria and other Middle Eastern countries.

Financial troubles prompted one of the world's wealthiest men, Warren Buffet, to start a campaign to increase the tax level on the super-rich. High unemployment, especially among young people and the few remaining workers with decent benefits (public sector employees), is causing waves of social unrest across the US and Europe as most people seem to be in a race to the bottom. Occupy Wall Street has appeared as a new kind of "movement" in the US. In London we had urban unrest in August 2011 dubbed the "because I'm worth it" riots, which many commentators tied to pervasive consumerist ideals that remain severely out of reach for an increasingly large segment of society.

Financial troubles and consumerism continue to blind us to real value, activism is alive and well, and designers are jumping into that fray. These are big topics that haven't often been discussed together before, making this book more like a draft than a polished argument. In that spirit it offers an initial draft of some tools for practice along with some possible agenda items for design activism in the context of consumerism and economic growth. I look forward to seeing how these either get polished further or redrafted, once they're out in the world.

Ann Thorpe
London, November 2011

Acknowledgments

A wide range of publications, conversations, conferences, lectures, and of course, design projects enriched the work leading up to this book. I would like to thank all who engaged with the work, both directly and indirectly, at various points.

I am particularly grateful to the many designers who have undertaken great projects over the years, and to the many who have contributed images for this book. Their contributions are credited with the images by chapter. They have all (whether or not projects and images are included here) given us a valuable body of work that we explore in these pages.

A number of people reviewed versions of written material that is reflected in the book. For the questions, comments and encouragement of these reviews I thank Jeffrey Chan, Emma Dewberry, Daisy Froud, Tim Jordan, Guy Julier, Peter Lloyd, Katie Lloyd Thomas, Paul Micklethwaite, Stephan Peake, Stephen Potter, Tatjana Schneider, Otto von Busch, Stefan White, and about seven anonymous reviewers of the book proposal and related articles.

For specific input on this manuscript I give my heartfelt thanks to Liz Ogbu, Ajay Revels and Kate Fletcher. Similar gratitude goes to Peter Victor, for thoughtful and encouraging replies to a number of my meaty economics enquiries.

In addition to reviewers, there were a number of important discussants and colleagues along the way, including Anne Biklé, Stacey Birkett, Jody Boehnert, Matthew Cook, Emma Dewberry, Clive Dilnot, John Gertsakis, Megan Arrivey Hall, Julian Lindley, Peter Owens, Miles Park, Stephen Peake, Peg Rawes, Helen Roby, Louise St. Pierre and Philip White.

Social media played a role in developing the book. In particular I participate in four email lists that I have very usefully canvassed from time to time on various research questions. These lists are PhD Design, Stanford Design Alumni, Contentious Politics (AMSOC) and, most recently, BESTS (Built Environment and STS). Flickr users generously came to my rescue with a number of diverse images from generic suburban sprawl to specific buildings or landscapes.

I also have to admit that twitter alerts have more than once put me on to useful sources (@atlasann). Writing for and getting responses to my blog, (DesignActivism.net) has also been very helpful and I thank my readers for that.

I was lucky to take part in a number of events that furthered ideas and interest in the project, and I am grateful to the organizers for creating these opportunities. In particular I would like to acknowledge Jeremy Till and Deljana Iossifova of the University of Westminster's project on Scarcity and Creativity in the Built Environment (SCIBE); Ben Campkin and the Urban Laboratory at University College London and the Cities Methodologies Event; Simon Guy and Albena Yaneva and the Politics of Design Conference at the Manchester Architecture Research Centre; Tim Jackson and the RESOLVE team at Surrey University and their two RESOLVE conferences; David Wang and the Design + Politics Conference at Washington State University Spokane; Guy Julier and Katie Hill and two design activism events at Leeds University School of Architecture, Landscape and Design; Ezio Manzini, Carla Cipolla and Jorge Frascara and the Turin Changing the Change Conference sponsored by the Milan and Turin Politechnic Universities (conference contents rivaled by a stunning outdoor conference dinner). For organizing book talks that helped springboard from my last book to this one, I am grateful to Jeff Hou and Joyce Cooper at the University of Washington, Louise St. Pierre at Emily Carr University of Art and Design, and Ben Croxford at University College London.

I interviewed a number of people at different points throughout the work; some before I really knew where it was going, and some with very focused, last-minute questions. But in *alphabetical* order they are: Anne Bottomley, William Davies, Pooran Desai, Kate Fletcher, Christine Gaspar, Robert Ivy, Karrie Jacobs, Jon Kolko, Julie Lasky, T. Luke Young, Blaine Merker, Liz Ogbu, Alix Ogilvie, Mathew Passmore, Cliff Pearson, Peter Victor and Susan Yelavich.

During the development of these ideas I taught an annual seminar at the Bartlett School of Architecture (on dimensions of sustainable design) at University College London and thank my students and my seminar faculty peers for many interesting discussion sessions. In addition, I ran a workshop at the Cities Methodologies event at University College London where I pressed innocent workshop volunteers into service on issues of consumerism and design. Thanks to attendees Joanne Bristol, Carolina Caicedo, Xavier Llarch, Alison Masters, Sinan Pirie (who also assisted), Monica Val and Essi Viitanen.

The section entitled 'Activism framed in design terms' in Chapter 5 is taken from a forthcoming journal article entitled 'Defining Design as Activism'.

As Earthscan came together with Routledge during the development of the book, I had three very supportive and enthusiastic editors and assistants including Claire Lamont, Michael Fell, Nicki Dennis and Alice Aldous. Other valuable contributions and assistance in production, from imagery to indexing, came from Geraldine Martin, Ann King, Philippa Mullins, Saxon Graphics, Megan Arrivey and Spencer Creelman (cover designer).

Finally, thanks to my friends (especially early mentors Stephanie Moulton and Sally Woodbridge) and family for past and present support—it takes a village to write a book!

Chapter 1

Design activism, movement society and a post-growth scenario

INTRODUCTION

Much design activist work, whether implicitly or explicitly, confronts problems that result from consumerism and economic growth. This is an underlying premise for the book, which connects social change through design activism to the broad idea that we need to move away from consumerism and growth as a central organizing principle in society. Although growth and consumerism are not, perhaps, the root of every social or environmental problem, there is arguably no problem that they don't exacerbate.

Still, a number of architects and designers may not see a way for their work to perform as activism, or to confront consumerism. They may think of their social design work in ethical rather than activist terms, or they may downplay any activist connotations. The chapters ahead attempt to show that most social or public interest design work can usefully be understood in political activist terms, whether the politics are cultural, spatial or governmental. Similarly, design activists may not see clear or "actionable" connections between their specific issues and consumerism and growth. For this reason the book aims to provide a better understanding of how design activism works, and to articulate how it is connected to consumerism and growth.

Activism, consumerism and growth are not the only framework for considering how design can contribute to solving many of society's pressing problems. However, this book argues that this framework is a very useful and under-explored way that architects and designers can confront growth. The book sets out to explore and illustrate this usefulness, particularly through the context of social movements.

The history of social movements is one of developing methods for building power to bring about change in situations where those who seek change are

The history of social movements African American civil rights marchers in 1963. Photo Warren K. Leffler, courtesy of the Library of Congress.

poorly resourced and lack conventional forms of power. Further, political scientists and sociologists have suggested that social movement activity is an accepted and even significant means of influencing political process and change; in that sense many western democracies have become "movement societies."[1]

To make the argument that the activism/consumerism/design framework is useful, this book is located at the nexus of three strands of thought. The first is design, the second is social change, and the third is consumerism and economic growth. Each of these are large areas, necessarily making the book more akin to a sketch than a tightly specified technical drawing, more akin to Handvetica than Helvetica, more prototype than finished structure. As a prototype framework for the issues, it attempts to lay out some terms for debate, put some topics and questions on the agenda, and frame design activism in post-growth terms.

A key concern in the book is to answer the question for designers: "What can I do about consumerism and growth?" For so long design has been connected to consumerism as one of its key engines. The challenge now is to link the broad, often abstract ideas about economic growth and its problems (such as climate stability) to methods of change that are relevant to architecture and design. The book does this in eight chapters. This first chapter clarifies terms and situates the book within the areas of design, social change and economics. It explores some of the tensions inherent in design activism.

The argument of the book, its exploration and illustration of the usefulness of an activism/consumerism/design framework, then comprises several parts. Chapter 2 outlines the systemic issues of consumerism and growth, noting how these pressures both shape and are shaped by design. This chapter argues that we can understand the relatively abstract problems of consumerism and economic growth in terms of four specific challenges.

Chapter 3 uses the articulation of these challenges to link issues of consumerism and growth to project-level design activism. This chapter also reviews the problem of how we measure the results of activist work, particularly through social metrics. Currently there are no systematic ways of measuring social value, which informs the broader fact that there is as yet no blueprint for a sustainable economy. Instead, the chapter argues, activists are engaged in a number of political struggles across disciplines that converge on the four challenges we have identified.

Chapter 4 picks up on some of the broader issues of a sustainable economy, reviewing efforts to normalize the inclusion of social values through market mechanisms. The chapter argues that, alongside the market, there is probably a need for other institutions of value creation and exchange that are recognized, supported and protected. The chapter closes with a review of how design activist practices are financing their work against the odds—how they fund work that appears to "soak up" income without increasing economic growth.

Chapter 5 presents the classic activist methods for seeking change and, using a range of design examples, argues that these methods also usefully describe design activism. The methods such as organizing, advocacy and mobilization shine a useful light on design activism.

Chapter 6 investigates the power dynamics underlying activist methods. The chapter then considers the capacities that activists, typically working on low budgets, have to build power. These capacities include disruption, framing and targeting. The chapter argues that these capacities also help us describe design activism's capacities to build power for change.

Chapter 7 jumps to a future point in time and speculates on a post-growth scenario. In this scenario new organizing principles of health, infrastructure and social capital replace the old organizing principles of consumerism and economic growth. Chapter 8 offers a brief conclusion.

The book is best read sequentially, since examples and concepts explained in earlier chapters are used to illustrate points in later chapters. Next we turn to the tasks of this chapter, including defining some terms, situating the book within the topic areas and examining some tensions inherent in design activism.

WHAT IS ACTIVISM?

Activism involves taking action that calls for change on behalf of a wronged, excluded or neglected group (or issue)—it is driven by the identification of a wrongdoing or problem that needs changing.[2] Typically operating on low budgets, activism is also known for its unconventional political approaches, particularly collective action and loose coordination through social movements.

Sociologist Tim Jordan describes activism as a moral undertaking because it seeks to put forward a vision for a better society.[3] This poses a question. Since most design seeks to improve the conditions of life for people, isn't most of design, in some senses, activism? The view that most design *is* activism is sometimes bolstered by the idea that architecture, in particular, has long been influenced by arts and intellectual movements, such as modernism, that contain ideas about a better society.

Although these movements had some broad proposals for how society should be organized, they were also closely bound to commerce and aesthetics.[4] Consider the contrast between the idea of "modernism" and a particular instance of activism. Modernism's idea was that people could be made more equal and society made more fair through "truthful forms" in buildings and objects that united workers, designers and users. Contrast that with the bus boycott in 1950s America through which blacks demanded an end to segregated seating on buses.[5] The former is an abstract ideology whereas the latter is targeted activism.

Although "good" design does typically work to bring about change, in its dominant forms, good design (usable, profitable, beautiful, meaningful) doesn't usually constitute activism on behalf of excluded or neglected groups. Rather, it constitutes general improvements to daily life that are most often gained through private consumption, accessed according to the consumer's ability to pay.

WHAT SHOULD WE CHANGE?

It is useful to be more specific about the range of neglected or excluded groups and issues for which we undertake activism. Although activism can be regressive and champion issues such as white supremacy or religious fundamentalism, the focus of this book is on progressive activism that falls broadly within the framework of sustainable development. Pressing issues in this view include harmful degradation of the natural environment, gross and rising income inequality within and among countries, and vulnerability of many diverse cultures and a range of human rights to a commercial monoculture. (These issues are summarized in Figure 1.1). Most of the problems within these broad categories are linked in some way to constant pressure for economic growth driven by consumerism.

Currently our economy must either continue spiraling upward, with growth, or crash downward if growth fails. All the social and environmental problems of growth, in this view, are a necessary cost of necessary growth; but recently economists have made a startling suggestion: we could redesign our economy for a post-growth era. The economy wouldn't have to either spiral up or down; instead we could thrive in a steady state, a state that would allow us to improve real well-being by rebalancing spending and costs.

The past two decades have indicated that architects and designers want more social and environmental relevance in bringing about change. For example, architect Hashim Sarkis comments:

> Calls for alternative practices in architecture have multiplied in the past few years, appearing to rise in unison from publications across academia and the profession. … Additionally, experimental and integrated practices, previously relegated to a marginal position, are appearing more frequently in lecture circles, professional workshops, and competition highlights.[6]

Designers have been asking if they are contributing enough to a wide range of important issues such as climate change, poverty, humanitarian aid, education or health, to name a few. But seen in the light of society's singular objective of economic growth, these issues are all cost and no profit. They don't contribute to economic growth. Sure, they may contribute to economic growth very indirectly and over the very long term, but this contribution is all too easily brushed aside in quarterly growth reports and short-term re-election campaigns.

Money and investment continue to flood into economic growth initiatives—most driven by consumerism—while only trickling into vital social and environmental agendas. In this context designers who seek to be change agents must work under conditions of dwindling resources (especially money) to build power to bring about change. It turns out that the tools to do this have long been around in the social movement arena.

Figure 1.1 Pressing issues for activism

1a Share of total income going to Top 10%, 1917-2007

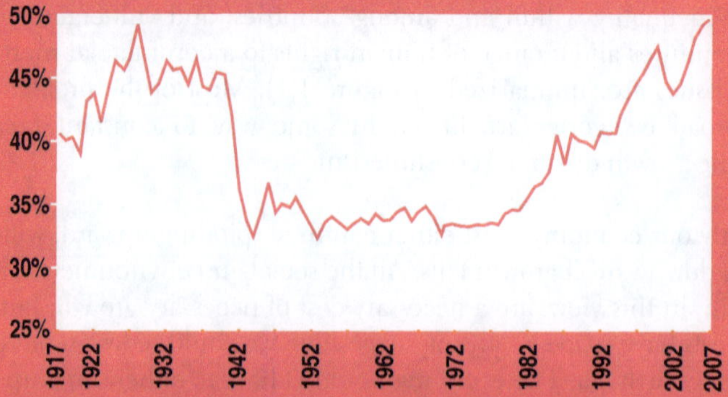

Studies of tax data in the United States show that the share of total income going to top income groups rose dramatically in recent decades.

1b Living Planet Index 1970-2007

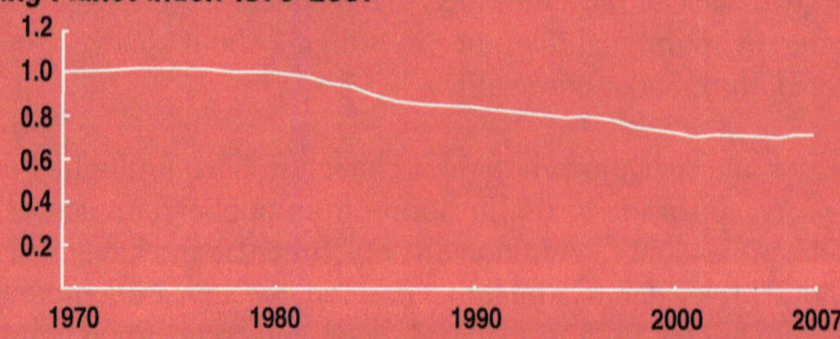

The index shows roughly 30 percent decline based on trends in 7,953 populations of 2,544 mammal, bird, reptile, fish, and amphibian species.

1c Language Loss in North America

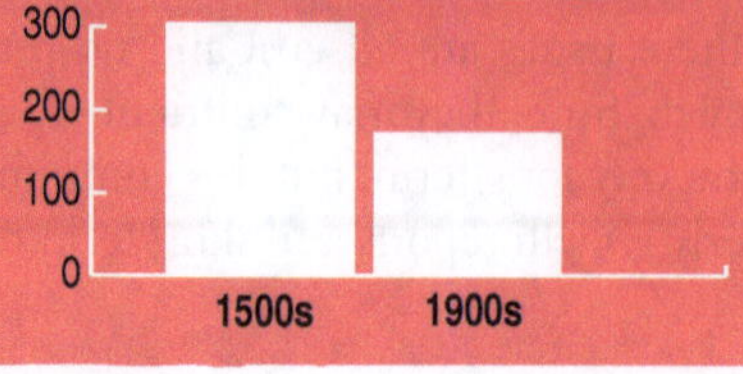

The pace of language loss is increasing. Estimates are that half of the world's more than 6,000 languages will be extinct by the end of this century.

Sources: 1a Anthony B. Atkinson, Thomas Piketty, and Emmanuel Saez, "Top Incomes in the Long Run of History", *Journal of Economic Literature* 2011, 49:1, 3–71. 1b Duncan Pollard (ed.) *Living Planet Report 2010* (WWF in conjunction with Zoological Society of London and Global Footprint Network; Gland, Switzerland, 2010), 20. 1c Jack Hitt, "Say No More", The New York *Times*, February 29, 2004.

SITUATING THE TOPIC

This book takes an interdisciplinary view, looking at design, economics and the politics of social change. Recognizing that each of these is a large area in itself, we begin by situating the book within each of these topics.

Design

In situating the topic of design activism within the broader field of design, it is perhaps useful to consider two views. The first is a view from within design. This interior view includes the discussions designers have about their own profession, academic systems and practice. The second view is of design from outside itself.

The first point of order is to discuss the scope of design covered in this book. Design here is anchored *primarily* to physical, material and visual aspects of the built and manufactured environment. This is not an assertion that design's manifestation is or should be primarily through the production of stuff. Clearly there are a number of interesting approaches to design that focus on service and process design.[7] But physicality and spatiality give the book a specific and useful niche, and allow for more explicit analysis of levers for change. Although the broad topics of communication and interaction design, what might formerly have been thought of as graphic design, are not entirely excluded, neither are they a focus.

The scope of the built and manufactured environment, which reasonably contains architecture, product and landscape design, may even seem too broad. But examination of many cases of design activism shows that there is fluidity across these disciplines.[8] Architects take on product design; product designers create portable structures; landscape designers develop outdoor furniture. Broad spatial and material aspects of design activism provide a good starting point and help focus arguments and discussion.

Within design

In the first view, the largest practical context for design is commerce. For this reason, one prominent strand of design activism focuses on making the business case for social and environmental design. Many readers will be familiar with the efforts of companies, such as Interface, Patagonia, and even Walmart, to pursue a triple bottom line that includes social and environmental "returns" as well as economic ones.[9] These companies have often pursued their objectives through the lens of design—through structures, products and design processes.

Alongside the business context, design activism also arises in nonprofit groups as well as public, or government, arenas. Architecture for Humanity, Design

Corps or the Living Future Institute are examples of nonprofit organizations pursuing social and environmental work through architecture and design. In the government arena, cities and states have developed a range of "demonstration buildings", such as Chicago city hall's green roof or the Lewis and Clark state offices, a LEED platinum building that houses the Missouri Department of Natural Resources.

The academic context is also important for design activism. Many university design-build studios pursue social design work. Some academic work is led by faculty, such as Politecnico Milan's establishment of the DESIS network (Design for Social Innovation and Sustainability), and some is led by students, such as the recent Treads project bringing shoe design to an inner Cincinnati school.[10]

As these examples suggest, the work of design activists cuts across a wide swathe of issues. The design activism timeline shown in Figure 1.2 gives an indication of the range of issues for design activism stretching back to the 1930s and 1940s, as well as the changing character of activity over the past few decades.

Lewis and Clark State Office Building designed by BNIM Architects. Photo Scott Myers, courtesy of Missouri Department of Natural Resources.

Figure 1.2 Design activism timeline

1930s & 40s

housing and furniture
- Bauhaus and the social potential of design
- Buckminster Fuller dymaxion car and house
- R.M. Schindler's shelters: low cost, pre-fabricated housing

1950s

housing
- Buckminster Fuller geodesic domes
- Walter Segal self build system

accessibility
- "barrier free" movement (forerunner to universal design) for disabled veterans

1960s

counterculture

1960s design groups: Situationists International, Superstudio, etc.
1966 Drop City community founded
1968 Whole Earth Catalog, Stewart Brand

environment

1969 **Design with Nature** by Ian McHarg
1969 Sym van der Ryn establishes Ecological Design Institute

community design & appropriate tech

1961 First American Barrier Free Design standard is published
1961 Lawrence Halprin begins planning the Sea Ranch community, California
1962, Findhorn Foundation created by Eileen Caddy, Peter Caddy and Dorothy Maclean in Scotland
1965 Intermediate Technology Development Group (Appropriate Technology) founded
1968-69 Community Design Center of Minnesota founded 1969, Los Angeles Community Design Center founded 1968

1970s

design for development/humanitarian

1971 **Design for the Real World** by Victor Papanek
1972 Nathan Shapira develops exhibition on design for low income economies
1976 Habitat for Humanity founded
1977 Association for Community Design founded
1979 Ahmedabad Declaration on Industrial Design for Development issued

enviroment

1970s Co-evolution Quarterly began
1970 Cosanti Foundation initiated by Paolo Soleri began building Arcosanti, an experimental town (ongoing)
1971 New Alchemy Institute founded by John Todd, Nancy Jack Todd, and William McLarney (operational until 1991)
1973 American Institute of Architects Energy committee founded
1973 Centre for Alternative Technology founded (Wales) by Gerard Morgan-Grenville
1975 Center for Maximum Potential Building Systems established by Pliny Fisk III and Gail D. A. Vittori
1972 Earthship biotecture's Thumb House, completed by Michael Reynolds
1975 construction begins on Village Homes, with principal designer Mike Corbett
1977 **Soft Energy Paths** by Amory Lovins
1977 **A Pattern Language: Towns, Buildings, Construction** by Christopher Alexander, Sara Ishikawa and Murray Silverstein
1979 **Passive Solar Energy Book** by Ed Mazria

diversity: religion

1977 Aga Khan award established for architecture recognizing good design in Islamic contexts (ongoing)

1980s

social responsibility

1981 Architects/Designers/Planners for Social Responsibility founded

1987 Homeless Vehicle Project, Krzysztof Wodiczko design collaboration with homeless people to develop a cart-like shelter/vehicle (through 1989)

environment

1981 Structural failure at a major US hotel prompts the conversion of Bob Berkibile to one of the first sustainable design champions in architecture

1982 Founding of the Rocky Mountain Institute by Amory and Hunter Lovins

feminism

1984 **Redesigning the American Dream: Gender, Housing, and Family Life**, by Dolores Hayden

1990s

humanitarian

1999 Architecture for Humanity founded by Cameron Sinclair and Kate Stohr

1999 Architects without Frontiers, founded by Esther Charlesworth, Garry Ormston and Beau Beza

affordability/accessibility & diversity

1993 Rural Studio founded by Samuel Mockbee and Dennis K. Ruth at Auburn University in Alabama, design focusing on poor local communities

1993 Congress for the New Urbanism established

1994 Sphere Magazine begins publication by World Studio (through 2003)

1995 Merrima Aboriginal Design Unit established within the Australian government's Department of Public Works, Sydney

1999 Design Corps founded by Bryan Bell, focusing on US community focus, often rural or migrant groups

1999 The Glass-House Trust begins evolving into The Glass-House Community Led Design in 2006, UK

environment

1990 A Scandinavian Design Council Manifesto issued on Nature, Ecology, and Human Needs for the Future

1990 formation of the AIA Committee on the Environment

1991 Ecodesign Foundation incorporated, Australia for re-creation for ecological and social sustainment

1992 The Hannover Principles developed by William McDonough

1993 founding of the US Green Building Council

1993 **Design for Society**, critiques of consumerist design by Nigel Whitely

1994 **Remakings: Ecology, Design, Philosophy** by Tony Fry

1996 **Ecological Design** by Sim van Der Ryn and Stewart Cowan

1997 continued formalization of eco design with publications such as John Gertsakis, Helen Lewis, and Chris Ryan **A Guide to EcoReDesign**, Han Brezet and C. van Hemel's **Ecodesign: A Promising Approach to Sustainable Production and Consumption**, and Ken Yeang's **The Skyscraper: Bioclimatically Considered**

1996-97 exhibitions of recycled material such as "Re- Materialize" and "Hello Again"

1999 **Natural Capitalism: Creating the Next Industrial Revolution** by Paul Hawken, Amory Lovins, and L. Hunter Lovins

feminism

1992 Women in Design section founded, IDSA (Industrial Designers Society of America)

1999 **Design and Feminism** Joan Rothschild

1996 **Architecture and Feminism**, Debra Coleman, Elizabeth Danze and Carol Henderson, eds.

alternative education

1996 Ecosa Institute founded by Antony Brown

2000-2011

humanitarian (becoming social design or design for social impact)

2001 Designers without Borders founded as a US-Ugandan organization to assist with communication design

2001 Designers without Borders (Norway) founded by the Foundation for Design and Architecture in Norway and the office of Peter Opsvik, to deploy design as a development tool

2002 Social Design Notes website begins
2003 Design that Matters founded by Timothy Prestero to design new products and services for the poor in developing countries
2004 Article 25 (formerly Architects for Aid) founded by Maxwell Hutchinson and Victoria Harris
2007 MASS founded by Michael Murphy and Alan Ricks, for well built environments to empower in developing economies
2008 Socialdesign "we cannot not change the world," website launched to foster discussion on social design
2008 Project H Design founded by Emily Pilloton to use design for positive transformation of communities
2008 Change Observer blog initiated following on Rockefeller Bellagio conference on design for social impact
2009 Design Impact and Fellows
2008 Rockefeller Foundation publishes Design for Social Impact by IDEO
2009 Human Centered Design Toolkit by IDEO, bringing innovation to the base of the pyramid
2009 Design Ignites Change programs on social design for high schools and colleges
2009 Design with Africa grows out of the Network of Africa Designers (founded 1999)
2009 Design for Dictators website founded offering fictional products for dictators
2010 IDEO.org, social design offshoot from IDEO
2011 The Policy Lab founded, design application to policy for peace, disarmament, conflict resolution and other international policy

accessible/public interest/diversity

2002 Public Architecture founded by John Peterson for wider positive social impact in the local community
2002 UK Design Council begins work on design-led solutions to social problems
2004 [Re]design founded by Sarah Johnson for sustainable design, making and learning, UK
2005 the 1%, Public Architecture's initiative to professionalize pro bono work
2005 University of California Berkeley, College of Environmental Design publishes Frameworks, themed on Design Activism Issue 1 Spring 2005
2005 SEED (Social Economic Environmental Design)
2007 INDIGO, the International Indigenous Design Network, forms out of projects at Monash University, Australia
2008 SEED Foundation social enterprise and design, UK
2008 **Expanding Architecture: Design as Activism** edited by Bryan Bell and Katie Wakeford
2009 **Design Activism: Beautiful Strangeness for Sustainable World** by Alistair Fuad-Luke
2009 Design for America, extra-curricular student-led studios creating local and social impact through interdisciplinary design
2010 Community Oriented Design (CO Design) founded by Lucinda Hartley, Australia, nonprofit design services to disadvantaged communities
2011 International Network of Indigenous Architects founded

prizes and conferences

2000 Rose Architectural Fellowships introduced (after Frederick P. Rose), three-year partnerships between emerging architects and community-based organizations
2000 Structures for Inclusion 1 conference organized by Design Corps
2006 "ecodesign" category added to IDSA / BusinessWeek IDEA awards program
2007 The Buckminster Fuller Challenge for $100,000
2008 Curry Stone Prize, for design emphasizing social good, reaching wider segments of society, for $100,000
2008 Ulm Foundation (Germany) international competition "Designing Politics-the Politics of Design" to investigate the social responsibility of designers to promote democratic quality of design
2008 A Better World by Design Conference initiated
2008 Rockefeller Bellagio conference on design for social impact

environment

2002 Architecture 2030 founded by Edward Mazria: getting to zero carbon emission buildings by 2030

2002 **Cradle to Cradle** By William McDonough & Michael Braungart

2006 EcoLabs founded by Jody Boehnert (developed ecoliteracy teach-in for designers in London 2009)

2007 Designers Accord originally climate driven, now expanded

2008 Kyoto Design Declaration signed, committing to building sustainable, human-centered and creative societies

2009 Living Building Challenge launched by Cascadia Chapter of US Green Building Council

2009 Platform 21=Repairing, repair is underestimated as creative, cultural and economic force, leads to publication of the Repair Manifesto

2009 **Design Futuring: Sustainability, Ethics and New Practice** by Tony Fry

alternative education models & politics in design education and research

2001 Designmatters founded at Art Centre College of Design by Mariana Amatullo to harness design for more equitable and sustainable world

2003 The Institute without Boundaries founded by George Brown College and Bruce Mau Design (Canada) with inaugural project, **Massive Change**

2004 Global Studio spearheaded by United Nations Millennium Project Task Force on design education to facilitate inclusive, sustainable city building

2005 Biomimicry Institute founded by Janine Benyus, offers educational programs

2005 Center for Architectural Research founded at Goldsmiths, University of London with a strand on design and politics/spatial politics

2006 Manchester Architecture Research Center founded at the University of Manchester with a strand on design and politics/spatial politics

2007 The Agency research group founded at Sheffield School of Architecture, with a theme of Transformative Research into Architectural Practice and Education

2008 Leeds School of Architecture, Landscape and Design at Leeds Metropolitan University hosts “Mapping Design Activism” followed by Leeds Festival of Design Activism in 2009

2009 Wouter Vanstiphout takes up a Chair in Politics and Design at TU Delft, the Netherlands

2009 Academic network DESIS: Design for Social Innovation towards Sustainability initiated

2010 IMPACT! Design for Social Change summer residency (includes product and fashion along with visual arts) School for Visual Arts 2010 by Mark Randall and Steve Heller

2010 Doina Petrescu becomes Professor of Architecture and Design Activism at Sheffield School of Architecture, University of Sheffield

2010 Austin Center for Design founded by Jon Kolko to educate designers for social enterprise

2011 Public Interest Design Institute founded by Bryan Bell, offers multi-day training on pro-active community-based design

From "within" design there is also a tendency to view design activism through the lens of the major design movements of the past 100 years, such as arts and crafts, modernism, postmodernism, community design, and systems design. In the past decade or so we have seen terms emerging that perhaps suggest new design movements. The terms include social design, design for social impact, architectural agency, spatial agency, and public interest design.

The concept of public interest design seems to be emerging from within architecture; for example, architect Bryan Bell of Design Corps has formed the Public Interest Design Institute.[11] Public interest design differs from community design, according to Bell, in that it is a professional track, not volunteer or academic.[12]

In the UK, there have also been recent discussions of architectural agency or spatial agency. Spatial agency, according to architect Tatjana Schneider, argues for an indeterminate approach to architecture, such that the processes and contexts through which space is developed are flexible—the possibilities of space are opened up to agency on the part of a wider range of concerns than might be typically present in architecture. It is a form of spatial engagement for which success is not necessarily measured in the traditional way, by a "built object."[13]

The concept of "social design" seems more common in product design, perhaps stemming from investment by the Rockefeller Foundation in pioneering work by both IDEO and Winterhouse Design in improving product design relevance to the "social sector", particularly in the context of developing countries.[14]

From outside design

If we look at design activism from outside design itself, a different picture emerges. In this picture the issues that design activism pursues are almost all part of larger social movements which concern issues such as environmentalism, health, disability, aging, poverty, education, transportation or justice, to name a few. Each movement is made up of a range of organizations and individuals engaged in struggles for change that cross a spectrum of issues under one banner. For example, some environmentalists are focused on reducing household waste in cities, whereas others are focused on protecting wilderness or restoring habitats. Social movements are full of complexities and even contradictions.

Different "actors" within movements form specific campaigns for change, through which they diagnose the problem, identify solutions, and then act towards making the changes necessary to reach the solutions. Sometimes designers and design organizations are central actors in movements. For example, architect Ed Mazria's organization Architecture 2030 has arguably sped up the pace of commitment to carbon-neutral building.

Although other, non-design actors in these movements may have some sense of how their struggles relate to materials and spaces, they may only rarely, if at all, be aware of the potential for material and spatial design to contribute to their struggles. Even in some movements that appear ostensibly based on spaces and materials, such as affordable housing, alternative energy or green building, there are many movement actors who view the issues through different lenses. Lawyers and public agencies may view the issue through regulation and taxation, seeing these as central. Sociologists and community groups may view the issue through a social behavior lens, pointing out that some super-green housing projects don't perform as well as expected owing to the behaviors of the tenants. In this view, if design is seen at all, it is a useful, perhaps necessary, element of change, but it is not sufficient on its own.

Social change

There are many ways to look at social change. For example, it is possible to view social change entirely through the lens of business and commerce. Here, efforts such as "corporate social responsibility" exist to facilitate businesses acknowledging the wider components of profit and loss. At the same time, consumer education aims to help consumers "demand" better social performance from business, for example, by introducing labeling schemes such as "energy star" for lighting or appliances.

It is also possible to view social change through the lens of information and communication. This lens focuses on the community and civic purposes of information and communication technology, among other things.[15] Here, "transparency," or making information accessible, is central, along with freedom of information, and useful analysis and interpretation of information. Communication (but not necessarily visual communication) is posed as the central aspect of any collective enterprise.

Depending on the issues, it is also possible to look at social change from the perspective of cultural identity and social behavior. For example, recent efforts to pioneer "social innovation" as a means to social change rely on altering the patterns in social relationships. These social innovations "simultaneously meet social needs and create new social relationships or collaborations."[16]

These examples from business, sociology and information science (and we could pick many others) make the point that we can locate social change in many contexts. Indeed, Alastair Fuad Luke's book *Design Activism* looks at social change through the lens of design, and, parallel to the examples above, frames social change in design terms. By contrast, in this book we frame design in social movement activism terms.

Before exploring the social movement context further, it is also useful to consider how we can look at social change from the point of view of structure and agency. The examples above suggest structures, such as the marketplace, the level of information technology, or cultural norms, that guide how any individual or group can act. For example, if you are poor, it is harder for you to engage in consumer mechanisms for change.

Knitfiti The urban environment as a canvas, agency in response to structure.

In the view of agency, individuals and groups make many strategic choices when navigating structures such as the marketplace or an information technology. Groups or individuals, as agents, create "meaning" that can change structures. For example, a group of children might appropriate a park for skateboarding, uncovering potential that was never intended. Graffiti, even knitfiti (knitted graffiti), use urban structure as a canvas. Further, as agents we bring our own goals, motivations and emotions to any situation, which also guides the choices we make when faced with a structure to navigate. Neither structure nor agency can wholly explain any one outcome of change.

Relevance of movements to contemporary society

To some observers, social movement activism may seem old-fashioned, perhaps trapped in a narrow 1960s stereotype. Some people working on issues of social change have turned to more expansive, perhaps less politicized terms, such as "social innovation" or "alternative pathways," to describe efforts for change (Figure 1.3). David Hess, preferring the term "alternative pathway," comments:

> Some alternative pathways exhibit complex mixes of social-change goals with goals of profitability, faith-based charity, or even leisure-time hobbies such as gardening and home tinkering. Although some organizations may mix social-change goals with other goals, they may not view themselves as engaging in contentious politics, and they may not see themselves as belonging to a social movement. Furthermore, organizations that were originally dedicated to social change sometimes shift their goals.

But he does conclude: "However, because alternative pathways often take the form of social movements, theories of social movements provide a good starting point for the study of alternative pathways."[17]

Hess's conclusion reinforces the point of this book as well—that social movement concepts and frameworks provide a good starting point for thinking about design activism in the context of consumerism and growth. In terms of architecture and design, arguably the political aspect of social movements is the very thing that makes them interesting.

Designers have been involved in various social movements, particularly those that Hess calls product-oriented movements.[18] These are movements that involve struggles over the definition and configuration of alternative technologies and products, such as organically grown cotton or energy from renewables. An example is architects' involvement in the environmental movement, particularly in terms of technology such as passive energy structures and energy conservation methods of the 1970s. More recently architects have been

Figure 1.3 Alternative pathways

Is this a social movement?

Contentious politics

Traditional social movements: anti-war demonstrators at the White House 1968. (Photo Warren K. Leffler, courtesy of the Library of Congress).

Compared to...

Lifestyle politics

Localism: apple season, community juice-making 2011.

heavily involved in green building movements aimed at reducing the overall environmental footprint of buildings. Industrial designers have been involved in "universal design" movements aimed at making products and packaging accessible to people with different physical abilities, including children and the elderly. Other examples are found on the design activism timeline.

The continued relevance of social movements is signaled today by a number of factors. To the extent that social movements and activism hinge on "collective action" they are reinforced by the rise of "collaboration"; for example, in social networking, open source development platforms and collaborative consumption. In addition, people increasingly feel the limitations of individual action and the illusion of personal choice. Michael Maniates and John Meyer describe a common perception of our current catch-22. If individuals in the affluent countries won't sacrifice by consuming less, then we need either a catastrophe or an expert dictatorship to bring about change.[19] But as we stop thinking in terms of individuals and instead work collectively, social movements and collective action provide a viable alternative to the catastrophe/dictator dilemma.

Social movements also maintain relevancy by evolving. Older movements were often defined in terms of a central *class* struggle (for example, the "working class" and labor union struggles).[20] These movements sought to extend the coverage of citizens' rights, such as voting, legal protections, and access to resources. Newer social movements, arising in "post-industrial" or "new economy" conditions, often form around cultural, moral and identity issues.[21] Examples include environmentalism, alter globalization or peace/nuclear freeze movements.

Although evidence suggests that the new economy may lead to different types of movements, it has not overcome the need for movements. Geographer Edward Soja contends that the new economy has intensified spatial and social injustice. He ties the rise in inequality to:

> deregulation, privatization, and promoting the intrinsic values of small government versus big government; the reorganization of the New Deal; the reassertion of trickle-down notions to rationalize growing tax breaks for the rich; the increasing acceptance if not encouragement of corporate greed; and the massive decline in industrial unionism.[22]

Perhaps the biggest challenge for social movements arises from the recognition of the systemic nature of many contemporary movement issues. The globalized economy creates a more complex range of contexts, from local to global, within which to act. There are many players whose position is shifting.

For example, some view national governments as weakening. National governments are increasingly tied to international governing and trade groups (such as the European Union or the World Trade Organization), at the same time they are under pressure to redirect national budgets and rule-making to the local level, a process of devolution giving regions and cities more power.[23]

Another aspect of the systemic nature of contemporary movements is the connection across issue areas. For example, the US labor movement has come to see a positive connection between the goals of environmentalism and jobs.[24] Not only does forest clear-cutting or unmanaged fishing ultimately and permanently end jobs, but also, lax environmental laws in developing countries draw jobs away from developed countries such as the US.

Growing scientific evidence links issues across movements, making boundaries blurry at best. For example, suburban development patterns, blamed for increasing our automobile dependence and thus damaging the environment (through carbon emissions, loss of habitat, etc.), are now also empirically linked to a wide range of health issues such as obesity, depression and high blood pressure.[25] Similarly, research increasingly shows links between climate change, food production and diet.[26] Although in the past diet and food may have been seen as human health issues and suburban sprawl may have been seen as an environmental issue, these two areas now share a lot of common ground. They can each be seen as both environmental and human health issues.

Climate change and food Energy- and land-intensive food production, dietary preferences, food transport.

When we think about the types of changes sought by social movements, we can see that older movements perhaps sought reform. They looked to change things by reforming the current systems and institutions; for example, by reforming gun control laws, or voting laws. Yet for tackling health, suburban development and climate issues together we have no specific basis for reform, since few, if any, policies or laws currently address these areas as linked.

In this context, sociologist Tim Jordan suggests that some activist campaigns are seeking to change things by transforming the current systems and institutions; for example, by inventing new alternatives and relationships.[27] Transformative movements cut across old boundaries.

Economics/Sustainable Consumption

Our third concern is economic growth and consumerism. Here economic growth means growth in the productive outputs of an economy and in the financial transactions that surround production and consumption.

Although issues of globalization, migration and uneven development make it difficult to separate the geographies of over-consumption and under-consumption entirely, this book takes as its main geographical context the over-consuming countries, and primarily the two English-speaking countries in which the author is most situated, the US and the UK. Although there are significant differences between these two counties, in a number of ways the UK has developed cultural characteristics that make it more similar to the US than to the rest of Europe. Compared to the rest of Europe, for example, the UK has longer working hours, higher levels of poverty, higher levels of personal debt and higher teenage pregnancy.[29] The UK also has higher levels of income inequality than most European countries, putting it closer in these terms to the US than to its European neighbors.[30]

CONSUMERISM

There is probably no one definition of *consumerism* upon which everyone can agree, but many people would recognize consumerism as a social and economic pattern that emphasizes two main areas. The first is the pursuit of material wealth, the frequent acquisition and accumulation of things. The second is the portrayal of oneself and one's family in ways that compare favorably with commercially driven norms and ideals—the right "image." Image is always constructed through material means such as clothing, accessories, houses, cars and the like.[28]

Contexts of consumerism Emphasizing the frequent acquisition and accumulation of things. Photo Steve Brandon.

Since around the 1950s, economic growth has been a central organizing principle in many countries. Growth, driven by consumerism, is seen as the key to adequate levels of employment among other things. The market is viewed as the best decision maker, governed by rational individual consumers making free market choices. Economic growth has been taken as a proxy for overall well-being. Over the last few decades however, research and practical experience has led many people to question the idea that continuous economic growth is entirely beneficial.

For example, every unit of growth uses up resources and creates waste. The hope has been that better forms of production and consumption could create new norms for green, ethical consumerism or that improved efficiency could outrun effects of growth and consumerism. Better forms of consumption have, in the past decade or so, entered the marketplace and *grown rapidly*. It is not surprising to hear about sectors experiencing 100 percent or more growth in a few years' time. Given the emphasis society places on economic growth, this is big news. The amount of press spurred by rapid growth in these sectors can almost give the impression that they are, in fact, becoming new "norms."

But when we scrub away the frenzy over high growth rates, we get a different picture. None of these sectors experiencing forms of better consumption are anywhere near becoming new norms, as Table 1.1 indicates.

Table 1.1 Better forms of consumption not becoming "norms"

Form of better consumption	US market share
Organic food[31]	3.7%
Organic cropland and pastures[32]	0.6%
Organic cotton crops[33]	0.14% of all cotton crops
Fair trade products[34]	4%
Green energy programs[35]	7% of energy consumers subscribe to green energy options
Green building[36]	25% of new construction
Hybrid (alternative fuel) cars[37]	About 1% of current passenger car fleet (assumes 95% of hybrids sold in past five years are still on road)

Similarly in the UK, the Cooperative Bank tracks ethical consumption at the household level in categories such as food and drink, home hardware (light bulbs, boilers, paper, cleaners, etc.), travel, personal products (clothing and cosmetics), and finance. They track various aspects of "ethical" such as fair trade, organic, energy efficient, free range and second hand/reuse, to name a few. The most recent report notes that although ethical household consumption in these categories has almost tripled in the past ten years, it still represents less than 1 percent of total household expenditure.[38]

In addition, although resource use has become much more more efficient over the years, efficiency gains have not enabled us to "outrun" increasing resource use required by growth. We have not been able to "decouple" (or detach) economic growth from growth in resource consumption. Consider, for example, how automobile travel outpaces gains in efficiency. Jack Manno reports that between 1970 and 1990 automobile fuel efficiency increased by 34 percent, but total fuel consumption rose by 7 percent. Several factors offset the savings from fuel efficiency: high levels of car ownership (more cars per household), larger vehicles and more miles driven per car.[39] Peter Victor also notes that "if the adverse effects on the environment [from growth] are cumulative, decoupling slows down the rate at which things get worse, but it does not turn them around."[40]

There is also some evidence that at the individual consumer level, efficiency gains can actually generate more consumption, an effect known as "rebound."[41] For example, if you get a more efficient car, you may use the money you save to take a cheap airline flight.

Although economic systems put the focus on individual consumers, recent thinking is that, at best, individual consumer choice can influence about

INNOVATION EFFECT

In addition to rebound effects, there is also what we might call an innovation effect that makes electrical products, in particular, short-lived. The average lifespan for a computer in industrialized countries has dropped dramatically over the past decade. Estimates are that mobile phones "live" for barely two years.[42] There are also more of these electronic products around as they become more affordable as well as more essential to daily life. One measure of this innovation effect is the UK Energy Saving Trust's estimate that electricity consumed by electrical appliances, such as TVs and computers, doubled between 1972 and 2002. The Trust estimates that due to increasingly essential personal electronic tools, the figure will double again by 2012.[43]

one-third of consumption; the remainder is determined by both regional and national infrastructure.[44] Further, research also suggests that individuals, even in areas of consumption that they purportedly control, are plagued by temptation, peer pressure, and habit. In addition, individual consumers who are not among the super-rich face a steadily declining financial position. These problems mean that old assumptions which justified the benefits of economic growth are not holding up to scrutiny.

Despite the troubles with economic growth, it remains central and is rarely challenged; but two recent reports suggest that there is another way. Tim Jackson's *Prosperity without Growth* (2009) examined key issues around the idea of maintaining well-being ("prosperity") in conditions of a steady state economy. Jackson's work was based in part on Peter Victor's *Managing without Growth* (2008), in which Victor reports on a model for a steady state, or low-growth Canadian economy. These authors are both suggesting that it is possible to have an economy that works on principles different than continuous, consumerist-led economic growth—this is the idea of a "post-growth" era.

As this book is written, international calls for governments to "get the economy growing again" are reaching fever pitch. Whether or not the concern over economic recovery has died down by the time of the book's publication, the main point remains the same. We need to find a way to transition from this system reliant on growth to one that better addresses real well-being—we need to get from here to there. As the UK's Sustainable Development Commission argues:

> from a sustainable development perspective, the notion of "economic recovery" is itself a problematic one, because recent patterns of virtually worldwide economic growth, if resumed in a year or two, will have a devastating impact on eco-systems, and on the capacity of the planet to provide the foodstuffs, metals, and other natural and environmental resources on which the world economy depends.[45]

Although this book won't detail economic and policy aspects of how we should get from here to there, we pause here and in Chapter 4 to look at some of the broad-brush issues.

Several policy documents have used the recent economic crises as an opportune time to set out basic ideas for getting from here to there.[46] In response to current calls for growth, the Sustainable Development Commission argues that government packages of economic "stimulus" must be bigger but tightly focused on the transition to a green economy—priority areas include:

- renewable energy;
- retrofitting existing buildings for efficiency;
- directed help and support for greening operations in the public and private sector;
- sustainable mobility/transport;
- skills training for a sustainable economy.

For accomplishing this stimulus, the Commission suggests, "four broad options present themselves: deficit spending; raising money through environmental taxation or the auctioning of carbon permits; issuing green bonds; or increasing the public ownership of energy-related assets."[47] This stimulus lays some of the groundwork toward transition to a sustainable economy, which we discuss further in Chapter 4.

WIDENING THE RANGE OF BENEFICIARIES OF ACTIVISM

Positioning this book's discussion of social movements and design within the context of consumerism and growth puts our focus on the question of exactly who is excluded and neglected. Historically, movements have focused on poor and socially excluded populations. The lens of economic growth shows that increasingly a much wider group of average, perhaps middle-class people have their futures, as well as their current well-being, compromised by the costs of economic growth. Further, the entire population, as well as future generations, suffers from the effects of environmental degradation and cultural disintegration.

Yet due to the systemic nature of growth, most of us have a limited voice in this aspect of public life. We are effectively excluded. A key idea is that tackling consumerism and economic growth involves recognizing that in many ways, a wide swathe of consumerist society falls into the category of a neglected or excluded group. This wider swathe of society is then potentially both a target and a beneficiary of social movement work for a post-growth economy. This group does not replace other excluded groups but rather joins them, perhaps recognizing what they have in common.[48]

We have already begun to see efforts, particularly in the US, to mobilize wider segments of society under calls to renew the American dream. Organizations such as the "Center for a new American Dream" and "Rebuild the Dream" led Van Jones to call this the American Dream Movement based on the idea that "hard work pays in our country; that you can make it if you try; that America remains a land committed to dignity, justice and opportunity for all."[49] Similarly, there is a proposal that the United Nations (UN) develop a set of Millennium Consumption Goals to guide rich countries toward reducing consumption. This set of goals would be a sister to the UN's Millennium Development Goals for improving conditions for many of the world's poorest people.[50]

The notion of development goals suggests that over-consumption is a problem in countries where there is relatively little shortage of material goods, where the wealthiest 20 percent of the world's population make 86 percent of consumption expenditures.[51] These over-consumers need to cut back, but many people in poor countries will have to consume more to reach acceptable standards of living. The poorest 20 percent of the world's population make just 1.3 percent of consumption expenditures. Of course, needed increases in consumption in these countries can be smarter and better planned, learning from the mistakes of over-consuming countries and utilizing better technology. But under-consuming countries are likely to aim for—and are already adopting—lifestyles modeled on over-consumption, unless we in over-consuming countries can demonstrate something better.

These last paragraphs also raise the broad issue of population size. Clearly one way to reduce consumption is to reduce the number of people consuming. During the writing of this chapter the world population officially hit 7 billion. Currently world population isn't expected to level off until it reaches about 9 billion. Population control is a thorny issue and beyond the scope of this book; however, Tim Jackson offers an interesting perspective for consideration.

In addition to population numbers, he suggests, levels of affluence also drive consumption, and "in recent years, the affluence factor has exceeded the population factor in driving growth."[52] Although advocating for increases in affluence through growth is seen as synonymous with improved well-being, advocating for population limits is seen as interfering with basic liberty. Jackson points out that these perceptions are wrong. Higher incomes don't guarantee well-being, and population growth has been highest among the least "free" populations—the world's poorest people who lack education and access to contraception.

TENSION: DESIGN AND POLITICS

We enter into the book's topic acknowledging that neither economics nor politics are favorite design topics. Indeed there is an uneasy relationship between architects and designers and the topic of politics, in particular. Critics have consistently lamented the lack of politics in design. For example, architect Jeremy Till notes, "architecture exists in denial about the political implications of the processes and products of practice."[53] Kim Dovey also comments, "When confronted with arguments about damage to the public interest, architects are often genuinely offended and deny the importance of political, commercial or personal imperatives."[54]

For some, the apolitical tendency has increased in the past few decades, and Jose Gamez and Susan Rogers note, "Not only have American architectural efforts in the last fifty years been largely aesthetic exercises, but they also have flirted only briefly with the political—and then only in symbolic form."[55] Kenneth Frampton highlights the absence of politics from architecture, noting:

> At this juncture one can hardly emphasize enough how the substance of political process needs to be articulated within the field, both pedagogically and otherwise, not only in relation to the big politics of large-scale environmental policy, to be argued for agonistically in the public realm, but also in the small politics of psycho-social well-being and sustainability as these factors may be incorporated at a micro-scale into environmental design.[56]

Design practitioners embrace activism but still seem uneasy about politics. For example, activist architect Bryan Bell comments, "I prefer simply to think of it as the practice of architecture, just broader than before. Most of us doing this work do not need to decide whether we are in a movement or not."[57] Similarly, Natalie Jeremijenko explains that in her work on design interventions for neighborhood health concerns, her team finds it useful to avoid politics, "We have sidestepped the whole label of politics by framing the project in terms of health, detaching environmental issues from what people recognize as being big 'P' Politics."[58] Cameron Tonkinwise echoes this thought in terms of his school's action research, noting how the politics of design often tries to seem apolitical.[59]

With societal frustration over government gridlock, it's easy to understand why politics has a bad name, but it's important to keep in mind the fact that politics is wider than just government. Politics as *patterns of power* exist across all different domains of society, crossing boundaries from cultural to spatial, and from religious to democratic politics (see box on p. 28). Struggles to change existing patterns of power cross these boundaries as well. The current bad reputation of government politics shouldn't cloud our thinking about why it's important to understand patterns of power on many levels and to see their connection to economic growth as a centrally dominant pattern of power. This is not to say that designers need to advertise politics in their work, but rather that they might benefit from working consciously with patterns of power.

PATTERNS OF POWER

Power has meaning as the ability to make and influence decisions between alternative visions of the future.[60] Power arises in relationships, for example, among groups or individuals. Patterns of power describe the fact that institutions and systems of society often guide decisions to maintain things as they are, in stable patterns.

Stewart Brand and a number of other authors have documented a dominant pattern of power that prioritizes speed and short-term results while thwarting slow processes and long-term results.[61] In terms of cultural politics, power struggles to change this pattern concern efforts to preserve heritage, to nurture slow processes, and to find ways of representing long-term considerations more compellingly in the present.

Patterns of power are also enacted spatially, for example, in the spatial distribution of public services, amenities and undesirable facilities. Although the ideal is for everyone to have fair access to location-related advantages that result from public decisions (for example, housing, schools, hospitals, parks or transportation) an existing pattern finds that cities arguably favor the wealthy with more spatial and location-related advantages.[62] This situation has given rise to movements such as "environmental justice" and "right to the city."

Some of the broadest patterns of cultural power concern gender, religion, age, race and ethnicity, where one or more of these factors is seen to be the basis of privilege.[63] When such patterns of privilege are recognized as pervasive they are described as forms of discrimination. Struggles against discrimination may be most familiar in the form of mass movements for rights, such as civil rights or women's rights.

Racial and ethnic patterns of power often unfold spatially in terms of the control of certain places. Related power struggles to change these patterns of power have resulted in violence in many countries over the past few decades, including Africa, Eastern Europe and the former Soviet Union. However, ethnic struggles also persist in places such as the UK, for example, in the effort to preserve the Welsh language. Similarly, struggles persist in many countries concerning "native peoples" such as Native American Indians and Australian Aboriginals.

Professional tensions also arise for architects and designers concerned with politics. How should particular designers and design organizations, as well as other professionals, balance political commitment with professional responsibility? Tension arises partly because professions represent centers of power that typically legitimate existing power structures. In design terms, we might view professional design associations and licensing boards as dominant groups that uphold and attempt to extend the status quo. These groups have the power to decide who can practice design, they put resources into keeping the professions distinct and exclusive, and they attempt to extend the status quo in favor of those who already benefit from it, such as the existing cohort of licensed architects.

Other tensions arise related to the layered content in any given action. Rarely is the activist agenda of any design project "pure," as design unfolds across a range of criteria and contexts. Sociologists Tim Jordan and Paul Taylor explore this territory in terms of "hacktivism" or the use of computer hacking as a means of activism.[64] They describe the tensions between "the joy of the hack" (the pleasure involved in using a skill or craft), the hack's often commercial potential (whether intended or not), and the activist agenda.

While hacktivism is distinct in its commitment to reappropriate information technology for society's benefit, as with design activism, few can be full-time hacktivists. How the lines are drawn among elements of personal fulfillment through application of a skill, political agenda and material subsistence (i.e., through employment) is not always clear and distinct. It's also sometimes frustrating that any piece of design has conflicting content and usually doesn't reflect pure activism. A building, for example, has many different types of "content" such as aesthetic and functional content. Intentional activist or political elements may be incorporated into only one of these forms of content or it may cut across a project more broadly; it may even be in conflict with other aspects of the same project.

Architecture's starkly commercial context, in particular, has recently been contrasted with other service professions, such as medicine and law. These professions have much larger public service dimensions built into their practices through formalized pro bono mechanisms, internships, and other formal public service structures such as large public or teaching hospitals.[65] In 2005, the nonprofit group Public Architecture set up "The 1%," a campaign urging design professionals to adopt the goal of allocating 1 percent of their work hours to pro bono clients.[66]

Meanwhile, some larger product design firms, notably IDEO and Frog Design, have developed "social design" groups and have started giving away design tools such as IDEO's human-centered design toolkit, aimed particularly at developing world contexts.[67] IDEO recently developed Ideo.org to pursue social and public design.

Despite these potentially useful comparisons, Tom Fisher highlights some of the very real barriers to social or public interest work in the design profession. Against tremendous economic pressure, designers are without many of the features of professional practice that enable doctors or lawyers to temper commercial demands. Fisher cites insurance, organizational infrastructure, and project size and frequency as some of the reasons why architecture has failed to develop a public interest dimension that parallels law or medicine. He notes:

> Although the traditional practice of architecture parallels those of medicine and law, architects do not have the benefit of an insurance system that protects patients from paying the high fees of doctors, or the contingency-based fee agreements of lawyers who get paid only if they win the case. Nor do most architects have the ongoing relationships and repeat business that many doctors have with their patients or lawyers with their clients. In the area of public service, medicine and law have created an infrastructure within the profession that allows its practitioners to provide services to the needy, but architecture has no such infrastructure... . Medicine has spun off the field of public health, and law has created the public-defense system.[68]

The tensions outlined here constitute a backdrop for the explorations ahead.

EXAMPLES AND SOURCES

A final note concerns the audience for the book and the material from which the book is constructed. The social movement arena, like the design arena, is populated by practitioners as well as scholars. Accordingly, and drawing from across disciplines, the examples, arguments and background presented throughout this book are woven together from both practitioner experience and scholarly thinking, from both trade press and academic articles, from interviews with theorists and practicing design activists. However, the book's tone and style favor accessibility to practitioners over academic pedigree and rigor.

The development of the ideas in this book included reviewing hundreds of design projects in an effort to look for broader patterns. As a result the following chapters use some of these projects to illustrate concepts and ideas. These projects, worthy though they may be individually, are not highlighted as best or latest examples, but rather are included to represent types of projects. Together, the examples begin to show broader patterns of design activism and its connection to consumerism and growth.

Typically—fortunately—there exist more illustrative examples than can be included here, more than any one author can know about. Ideally the examples that are included will trigger in the reader's mind the reader's own knowledge of similar examples that extend the concept's or argument's validity.

In Chapter 2 we turn to the question of economic growth and consumerism, and how they shape and are shaped by design.

NOTES

1 See, for example, Dieter Rucht and Friedhelm Neidhardt, "Towards a 'Movement Society'? On the Possibilities of Institutionalizing Social Movements", *Social Movement Studies*, Vol. 1, no. 1 (2002), pp. 7–30; and Sarah A. Soule and Jennifer Earl, "A Movement Society Evaluated: Collective Protest in the US, 1960–1986", *Mobilization: An International Journal*, Vol. 10, no. 3 (2005), pp. 345–64.
2 Charles Tilly, "Contentious Repertoires in Great Britain, 1758–1843", in *Repertoires & Cycles of Collective Action*, ed. Mark Traugott (Durham, NC: Duke University Press, 1995).
3 Tim Jordan, *Activism! Direct Action, Hacktivism and the Future of Society* (London: Reaktion Books, 2002).
4 Jose L. S. Gamez and Susan Rogers, "An Architecture of Change", in *Expanding Architecture: Design as Activism*, ed. Bryan Bell and Katie Wakeford (New York: Metropolis Books, 2008).
5 Doug McAdam, "Tactical Innovation and Pace of Insurgency", *American Sociological Review*, vol. 48, no. 6 (December 1983), pp. 735–54.
6 Hashim Sarkis, "Alternative A", *Journal of Architectural Education*, Vol. 62, no. 4 (May 2009), pp. 93–4.
7 Lucy Kimbell, "The Turn to Service Design", in *Design and Creativity: Policy, Management and Practice*, ed. G. Julier and L. Moor (Oxford: Berg, 2009), pp. 157–73.
8 Research on design activism included a review of more than 1400 cases in Ann Thorpe, "Design and Political Resistance: Tactics, Power and Transformation", Design and Innovation Group (Milton Keynes: Open University, 2010).
9 See, for example, Businesses for Social Responsibility, "The New Frontier in Sustainability: The Business Opportunity in Tackling Sustainable Consumption" (2010); and World Economic Forum, "Redesigning Business Value: A Roadmap for Sustainable Consumption" (Geneva: World Economic Forum, 2010).
10 Charley Hudak, Jince Kuruvilla, and Vanessa Melendez, "Start an Education Revolution in Seven Steps", Fastcodesign.com, 19 August 2011. Available at http://www.fastcodesign.com/1664773/start-an-education-revolution-in-seven-steps (accessed 20 August 2011).
11 Public Interest Design Institute, *2011–2012 Series Handbook*.
12 Bryan Bell, email to the author, 23 September 2011.

13 "Spatial Agency: A Conversation with Tatjana Schneider on Architecture as a Quietly Revolutionary Practice" (Turin, Italy: Cluster, 2011). Available at http://www.cluster.eu/2011/04/21/spatial-agency-a-conversation-with-tatjana-schneider-on-architecture-as-a-quietly-revolutionary-practice/ (accessed 28 August 2011); see also Nishat Awan, Tatjana Schneider, and Jeremy Till, *Spatial Agency: Other Ways of Doing Architecture* (London: Routledge, 2011).

14 *Design for Social Impact Workshop* (Rockefeller Foundation and Continuum: 2008).

15 A good view of social change from the perspective of information and communication is found in Douglas Schuler, *Liberating Voices: A Pattern Language for Communication Revolution* (Cambridge, MA: MIT Press, 2008).

16 Robin Murray, Julie Caulier-Grice, and Geoff Mulgan, *The Open Book of Social Innovation* (London: The Young Foundation; NESTA, 2010) p. 3.

17 David J. Hess, *Alternative Pathways in Science and Industry: Activism, Innovation, and the Environment in an Era of Globalization* (Cambridge, MA: MIT Press, 2007), p. 4 (both quotes).

18 David J. Hess, "Product-Oriented Movements: Approximating Social Movement Studies and Science and Technology Studies", *Science, Technology, and Human Values*, Vol. 30, no. 4 (2005), pp. 515–35.

19 Michael F. Maniates and John M. Meyer (eds), *The Environmental Politics of Sacrifice* (Cambridge MA: MIT Press, 2010), pp. 1–2.

20 Tim Jordan and Paul A. Taylor, *Hacktivism and Cyberwars: Rebels with a Cause?* (London: Routledge, 2004), p. 46.

21 See, for example, Francesca Polletta and James M. Jasper, "Collective Identity and Social Movements", *Annual Review of Sociology*, Vol. 27 (2001), pp. 283–305; Rhys H. Williams, "The Cultural Contexts of Collective Action", in *The Blackwell Companion to Social Movements*, ed. David A. Snow, Sarah A. Soule, and Hanspeter Kriesi (Oxford: Blackwell Publishing, 2007); and James M. Jasper, *The Art of Moral Protest: Culture, Biography and Creativity in Social Movements* (Chicago, IL: The University of Chicago Press, 1997).

22 Edward W. Soja, *Seeking Spatial Justice* (Minneapolis: University of Minnesota Press, 2010), p. 120.

23 Lesley J. Wood and Kelly Moore, "Target Practice: Community Activism in a Global Era", in *From Act Up to the WTO: Urban Protest and Community Building in the Era of Globalization*, ed. Benjamin Shepard and Ronald Hayduk (London: Verso, 2002), pp. 22–3.

24 Benjamin Shepard and Ronald Hayduk (eds), *From Act Up to the WTO: Urban Protest and Community Building in the Era of Globalization* (London: Verso, 2002).

25 Jeff Speck, "Our Ailing Communities: Public-health Advocate Richard Jackson Argues That the Way We Build Cities and Neighborhoods is the Source of Many Chronic Diseases", *Metropolis* (October 2006); and Sam Lubell, "Researchers Explore Link Between Sprawl and Poor Health", *Architectural Record* (December 2003).

26 E. Audsley, M. Brander, J. Chatterton, D. Murphy-Bokern, C. Webster, and A. Williams, "How Low Can We Go? An Assessment of Greenhouse Gas Emissions from the UK Food System and the Scope for Reduction by 2050" (WWF-UK, 2009).

27 Jordan, *Activism!*

28 Tim Kasser, *The High Price of Materialism* (Cambridge, MA: MIT Press; 2002), p. 1.
29 Barrie Clement, "Britons Work Longer Hours than Anyone in Europe", *The Independent*, London (2006); and The Cabinet Office, *State of the Nation Report: Poverty, Worklessness and Welfare Dependency in the UK* (London: Cabinet Office, 2010).
30 John Hills, *An Anatomy of Economic Inequality in the UK: Report of the National Equality Panel*, ed. London School of Economics Centre for Analysis of Social Exclusion (London: Government Equities Department, 2010), p. 53.
31 Organic Trade Association, "Organic Food Facts", June 2010. Available at http://www.ota.com/organic/mt/food.html (accessed 11 March 2011).
32 USDA Economic Research Service Data Sets: Organic Production, Table 3: "Certified Organic and Total US Acreage, Selected Crops and Livestock, 1995–2008" (2010).
33 Ibid.
34 Ned Smith, "Strong Sales Perk Up Growth Forecast for Fair Trade Goods", *Business News Daily*, 9 March 2011.
35 David J. Hess, Alternative Pathways in Science and Industry: *Activism, Innovation, and the Environment in an Era of Globalization* (Cambridge, MA: MIT Press, 2007), p. 143.
36 A McGraw Hill Construction report suggests that in 2010 green building in the US accounted for 25 percent of all new construction as reported by Timothy Hurst in "Despite Recession, Green Building Soars in U.S", *Earth & Industry*, 15 November 2010. Available at http://earthandindustry.com/2010/11/despite-recession-u-s-green-building-sector-soars/ (accessed 3 July 2011).
37 "Economic Downturn Spells Hard Times For Hybrids". Available at http://www.green-energy-efficient-homes.com/hybrid-car-sales-statistics.html, 2010 (accessed 10 July 2011).
38 The Cooperative Bank, *Ten Years of Ethical Consumerism: 1999–2008* (Manchester: The Cooperative Bank, n.d.).
39 Jack Manno, "Consumption and Environment in a Global Economy", in *Confronting Consumption*, ed. Thomas Princen, Michael Maniates, and Ken Conca (Cambridge, MA: MIT Press, 2002), pp. 67–99.
40 Peter A. Victor, *Managing without Growth: Slower by Design, not Disaster* (Cheltenham, UK: Edward Elgar, 2008), pp. 54–5.
41 Steve Sorrell, "The Rebound Effect: An Assessment of the Evidence for Economy-wide Energy Savings from Improved Energy Efficiency (UK Energy Research Centre, 2007), p. v.
42 Australian Mobile Telecommunications Association, "Mobile Telecommuni–cations Industry Statement of Commitment to Mobile Phone Recycling" (2008).
43 Jonathan Porritt, *Capitalism as if the World Matters* (London: Earthscan, 2007), p. 295.
44 Pooran Desai, *One Planet Communities: A Real Life Guide to Sustainable Living* (Hoboken: John Wiley & Sons, 2009).
45 Sustainable Development Commission, *A Sustainable New Deal: A Stimulus Package for Economic, Social and Ecological Recovery* (London: UK Government, 2009), p. 36.
46 In 2008 the United Nations Environment Program (UNEP) launched its global green new deal program and green economy initiative as reported in UNEP's

Annual Report 2008. In that same year the UK's Green New Deal Group published *A Green New Deal* (London: New Economics Foundation, 2008).

47 Sustainable Development Commission, *A Sustainable New Deal*, p. 34.

48 Tim Jordan and Paul A. Taylor, *Hacktivism and Cyberwars: Rebels with a Cause?* (London: Routledge, 2004), pp. 47–8.

49 Van Jones, "Introducing The 'American Dream' Movement", *The Huffington Post*, 22, February 2011. Available at http://www.huffingtonpost.com/van-jones/american-dream-movement_b_826477.html (accessed 22 August 2011).

50 Erick Assadourian, "It's Time for Millennium Consumption Goals", Worldwatch Institute, Transforming Cultures Blog, 2008. Available at http://blogs.worldwatch.org/transformingcultures/mcgs/ (accessed 22 August 2011); and Mohan Munasinghe, "Millennium Consumption Goals (MCG): How the Rich can Make the Planet More Sustainable", The Island Online (31 January, 2011). Availableathttp://www.island.lk/index.php?page_cat=article-details&page=article-details&code_title=17248 (accessed 22 August 2011).

51 Figures for richest and poorest levels of consumption expenditure are for 1998, from M. Fischer-Kowalski, M. Swilling, E.U. von Weizsäcker, Y. Ren, Y. Moriguchi, W. Crane, F. Krausmann, N. Eisenmenger, S. Giljum, P. Hennicke, P. Romero Lankao, and A. Siriban Manalang, "Decoupling Natural Resource Use and Environmental Impacts from Economic Growth, A Report of the Working Group on Decoupling to the International Resource Panel" (United Nations Environment Program, 2011).

52 Tim Jackson, *Prosperity Without Growth? A Transition to a Sustainable Economy* (London: Sustainable Development Commission, 2009), p. 53. Jackson's comments derive from a discussion of the IPAT equation that measures environmental impact (I) as a product of population (P), affluence (A) and technology (T).

53 Jeremy Till, "The Negotiation of Hope", in *Architecture and Participation*, ed. Peter Blundell Jones, Doina Petrescu, and Jeremy Till (London: Spon Press, 2005), p. 34.

54 Kim Dovey, *Framing Places: Mediating Power in Built Form* (London: Routledge, 2008), p. 16.

55 Jose L. S. Gamez and Susan Rogers, "An Architecture of Change", in *Expanding Architecture*, ed. Bryan Bell and Katie Wakeford (New York: Metropolis Books, 2008), p. 21.

56 Kenneth Frampton, "The Work of Architecture in the Age of Commodification", *Harvard Design Magazine*, no. 23 (Fall 2005/Winter 2006), p. 23.

57 Bryan Bell, "Expanding Design Toward Greater Relevance", in *Expanding Architecture*, ed. Bryan Bell and Katie Wakeford (New York: Metropolis Books, 2008), p. 16.

58 Benjamin H. Bratton and Natalie Jeremijenko, "Suspicious Images, Latent Interfaces", in *Situated Technologies Pamphlets* 3, ed. Omar Khan, Trebor Scholz and Mark Shepard (New York: The Architecture League of New York, n.d.), p. 30.

59 Cameron Tonkinwise, "Politics Please, We're Social Designers", *Core77*, New York, 1 September 2010. Available at http://core77.com/blog/featured_items/politics_please_were_social_designers_by_cameron_tonkinwise__17284.asp (accessed 20 October 2010).

60 Kenneth E. Boulding, *Three Faces of Power* (London: Sage, 1989).

61 Stewart Brand, *The Clock of the Long Now: Time and Responsibility* (London: Weidenfeld & Nicolson, 1999).
62 Soja, *Seeking Spatial Justice*, pp. 48–52.
63 See, for example, Gary Craig, *Civil Society Associations and the Values of Social Justice* (Dunfermline: Carnegie UK Trust, 2009).
64 Jordan and Taylor, *Hacktivism and Cyberwars*.
65 See, for example, Casius Pealer, "Practice Matters: Nonprofit Work Experience, Beneficial for All but Far too Rare", *Architectural Record* (August 2007), pp. 63–4; and Sam Lubell, "Record News: New Program to Encourage More Pro Bono Work in Architecture", *Architectural Record* (May 2005) n.p.
66 David Sokol, "The 1% Helps Do-Gooders Do More Than 1%", *Architectural Record* (September 2007) n.p.
67 Alissa Walker, "Open-Source Innovation: IDEO's Human-Centered Design Toolkit", in *Case Studies in Sustainability from the Designers Accord* (Fast Company, 2009). Available at http://www.fastcompany.com/blog/alissa-walker/designerati/human-centered-design-toolkit-shares-information (accessed 20 May 2011).
68 Thomas Fisher, "Public Interest Architecture: A Needed and Inevitable Change", in *Expanding Architecture: Design as Activism*, ed. Bryan Bell and Katie Wakeford (New York: Metropolis Books, 2008), pp. 11–12.

Chapter 2

Design in the shadow of the rise and fall of growth

Architect Alejandro Zaero-Polo of Foreign Office Architects comments that his generation emerged in a social and political context of "cheapness."[1] His generation of pragmatist architects is accused of abandoning any social or political program. He suggests that in the previous generation political discussions in society were about equality—of gender, race or class, for example—and the heroes were figures such as Mahatma Gandhi or Martin Luther King Jr. By contrast in his time, heroes of cheapness have brought cheap clothes, cheap travel, cheap software, cheap food and cheap structures to the market.

This societal pursuit of cheapness expresses a central strategy of economic growth— cost-cutting—one of several that are constant and pervasive, affecting our everyday lives. Ultimately, growth relies on increasing profits, and there are several common ways to grow profits, including reducing costs, increasing sales, expanding markets, and attracting investment. Table 2.1 outlines some common practices that achieve economic growth.

These constant pressures for economic growth color our day-to-day experiences. Economic growth is the ocean in which we all swim – and increasingly sink. All the practices associated with economic growth are so pervasive and routine that we almost accept them as a sort of natural order. In fact, growth is carefully cultivated through political priorities, cultural narratives, and even technical mechanisms.

In this chapter we explore the ideas underlying economic growth, their weaknesses, and consider, in the process, how growth shapes, and is shaped by, architecture and design.

Table 2.1 Approaches to cheapness

Cost-cutting	Increasing sales and expansion
• Use lowest cost materials and labor (often third world labor). • Shift from full-time employees to contract workers. • Reduce employee wages (for example shift from qualified, medium-wage workers to unqualified, low-wage workers such as from nurses to health assistants, from police officers to community police volunteers; eliminate older, better paid workers in favor of new younger and less well-paid workers). • Reduce employee benefits (for example, offer jobs without health insurance or retirement plans). • Emphasize short-term gain over long-term investment (for example, reduce maintenance and upkeep, reduce employee training). • Meet lowest allowable standards. • Automate and make remote (have intercoms instead of reception areas, surveillance cameras instead of real observers). • Minimize diversity and emphasize uniformity, standardization, and mass production.	• Expand markets via new offerings (expand into new territories, create new products). • Increase productivity (each person and process does more per unit of time). • Expand markets via hooking people into a brand or using lock-ins with product systems. • Generate "experiences" that are either profitable, or that persuade people to buy. • Make experiences, places and services into commodities, for example, merchandising children's television characters, or commercializing formerly social activities such as dating (see Box "Commoditization", p.38). • Increase proportion of space where commercial activities or advertising can occur (for example, in schools, in public spaces). • Process materials and goods (like processed food) so that they contain the highest proportion of low-quality contents while retaining surface appeal.

COMMODITIZATION

We make more use of commercial services than before because economic growth favors converting as many goods and services to commodities as possible. For example, rather than "self-provisioning"—taking care of children or cooking our own meals—we use commercial childcare services and buy prepared meals. Expenditures on food that we eat away from home have risen from 34 percent in 1972 to almost 50 percent in 2006, and the proportion of this spending in fast-food restaurants has risen from 21 to 38 percent in that same period.[2]

Jack Manno makes the observation that in industrialized economies, market driven "selection pressure" heavily favors commodity goods and services. The result is survival of the fittest, where the "fittest" are those things that can best be turned into profit-generating commodities. Manno calls this fitness "high commodity potential," noting that in transportation, for example, personal automobiles have the highest commodity potential. These "solutions" then generate economic growth, justifying public investment to improve them and soaking up most R&D funding. Benefitting from so much public and private investment, they appear to work better. Manno concludes that finally the proliferation of goods and services that have the highest commodity potential "becomes the very meaning of development. Low commodity potential approaches appear backward."[3]

Similarly, Ezio Manzini suggests that designers focus on product-based well-being, which stems from the idea of labor-saving technology.[4] He argues that saving labor was then extended to a general notion of bundling knowledge and skills into devices, reducing user involvement. He calls these "disabling" solutions, but we might also view them as commoditized solutions.

HOW GROWTH CAME TO BE GOOD

Economic growth's "goodness" is broadly linked to the idea of progress made through the efficiency of the market. In addition, pressures for economic growth are also tied to employment, national comparisons and increases in living standards that emerged in the last few hundred years, accelerating through the first half of the 1900s.

Economic growth is measured in terms of financial transactions, usually at the national level. Measures of national economic growth (usually called Gross Domestic Product or GDP) track how much people, businesses and governments are spending.[5] In turn, growing levels of spending are assumed to mean higher incomes that should lead to "better choices, richer lives, and improved quality of life for us all."[6] Economic growth becomes a proxy for well-being.

Progress

Economist Peter Victor suggests that positive ideas about growth are modern, and stem from the notion of "progress."[7] He reports, "Until the Enlightenment, if people thought about it at all, most believed either that life was lived pretty much as it always had been, as in traditional societies, or that humanity was on a downward path, descending from a previous Golden Age or Garden of Eden."[8] Only within the last few hundred years have people begun to see improvements in living standards in their own lifetimes. The emergence of science also contributed to the idea that change could unfold sequentially toward an improved human condition.

Over time, society's focus moved more closely toward *economic* progress based on market transactions. Not only are market transactions easily quantifiable, but also economists argued that markets are the most efficient way of distributing resources. Markets enable us to convert the "value" or "utility" of a product or service into a monetary price, then money offers a convenient, universal way for people to express their preferences, needs and wants—through consumer purchases ("consumer demand").

There are two assumptions underlying the idea of efficient markets. The first is the assumption that prices contain all information about value, enabling consumers to make accurate choices. The second is the assumption that consumers act rationally and freely to maximize their well-being when making consumption choices (Figure 2.1).

Figure 2.1 Assumptions of market efficiency

Prices include all information about value

People consume rationally and freely to maximize well-being

Efficiency in markets is a central piece of the model justifying economic growth as a measure of well-being. This view combined with pressure from employment and national comparisons further accelerated the quest for growth.

Employment

In affluent countries 60 to 70 percent of growth comes directly from consumer demand.[9] But most people can only "consume" because they earn income from jobs. So as long as the population grows, more jobs are needed to ensure steady consumption. Continuous economic growth is now often seen as the only path to providing those new jobs. Economic growth became especially important in the 1960s as many countries committed themselves to full employment policies.

Employment continues to be the central argument for growth, during a time when "the shortage of employment has become more important than the shortage of products."[10] But full employment is elusive, partly because the incentive for growth also provides an incentive to increase productivity—to reduce the amount of labor or material that goes into each unit produced.[11]

National comparisons

When systems of national accounting (that later became GDP) emerged in 1953, they facilitated real-time comparison among national economies, leading to competition among countries over which ones were growing the most. Avner Offer comments that for this reason, during the 1950s and 1960s, growth in GDP became "a normative benchmark for economic and even social performance, the higher the better."[12] Richard Norgaard adds, "Growth wasn't that important until we were racing the Soviets," noting that a Soviet threat to "bury" the US economically turned growth into an endless race, rather than a useful path toward some meaningful end.[13]

Over time notions of progress have become tied largely to a societal narrative of economic growth through market transactions. In this narrative consuming more is better. Further, mainstream economic narratives also treat ecological well-being as a luxury to be pursued only when we can afford it.[14]

The growth narrative is also amplified by cut-throat competition among nations in globalized markets and constant increases in productivity and efficiency that often eliminate jobs. At the same time, notions of individual well-being have become tied largely to incomes gained through employment, making full employment a central goal that, in itself, relies on economic growth.

NATIONAL ACCOUNTING

The calculation of GDP seems to be done by a calculator that can only add up transactions, but never subtract costs. A design-related example comes from crime. Although crime is ostensibly negative, the financial activity generated by prison construction contributes to economic growth. Design also contributes to numerous crime-prevention devices installed by fearful householders, as well as the products generated in "design-against-crime" initiatives, and the sales of anti-crime devices also contribute to economic growth. The GDP does not have a way to subtract for all the negative effects of crime.

Another example comes from flooding. Floods result from inappropriate building in flood plains, changes in land use (for example, increased levels of paving), and changes to weather patterns (some related to climate change). But there is no way to subtract the ecological and social costs of floods from GDP. Reconstruction and replacement after floods might even be counted as economic growth. In many cases, the government has tried and failed to make building in flood plains less appealing to residents and businesses.[15] Apparently architects, landscape architects and urban designers have also been unsuccessful in helping people avoid flood plains and consider alternatives to solid paving.

As these examples suggest, both social damage (such as crime) and environmental damage (such as flooding) aren't well captured in measures of "growth." These make GDP a poor measure of a nation's true well-being. That's why there is currently a range of projects underway looking for alternative measures, or metrics, for tracking real well-being. Efforts such as the genuine progress indicator and other "national accounts of well-being" suggest that new measures "are needed because the economic indicators which governments currently rely on tell us little about the relative success or failure of countries in supporting a good life for their citizens."[16]

THE FALL OF ECONOMIC GROWTH

Although growth has brought progress over the past few hundred years, in terms of living standards such as infrastructure, health and comfort, its weaknesses are becoming more apparent. A number of researchers from different fields have demonstrated weaknesses in the assumptions underlying the idea of efficient markets.

These researchers argue that prices don't capture all relevant information and individuals don't act so freely in making decisions based on price information.

These failings, both of national accounting systems and of efficient markets, mean that in fact, economic growth is not a good proxy for well-being. At the same time, a great deal of research shows that beyond a very low threshold level, increased income does not produce commensurate increases in well-being. Levels of material consumption actually have little to do with real well-being. All of these points should make us reconsider the "goodness" of growth.

In the following sections we reconsider growth in more detail. Woven throughout this exploration are examples of how architecture and design shape and are shaped by the pressures for economic growth and consumerism. We first consider the issue of prices and then the idea of individuals acting freely and rationally in the marketplace.

Prices

It is now widely understood that the market and its financial or capital resources (for example, money, buildings or equipment) sit within a much wider economy made up of ecological and social resources. A key problem is that the market doesn't adequately account for the value of these resources or the damages to them that occur from pressures for economic growth. Prices don't reflect these values and damages.

False price The price of this fabric doesn't include all the social or environmental benefits and costs of its production.

This problem is vivid in many ecological design solutions. Consider the story of Designtex fabric developed by architect William McDonough and chemist Michael Braungart and popularized in their book, *Cradle to Cradle: Remaking the Way We Make Things*. The environmental design (ED) version of Designtex is much better than a typical fabric, for the environment, for workers, and for the community where the manufacturer is located, but for many would-be consumers the fabric is prohibitively expensive. That is because the benefit to the environment isn't counted in the price. Designtex avoids a range of environmental effects—for example, on toxic waste (potentially spills), water treatment, or managing chronic illness stemming from worker exposure to chemicals. If these savings could easily be put into a dollar figure, they would bring the price down compared to less ecological choices.

At the same time, there are many other growth pressures in favor of using harmful chemicals to grow and process fabric fibers. For example, chemicals used in plastics and fibers make those materials more versatile, which allows for an expansion of market offerings—and consequent growth. At the same time, testing chemicals is expensive, and huge profits would be sacrificed if the 1000 or so new chemicals introduced each year had to be proven safe. It's a "multi-billion-dollar hornets' nest," so regulators keep their distance; most chemicals aren't tested; rather they are presumed innocent until proven guilty—92 percent of chemicals in use are unregulated.[17] Although evidence

Not "safe" anymore Bisphenol A (BPA) withdrawn from water and baby bottles in 2009.

mounts against many chemicals that were formerly thought to be "safe" (an example is Bisphenol A (BPA) withdrawn from water and baby bottles in 2009), no major university chemistry department in the US specializes in "green chemistry" (ecologically safe chemical development).[18]

Similarly, human costs associated with cheap labor are also not included in prices. At the time of *Cradle to Cradle*'s publication, Designtex was made in Switzerland by well-protected and fairly compensated workers. To achieve higher growth rates, however, it is usually smarter to use poorly protected overseas workers who are much cheaper than workers in richer and better regulated countries. If we had an easy way to convert the human costs of exploited overseas workers into financial costs, we could put these costs into the final goods to show they are expensive in terms of human life.

The example of Designtex is one of many that illustrate the problem with our economic system which ignores environmental or social costs and benefits. These costs and benefits are difficult to price, which is part of the reason why they are ignored. Prices do not reflect information about all the areas of value related to goods and services, and this is one problem with the model used to justify economic growth.

Other values that are not included in current systems of economic accounting are highlighted in Table 2.2.

Price of labor

Research suggests that if we begin to include the social and environmental values left out of typical calculations, the highest paid individuals rarely "return" to the economy anywhere near the value that merits their pay, while conversely lower paid service jobs such as teaching, nursing or childcare return to society values that far outweigh their pay.

When the New Economics Foundation studied the medium- and long-term impacts of various jobs, they found "that low-paid work often produces considerably more value than high-paid work and, indeed, that high-paid work can even incur a negative value, by having a destructive effect on society and/or the environment." In examples from the study, minimum wage earners in childcare, cleaning and recycling return somewhere between £7 and £12 for each £1 they earn. By contrast the study finds that a banker who earns between £500,000 and £10 million destroys £7 of value for every £1 of value generated.[19]

Table 2.2 Some values and costs excluded from the market

Ecosystem services

- Regulating services: benefits from regular natural processes (e.g., water filtration, waste decomposition, climate regulation, crop pollination).
- Cycling services: foundational cycles for all other ecosystem services (e.g., nutrient cycling, photosynthesis, soil formation).
- Cultural services: human benefits gained from relations with ecosystems (e.g., enriching recreational, aesthetic and spiritual experiences).

source: Living Planet Report 2010: Biodiversity, biocapacity, and development

Social production

- Care provided by family or friends.
- Social relationships.
- Lost leisure time.
- Excessive commuting time.
- Family breakdown.
- Income inequality.
- Education and creative expression.
- Intergenerational ties.

source: The Genuine Progress Indicator Report, 2000 update.

This is yet another way of assessing how the market (in this case for labor) also incorrectly accounts for value and cost when social and environmental factors are excluded. Since these studies didn't attempt to estimate what architecture and design jobs might return in wider social and ecological value (or debt) for each dollar earned, we have an open question.

Meanwhile recent research suggests that actual "base pay" rates are low on most workers' list of factors that motivate them on the job, as long as workers are earning a reasonable wage and are relatively job secure. This finding results from the Mercer global engagement scale, developed with thousands of workers across the globe. Factors that motivate workers the most include respect, being valued, type of work, providing good service to customers, co-workers and work life balance. Bonuses come bottom of the list.[20]

Architecture and design practices illustrate another force that affects labor in the profit driven marketplace. As in other industries, there is increasing pressure on architecture and design industries to hire cheaper, overseas labor, while at the same time opening overseas offices to expand their businesses. But business expansion also puts pressure on small architectural firms to be absorbed by larger ones, on the argument of cutting business costs and improving efficiency. In this case the prices typically don't reflect the loss of locally diverse practices and the cost of increasing standardization of environments.

Price of standardization

Standardized, mass-produced and uniform materials (or plants, where landscapes are concerned), especially when made into the same basic shapes (standardized forms), are typically cheaper than many environmentally or socially preferred options. Lack of diversity itself carries a social cost. Although designers and consumers alike may yearn for more diverse formal and material exploration, rarely does financial cost allow for it. Where cheap materials equate to short-term products, there are additional costs associated with the solid waste they generate, the time they waste, the stress or irritation they cause, and so on.

Standardized housing forms Cheap suburban sprawl. Photo Copyright 2007-2011 by Mark Zoetrope (MarkZoetrope.com), all rights reserved.

Cheap landscapes The road to big box retail. Photo Will Weaver, 2010.

Cheap goods are increasingly sold through standard "big box" or warehouse outlets in which the architecture typically has no connection to the social or environmental context of the location. Within these stores, customers are encouraged to buy "supersized" portions and multi-buy offers that in themselves escalate consumption.

In addition, the need for economic growth and reducing costs means that most entities contracting for construction or design work opt for the lowest financial bid rather than the best-value bid—where values include social and environmental consideration. Lowest bid projects then make use of many of the cheapest possible materials and standardized techniques, leading to a downward spiral in the quality of the built and manufactured environment.

Landscape effects: contracting out public space

If we think further about the pursuit of cheapness, we find other design-related areas where prices are low precisely because they don't capture social and environmental values. The pressure toward privatizing public services and public spaces illustrates the problem. There has been a strong trend toward cities contracting out the management of public spaces, along with other public services such as waste management.[21] Private companies compete to provide the lowest possible cost for services, while at the same time maximizing their own profit out of the deal. In these scenarios, civic values that a city may once have sought through design solutions are typically lost to the priority of maximizing profits in private "service" companies.

The trend toward private suburban communities is another example of the lure of low prices. Peter Cannavò notes that in a number of major cities (Las Vegas, Chicago, Dallas) new suburbs are required to form private communities and pay for their own services. The trend is increasing. In 1970 about 2 million Americans lived in private communities, but by 2005 that number had risen to 54 million.[22] These private entities manage neighborhoods as property, often severely limiting the variety of structures as well as the acceptable use of property. The idea is to cling to a suburban market ideal which typically necessitates higher consumption simply in its norms of big houses, big cars and conventional resource-intensive landscaping.

Cheap landscapes Optimized only for car travel.

Engineered solutions Use lowest cost approach to meet regulations rather than serve people.

Privatization Suburbs become commodities rather than communities. Photo Patrick Huber.

Prices also send the wrong signals through the mechanism of impact fees. Emily Talen describes how cities such as Phoenix and Chicago implement new parks and other public spaces not according to where they are needed, but rather, according to where developers have paid impact fees.[23] In the case of Phoenix this means that parks are planned for low-density, peripheral locations rather than strategic locations that might synergistically enrich the public landscape.

This effect is similar to "privately owned public spaces" funded through impact fees, which again are located where developers who provide the fees deem suitable, rather than where these spaces might best contribute to the broader public landscape. Whoever has money to pay impact fees determines location, whether or not the location adds wider value. The fee-based locations and contexts then dictate the benefit that any landscape or architectural design can bring to the site.

In general we can see how the relative cheapness of large-scale projects, mass production and privatization govern a number of aspects of architecture and design, typically at the cost of local scale and diversity.

Not all information can be expressed as "price"

Estimating monetary prices for social and environmental values is difficult and possibly inappropriate in many cases. For example, economist Peter Victor voices skepticism that we have the technical competence to make these monetary estimates, even putting aside ethical questions.[24] We have to ask whether monetary values are actually appropriate for representing the value of nature and human health, or social bonds.

Consider these examples. We see oily birds washing up on the beach after an oil spill. Imagine that the oil spill forces us to move to find work, or one of our children experiences health problems associated with the event. Would it ever be appropriate to put a monetary value on nature, family ties, friendship, or the compassion or anger that these examples might generate?

A number of methods exist for attempting to estimate these values in financial terms, such as asking people what they would pay to avoid certain outcomes or to access certain landscapes. Other studies might observe what people do (such as travel more frequently to see family and friends left behind) to compensate for loss, and estimate that the cost of travel represents the cost of a compromised relationship. The range of practical and ethical weaknesses of these methods ultimately limits their real applicability.[25]

Family ties Should we put prices on relationships or on nature?

The problem of excluding natural and social "resources" from market transactions, combined with the problem that some of these values are impossible to correctly "price", means that the "market" fails. Prices don't and may never be able to include necessary information about investment and purchase decisions. But what about the other assumption of efficient markets—the rational, free individual?

Limitations on rational, free, individual choice

It turns out that the assumption that individuals act rationally (to maximize their well-being over time) and make free choices in the market is also not correct. There are several areas where this assumption falls down, including the convenience and inertia of habit, the human weakness for temptation, and the effects of peer pressure and social networks. It is worth examining these areas in more detail.

At the start, we notice that the focus on "individuals" carries through to the individualization of consumption.[26] In design terms, increasing sales also means focusing on individual solutions rather than seriously examining how groups might share structures and objects. For example, we sell more power

Power tools Owned individually but rarely used.

Individual cars Rarely used to capacity.

tools, cars and washing machines when each individual or household owns their own private goods. Research shows, however, that during its lifetime the average domestic power tool is used for a total of only about 10 minutes.[27] Similarly, four- and five-seat automobiles are hardly ever used to capacity; most carry one passenger to work, sit parked all day, and return home with one passenger. Yet priorities of increasing sales filter into design research and design innovation that tends to concentrate on individualization and solutions for the individual or household.

Time and commitment

Avner Offer presents a detailed argument concerning how time is a very important aspect of "maximizing well being."[28] He outlines how we trade off choices we make now against their future impacts; for example, the trade-off between junk food now and a slimmer figure later. Similar trade-offs between immediate rewards now and bigger rewards in the future compromise our decisions about education, retirement, exercise, marriage and so on.

Offer's compelling analysis suggests two important ways in which these trade-offs have become problematic under the conditions of affluence found in most industrialized countries. First, the number, allure and frequency of immediate rewards have all increased. In design terms, Otto von Busch reports that the pace of fashion design is escalating so much that major retail brands such as H&M update their collections ever frequently, sometimes monthly.

Offer describes these immediate rewards as "psychic" rewards that stem from sensual stimulation, particularly novel stimulation such as a new phone, new blouse or new film (Figure 2.2). Von Busch describes this more viscerally:

> When confronted with new fashion we can find ourselves, almost unconsciously and often unwillingly, electrified by the brilliance of its very newness. This burst of intensity is how a new fashion "hits" us, how we are temporarily "blinded" by its luminosity, and how "immune" to it most of us are after the last epidemic craze has passed.[29]

At the same time, our ability to resist the temptation of immediate psychic rewards and to instead prudently study, save, or exercise (for example) has steadily deteriorated. Offer describes how our systems for making commitments to our own future well-being have eroded, while new systems (that account for the plethora of new consumerist temptations) have not yet evolved for maintaining commitments to future well-being.

Historically our methods of committing to the future involved both our own internal will-power (self-control or self-discipline), as well as social and

Figure 2.2 Sensual stimulation

Stimulation & novelty: body

Physically easy

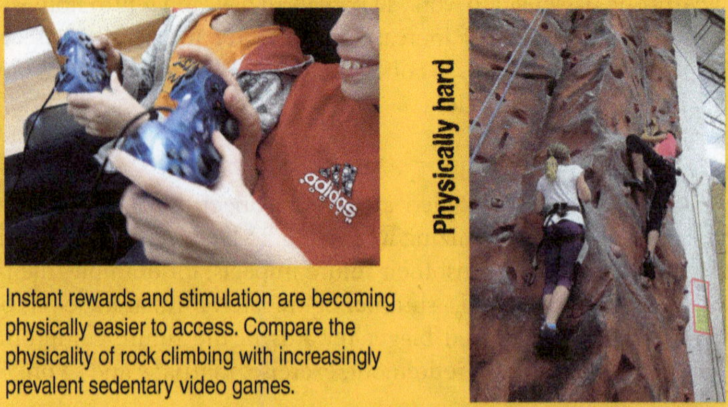

Physically hard

Instant rewards and stimulation are becoming physically easier to access. Compare the physicality of rock climbing with increasingly prevalent sedentary video games.

Stimulation & novelty: mind

Mentally easy

Mentally hard

courtesy Toulane University Public Relations

Instant rewards and stimulation are becoming mentally easier to access. Compare the prevalence and passivity of watching a screen to the challenge of learning to play a musical instrument or learning a foreign language.

community constraints related to family structure, social traditions, religion or other "social contracts" such as mortgages and deadlines. Recent design research and analysis suggests that physical and built infrastructure also plays an important role in our ability to commit to the future. For example, regarding physical activity, New York City's "Active Design Guidelines" suggest:

> Physical activity, once part of our normal lives, has been designed out of our daily routines. Sedentary jobs have taken the place of manual labor, cars have replaced walking or biking, elevators and escalators have supplanted stair climbing, and televisions, computers and video games have

Stimulation and novelty The brilliance of its very newness. Photo Josef Kubicek.

displaced active leisure pursuits, especially among children. The design of our buildings, streets, neighborhoods, and cities often makes physical activity unnatural and difficult to achieve.[30]

As our affluent society is faced with increasingly compelling immediate rewards easily accessible through cheap purchases, and reinforced by the infrastructure around us, our ability to maximize our well-being *across time* is failing.

One of Offer's key observations is that our strategies for committing to the future, whether internal or community based, are costly and difficult to cultivate. They take time to build up and often involve a process of social learning and education. The strategies require regular training to maintain. Alongside that, Offer outlines the problem of the diminishing returns of novelty. He suggests that there is a relationship between "stimulation" and "satisfaction" where more stimulation leads to more satisfaction, creating a "pleasure zone" but only up to a point. After that point, satisfaction is replaced by habituation—we become too used to the stimulation for it to yield much satisfaction.[31]

This idea is shown in Figure 2.3. As von Busch suggests, we become "immune." Further, research finds that we may be seeking this instant gratification, partly to ward off feelings of personal inadequacy.[32]

When we consider consumer culture we can see how people often attempt to increase satisfaction through material goods, food, or television watching, but as they reach habituation they move on to new levels of indulgence to regain satisfaction from stimulation. They acquire more and different material goods, they overdose on different kinds of unhealthy food, or they watch internet videos in addition to regular television. The ready availability of novel stimulation is overwhelming in consumer culture. The only way to maintain the

Figure 2.3 Diminishing returns of novelty and stimulation

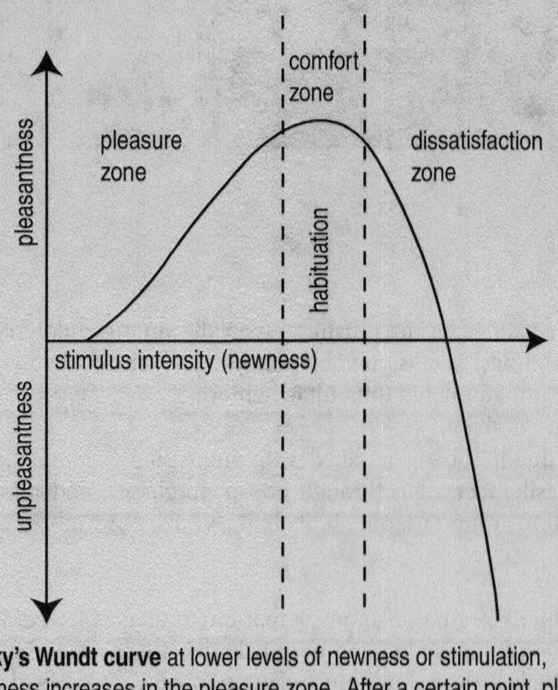

Scitovsky's Wundt curve at lower levels of newness or stimulation, pleasantness increases in the pleasure zone. After a certain point, pleasure levels off in a comfort zone, when we become habituated to the stimulation. After habituation, increasing amounts of stimulation are neutral or decrease satisfaction. For example, we can't eat more after we're full, in warming up from the cold we can become too hot if heat persists.

Source: Avner Offer, *The Challenge of Affluence*, p. 56.

satisfaction, however, is to keep escalating stimulation and moving on to new stimulations. This escalation fits well with profit motives and generates economic growth. The whole process is no doubt helped along by massive doses of advertising, which Offer also discusses.

In design terms, the need for constant new stimulation is apparent in how designers focus on short-term appeal at the cost of long-term function or performance. Industrial design and even architecture and landscape architecture are prone to preferencing surface features and other "point-of-sale" features. An example is the use of cheap, shiny plastics that start out looking good, but scratch and wear easily—that age poorly in both aesthetic and functional terms. Architects commonly discuss the problem of trying to package office exteriors for buildings that contain the cheapest possible standardized interiors.[33] It's almost like processed food. We increase the proportion of cheap or low-quality ingredients while offering surface, or short-term appeal. For example, we put a thin veneer of wood over particle board, or a photograph of wood onto plastic.

In addition, the focus on point-of-sale means that architectural design notoriously focuses on the building's initial completion and its presentation in photographs "out of time," with little attention to long-term performance, maintenance or adaptation. Indeed, architects very rarely go back to assess actual building performance. Ian Cooper suggests that there has been in architecture a 40-year neglect of evaluation, known in the field as "post-occupancy evaluation," of how buildings actually perform.[34] Meanwhile, real estate appraising assigns value based on square footage, meaning that dumb, toxic, inefficient, poorly constructed square footage is seen as worth the same as smart, healthy, wisely constructed square footage. Instead of a system of commitment to long-term building performance, we have instead a focus on the new and novel.

The design of the built environment also helps keep people focused on short-term stimulation. There is tremendous pressure to create and control environments that help maximize consumer spending. These environments often exclude or attempt to minimize any distracting or challenging aspects of broader public life. For example, designers are finding new ways to prevent people from sitting or lying down, often by making very narrow benches, or spiking ledges. In addition, there is pressure to increase sales by exploiting public places for private gain. For example, a café may use sidewalk space and limit the use of that public space to paying customers. Office buildings that provide "privately owned" public spaces as part of their permitting agreements are frequently tempted into increasing income by commercializing these public spaces.[35] And increasingly structures, objects, and spaces of every kind are being viewed as surfaces for advertising.

Unsittable bench.

The temptation of constant stimulation helped along by architecture and design is overwhelming many of us. One indication is the finding that as much as 15 percent of the population may fit the clinical definition of "compulsive shopper."[36] People tend to fall into this pattern as a way to deal with anxiety, stress or lack of self-esteem.[37]

Another indicator that instant rewards are overtaking long-term commitment may be found in patterns of household saving and spending over the past few decades. Although figures of debt and spending are somewhat complicated to interpret, and questions remain about the "right" level of savings, over time in industrialized societies we have generally seen household savings go down while unsecured debt (e.g., credit card debt) has gone up. Researchers at the Federal Reserve Bank found that by 1990, unsecured consumer debt had increased five-fold in just three decades. In the same period, personal bankruptcy filings increased by a factor of five as well.[38]

As Tim Jackson notes, an infrastructure for increasing credit (particularly through credit cards) has been a central means of expanding consumerism—and thus increasing economic growth—even in times when consumers don't actually have money to spend. He notes, "consumer debt served as a deliberate mechanism for freeing personal spending from wage income and allowing for consumption to drive the dynamics of growth."[39]

Strikingly, Offer argues that there is another option: "to scale back stimulation deliberately, and maintain it permanently at the lower level of increasing returns. At that level, every additional increment of stimulation provides increasing satisfaction." He quotes George Ainslie saying, "In conditions of plenty, the problem is not to maximize the flow of rewards, but to keep them under control, not to maximize consumption but to pace it. Scarcity itself becomes scarce."[40]

Yet the idea that we should pace consumption for better long-term results is often painted as an intolerable sacrifice of our current prosperity. In our current societal narrative, slowing down on consumption is seen only as "giving up" something, rather than in terms of what is gained over time. Countering this narrative, John Meyer and Michael Maniates argue compellingly: "The assumption that citizens are unwilling to forgo current prosperity for future gain rests on the rather implausible belief that most of us are wholly content with our lives and the society within which we live now."[41] Their volume of essays dissects the many ways in which current sacrifices are hidden, such as sacrifice of the environment, sacrifice of our health to chemical contamination and so forth, often in favor of the "goodness" of economic growth.

These authors suggest that sacrifice isn't "denying yourself"; rather, sacrifice is making a choice between two things that each offer you some value or reward. The result of a sacrifice isn't self-denial or loss; rather, it is the flow of one set of values and rewards in place of the other. We make these trading-off choices all the time, forgoing a new car in order to pay for education, or working stints of long hours in the anticipation of career advancement. This echoes Offer's point that pacing rewards evens out an individual's *own well-being* across time.

Offer provides evidence that commitment strategies for the future are failing, not least because they are often portrayed as intolerable sacrifices, and this is a key refutation that consumers act rationally in their own best interests.

Social networks and peer influence

Another challenge to the idea of an individual consumer acting freely arises from recent research on social networks and how they influence decisions that people make. Researchers Jonathan Rowson, Steve Broome and Alasdair Jones comment, "Subconsciously or otherwise, we end up aping what our friends do and this mimicry is in turn passed on to others in the chain, influencing people several degrees of separation removed from ourselves."[42] The authors characterize this as "contagion of behaviors" and note that undesirable behaviors (such as smoking) can be just as contagious as desirable behaviors (such as exercise).

In light of this social network effect, not to mention peer pressure, it is hard to conceive of consumers as "rational individuals" and it seems clear that market choices are not entirely free. Instead, choices are colored by what other people do, by how well we can resist temptation, and by society's social and physical infrastructure that facilitates habits, such as driving, eating fast food or exercising (Figure 2.4).

A related consideration is the common economic assumption that not only is the individual consumer rational, but she is also insatiable. That is to say, in pursuit of maximizing "utility" an individual will always consume more if she can.[43] This is somewhat related to Offer's discussion of the relationship between stimulation and satisfaction in the absence of self-command. Increasing consumption in this view improves satisfaction, but only up to a point, and maintaining satisfaction requires moving on to new areas of stimulation and novelty. This constant escalation does suggest insatiability.

Figure 2.4 Social networks and contagious behavior

If you know someone who smokes, eats a lot of fast food, or cycles (for example on London's rental bikes), you are more likely to do it too.

Yet research finds that increasing financial and material wealth only improves well-being at relatively low levels of income per person. Beyond a basic level, people's subjective well-being is only weakly linked to their material circumstances.[44] We want constant novelty and stimulation, but when gained through private accumulation it doesn't actually contribute to well-being. Rather, it begins to be a burden. Parallel research shows that people's notion of their own well-being is relative to those around them. In other words, we don't need much material wealth to be happy, but inequalities in wealth trigger social competition.

Victor comments, "what matters to people is their relative consumption, not their absolute consumption." Concern for relative income and consumption accounts for a problem that he identifies: "People think that a higher income will make them happier, but overlook the rising aspirations that will accompany such an increase." As people experience rises in income, they begin to compare themselves with a new, higher income group, which then requires a new round of positional consumption. Victor is describing here the notion of "positional consumption," the idea that we consume to gain and maintain particular social positions.[45] Victor argues that in the face of positional consumption, high-quality public goods and public spaces are a central component of "development" (as opposed to just "growth") in affluent countries where there are no shortages of goods and "positional consumption" is the dominant form of consumption.

Positional consumption arguably occurs all across society. Companies want to build the tallest office tower, and cities want the most spectacular architectural trophy. Victor suggests that a growing proportion of goods in modern economies are "positional goods." Escalating competition for social position takes up more of our incomes while providing little in well-being.

The problem of comparison is one thing that makes the current economic system's inequality and extreme concentrations of wealth so troubling. Economic growth favors the rich, and financial and material wealth has been steadily concentrating among the top richest percentage of the world's population. For example, the Institute for Public Policy Research reports that in the UK:

> The wages of people in higher-level occupations have risen faster than the wages of people in lower-level occupations, since the early 1980s. However, the top 10 per cent of earners is where pay has really shot up over the last three decades. Between 1975 and 2008, the top 10 per cent increased their share of the UK's total wage bill from 22 to 32 per cent. Within the top decile, the top 1 per cent of earners did particularly well, more than

doubling their share of the wage bill from 5 per cent in 1975 to 11 per cent in 2008.[46]

In the US things aren't any better. Economist Paul Krugman notes that for most people, salaries have increased by only about 10 percent over the past 30 years. By contrast, for the wealthiest 20 percent of families, income gains have steadily increased, especially for the top 5 percent of the wealthiest families. The Congressional Budget Office found that between 1979 and 1997, the incomes of the top 1 percent of families rose 157 percent. As Krugman concludes, "the reality of increasing inequality is not in doubt."[47]

The consequences of "keeping up" appear in architecture and design terms as well, resulting in an emphasis on "buying new" over repairing and maintaining existing buildings, landscapes and objects. For example, many modern appliances cannot be opened or repaired by their owners, and most are not "upgradable." To keep up with the newest benefits, consumers must buy new products and structures rather than upgrade what they have. Many of us will recognize this in its extreme form with electronic products such as computers and phones. Yet research also suggests that many buildings are outpaced by the changing contexts around them and are demolished long before their functional life has ended.[48]

Keeping up Computers and other electronic products are outdated quickly.

As mentioned above, cities also engage in a sort of positional consumption in terms of attracting economic growth. One approach is to prioritize public elements, such as historic town squares, or new spectacular architectural features, as assets for attracting new investment—new tax-paying companies, for example—rather than as serviceable public features for the community. In a sense these facilities should be seen and used by upscale consumers.[49] In this jockeying for position, cities are pressured to develop in ways that suit prospective companies and organizations which claim to be able to bring economic growth to a city. Companies already resident in the city, by contrast, threaten to leave unless they win concessions from a city, such as new sports stadiums, new roads, tax breaks or related elements (see Figure 2.5, p. 64). All of this maneuvering shapes the type and location of design projects throughout the built environment, often eclipsing the broader potential of good design.

The concept of a rational, utility-focused consumer also overlooks the notion, pioneered by Mary Douglas, that goods play a role in our social language. We use goods to operate daily life both socially and functionally.[50] We use our goods to express our identities in an otherwise large and potentially anonymous society. If goods gain us "status" they also help us belong, even avoid shame. One example of this is illustrated by research on children, families and consumption by Allison Pugh.[51] Even parents who could scarcely afford it often bought children consumer goods as a way of helping them fit into social groups and avoid teasing. In this sense social and emotional concerns, rather than rational utility concerns, often govern our purchase decisions.

In light of the social language of goods, we can return to the issue of standardization mentioned earlier. As standard commercial forms and programs in design become "norms" they allow us to both belong, by owning something that's the norm, but also distinguish ourselves through different "brands" of this norm. In this sense norms and standards in themselves serve social purposes, but become problematic when they are governed by profits. Important elements of social meaning and purpose are framed through the advertising, marketing and publicity of profit-maximizing entities.

Novelty (stimulation-as-reward) and anxiety (social striving for position or belonging through goods) are two key factors that drive consumerism. These factors suggest that individual consumers are not making "free choices" that maximize utility in a rational way. This finding, combined with the failures of pricing, suggests that consumerism and economic growth define a system that isn't working.

Building on this point and drawing on the work of Amartya Sen, Tim Jackson points out the social trap, in which, at the individual level it makes sense to

Figure 2.5 Threatening to leave

Sports companies that own professional teams threaten to leave unless old stadiums are replaced, a story played out in Seattle when the Kingdome (top) was demolished in 2000 to make way for baseball's Safeco Field and football's Qwest Field (bottom) located on and near the site of the old Kingdome. As of 2010 King County still owes more than $80 million on the demolished stadium.

Old stadium

Kingdome implosion. Photo Ian Edelstein, courtesy of the Seattle Municipal Archives.

Two new stadiums

seek social positions and avoid shame through the language of goods, but at the societal level it leads only to "fragmentation and anomie." He continues:

> Most worrying of all is that there is no escape from this social trap within the existing paradigm. While social progress depends on the self-reinforcing cycle of novelty and anxiety, the problem can only get worse. Material throughput will inevitably grow. And the prospects for flourishing within ecological limits evaporate.[52]

This social trap arises not from the current economic recession but rather from the economic model that perpetuates materialism.

Before moving on it's worth asking, if consumerism and growth aren't delivering real well-being, what can? The New Economics Foundation (NEF) has examined this question on behalf of the UK government. Reviewing the research of more than 400 scientists worldwide, the NEF found five evidence-based approaches to well-being. These five approaches include social connection, physical activity, reflection and awareness, continuous learning, and cooperation and giving. These are explained further in the box on p. 66.

Well-being Cooperation, connection and physical activity are a few of the essentials for well-being.

WHERE DOES WELL-BEING COME FROM?

NEF's five ways to well-being.

Connect

Social relationships are critical to our well-being. Survey research has found that well-being is increased by life goals associated with family, friends, social and political life, and decreased by goals associated with career success and material gain.

Be active

Exercise has been shown to increase mood and has been used successfully to lower rates of depression and anxiety. Being active also develops the motor skills of children and protects against cognitive decline in the elderly.

Take notice

In the US, research has shown that practicing awareness of sensations, thoughts and feelings can improve both the knowledge we have about ourselves and our well-being for several years. But the twenty-first century's never-ending flow of messages from companies advertising products and services leaves little opportunity to savor or reflect on our experiences.

Keep learning

Learning encourages social interaction and increases self-esteem and feelings of competency. Behavior directed by personal goals to achieve something new has been shown to increase reported life satisfaction.

Give

Studies in neuroscience have shown that cooperative behavior activates reward areas of the brain, suggesting we are hard wired to enjoy helping one another. Individuals actively engaged in their communities report higher well-being, and their help and gestures have knock-on effects for others. But it is not simply about a one-way transaction of giving. Research by the NEF shows that building reciprocity and mutual exchange – through giving and receiving – is the simplest and most fundamental way of building trust between people and creating positive social relationships and resilient communities."[53]

Source: Adapted from Juliet Michaelson, Saamah Abdallah, Nicola Steuer, Sam Thompson and Nic Marks, "National Accounts of Well-being: Bringing Real Wealth onto the Balance Sheet" (New Economics Foundation, London, 2009), p. 48.

CONCLUSION

This chapter's review highlighted four key reasons why consumerism and economic growth thwart real human well-being:

1 Many important values don't have prices.
2 Consumer society makes privately gained, instant rewards ever easier for individuals to access through cheap purchases.
3 The pace of instant rewards is speeding up, but commitment strategies that worked to pace the flow of rewards are being outmoded; updated commitment strategies aren't yet in place.
4 To a certain extent, private purchases form an element of our social language, turning some important aspects of societal meaning and purpose over to profit-seeking entities.

Several main ideas emerge from this picture of consumerism and growth. First, although consuming less is definitely important, it appears that not just the amount we consume is important; the way we consume and the infrastructure around it is also important. Our societal narratives about consumption need to change.

Peter Victor's modeling of a steady state economy showed that to move beyond endless cycles of positional consumption, affluent countries need to concentrate on providing a flourishing array of public or community resources, such as public spaces, shared goods and green spaces. Traditional public places such as libraries and schools need to be supplemented by innovative new forms of shared and public places. In high enough density, these public resources serve to lower the pressure on private consumption as the primary, and in some cases only, means of novelty, reward and position.

Second, it seems clear that individuals are unlikely, on their own, to be successful in making significant changes. The current societal narrative, hung up on individualization—the individual's unwillingness to change or sacrifice— traps us in a no-win situation. Change only comes when we either suffer a large environmental, even social, catastrophe or when a dictatorial government steps in to force change. By contrast, the narrative of social movements suggests something different. Rather than catastrophe or dictatorship, we have the possibility of collective citizen action across large-scale movements. Evidence suggests that in this context people view sacrifice differently, and have an easier time seeing deeper, longer term values that a movement pursues.[54]

Third, this chapter has highlighted what many of us already know, namely that architecture and design are bound up in systems of economic growth and consumerism. Design decisions, like many others, often exclude any real consideration of social and environmental value because many of these values are hard to price. Design contributes to individualization, commoditization, and the increasing pace of immediate rewards. Architecture and design are woven into a social language of position and status. Although we can look at these forces as structural barriers that prevent design from delivering any real change, these forces may also be read as a map of where to target collective action, a map for agency.

In Chapter 3 we examine this map for agency more closely, looking at how design activism confronts the four issues summarized above.

NOTES

1 Alejandro Zaero-Polo, "The Politics of the Envelope". Lecture presented at the Politics of Design Conference of the Manchester Architecture Research Centre, Manchester, 24 June 2010.
2 Sarah A. Rydell, Lisa J. Harnack, J. Michael Oakes, Mary Story, Robert W. Jeffery and Simone A. French, "Why Eat at Fast-food Restaurants: Reported Reasons Among Frequent Consumers", *Journal of the American Dietetic Association*, Vol. 108, no. 12 (2008).
3 Jack Manno, "Consumption and Environment in a Global Economy", in *Confronting Consumption*, ed. Thomas Princen, Michael Maniates and Ken Conca (Cambridge, MA: MIT Press, 2002), p. 72.
4 Ezio Manzini, *Design, Ethics and Sustainability: Guidelines for a Transition Phase* (Milan: Politecnico di Milano, 2006).
5 Andrew Simms, Victoria Johnson and Peter Chowla, *Growth Isn't Possible: Why We Need a New Economic Direction* (London: New Economics Foundation and Schumacher College, 2010), p. 6.
6 Tim Jackson, *Prosperity without Growth? A Transition To a Sustainable Economy* (Sustainable Development Commission, 2009), p. 8.
7 Peter A. Victor, *Managing Without Growth: Slower by Design, not Disaster* (Cheltenham, UK: Edward Elgar, 2008).
8 Ibid., p. 5.
9 OECD, *National Accounts of OECD Countries 2009*, Volume I, Main Aggregates, "Household Consumption". OECD Publishing, OECD Library. Available at http://dx.doi.org/10.1787/na_vol_1-2009-en-fr (accessed 26 August 2011).
10 Victor, *Managing without Growth*, pp. 12–13.
11 Ibid., p. 156.
12 Avner Offer, *The Challenge of Affluence: Self-control and Well-being in the US and Britain since 1950* (Oxford: Oxford University Press, 2006), p. 15.
13 Richard Norgaard is quoted in Nathanael Johnson, "Toward a Common Wealth", *California Magazine* (Winter 2009).
14 Juliet Schor, "Time for a Change: The Role of Working Hours in the Transition to Sustainability". Keynote speech at RESOLVE Conference of Surrey University, "Living Sustainably: Values, Policies and Practices", London, 15 June 2011.

15 Environment, Food and Rural Affairs, Seventh Report section *The Agency's Role in the Planning System*. Available at http://www.publications.parliament.uk/pa/cm200506/cmselect/cmenvfru/780/78006.htm#a22 (accessed 12 December 2010).
16 Juliet Michaelson, Saamah Abdallah, Micola Steuer, Sam Thompson and Nic Marks, *National Accounts of Well-being: Bringing Real Wealth onto the Balance Sheet* (London: New Economics Foundation, 2009), p. 2.
17 Marilyn Berlin Snell, "Mr. Clean: Michael Wilson Wants the Chemical Industry to Make Products Safe Before they Get to the Market", *California Magazine* (September/October, 2008).
18 David J. Hess, *Alternative Pathways in Science and Industry: Activism, Innovation, and the Environment in an Era of Globalization* (Cambridge, MA: MIT Press, 2007), p. 65.
19 The direct quote and statistic come from Anna Coote, Jane Franklin and Andrew Simms, "21 Hours" (London: New Economics Foundation, 2010), p. 14.
20 Cary L. Cooper and Stephen Wood, "Happiness at Work: Why it Counts", *Guardian*, London (15 July 2011). Available at http://www.guardian.co.uk/money/2011/jul/15/happiness-work-why-counts.
21 Claudio de Magalhães, "Public Space and the Contracting-out of Publicness: A Framework for Analysis", *Journal of Urban Design*, Vol. 15, no. 4 (2010), pp. 559–74.
22 Peter Cannavò, "Civic Virtue and Sacrifice in a Suburban Nation", in *The Enironmental Politics of Sacrifice*, ed. Michael F. Maniates and John M. Meyer (Cambridge, MA: MIT Press, 2010), p. 230.
23 Emily Talen, "The Spatial Logic of Parks", *Journal of Urban Design*, Vol. 15, no. 4 (2010), pp. 473–91.
24 Peter Victor, "A Few Follow-up Questions". Email (12 June 2011).
25 A number of ecological economists have critiqued these methods, such as John M. Gowdy, "The Revolution in Welfare Economics and its Implications for Environmental Valuation and Policy", *Land Economics*, Vol. 80, no.2 (2004), pp. 239–57.
26 Michael Maniates, "Individualization: Plant a Tree, Buy a Bike, Save the World?'" in *Confronting Consumption*, ed. Thomas Princen, Michael Maniates and Ken Conca (Cambridge, MA: MIT Press, 2002), pp. 43–66.
27 Porritt, *Capitalism as if the World Matters*, p. 192.
28 Offer, *The Challenge of Affluence*.
29 This and the previous paragraph from Otto von Busch, *Fashion-able: Hacktivism and Engaged Fashion Design* (Gothenburg: Camino Forlag, 2009), pp. 31–4.
30 City of New York, *Active Design Guidelines: Promoting Physical Activity and Health in Design* (New York: City of New York, 2010), p. 26.
31 Offer, *The Challenge of Affluence*, p. 56.
32 Tim Kasser, *The High Price of Materialism* (Cambridge, MA: MIT Press, 2002).
33 Margaret Crawford, "Can Architects Be Socially Responsible?", in *Out of Site: A Social Criticism of Architecture*, ed. Diane Ghirardo (Seattle: Bay Press, 1991).
34 Ian Cooper, "Post-occupancy Evaluation — Where Are You?", *Building Research & Information*, Vol. 29, no. 2 (2001), pp. 158–63.
35 Alex Ulam, "Unlimited Access: APOPS Protects Democrative Spaces from Garbage, Padlocks, and Commercial Takeover", *Metropolis*, January 2003.

36 Helga Dittmar, "Understanding and Diagnosing Compulsive Buying", in *Handbook of Addictive Disorders: A Practical Guide to Diagnosis and Treatment*, ed. R Holman (Hoboken, NJ; John Wiley & Sons, 2004).

37 A.J. Armstrong, B. Gatersleben, and T. Jackson, "Can Mindfulness Help Reduce Consumption?" Paper presented at the eighth Biennial Conference on Environmental Psychology, Zurich, September 2009.

38 Song Han, Benjamin J. Keys and Geng Li, "Credit Supply to Bankrupt Consumers: Evidence from Credit Card Mailings", in *CFAP Annual Conference: Consumer Credit & Bankruptcy* (Cambridge: Centre for Financial Analysis and Policy, 2011).

39 Jackson, "Prosperity without Growth?", p. 22.

40 Direct quotes in this paragraph come from Offer, *The Challenge of Affluence*, pp. 56 and 58.

41 Maniates and Meyer (eds), *The Environmental Politics of Sacrifice*, p. 5.

42 Jonathan Rowson, Steve Broome and Alasdair Jones, "Connected Communities: How Social Networks Power and Sustain Big Society" (London: RSA, 2010), p. 30.

43 Tim Jackson, Wander Jager and Sigrid Stagl, "Beyond Insatiability: Needs Theory, Consumption and Sustainability", in *ESRC Sustainable Technologies Programme Working Papers* (Guildford: Centre for Environmental Strategy, University of Surrey, 2004), p. 5.

44 See, for example, arguments in Juliet Michaelson, Saamah Abdallah, Micola Steuer, Sam Thompson and Nic Marks, *National Accounts of Well-being: Bringing Real Wealth onto the Balance Sheet* (London: New Economics Foundation, 2009), pp. 12–14; and Offer, *The Challenge of Affluence*, pp. 22–3.

45 Peter A. Victor, *Managing without Growth*, p. 128.

46 Tess Lanning and Kayte Lawton, *Getting What We Deserve: Attitudes to Pay, Reward, and Desert* (London: Institute for Public Policy Research, 2011), p. 2.

47 Paul Krugman, "For Richer: How the Permissive Capitalism of the Boom Destroyed American Equality," *New York Times Magazine* (20 October 2002).

48 See, for example, Jennifer O'Connor, "Survey on Actual Service Lives for North American Buildings", in *Woodframe Housing Durability and Disaster Issues* (Las Vegas, 2004), pp. 1–2; and John E. Fernandez, "Design for Change: Part 1: Diversified Lifetimes", *arq: Architectural Research Quarterly*, Vol. 7, no. 2 (2003), pp. 169–82.

49 Stephan Schmidt and Jeremy Nemeth, "Space, Place and the City: Emerging Research on Public Space Design and Planning", *Journal of Urban Design*, Vol. 15, no. 4 (2010), pp. 453–7.

50 Mary Douglas and Baron Isherwood, *The World of Goods* (London: Routledge, 1979); and Mary Douglas, "Relative Poverty, Relative Communication", in *The Earthscan Reader in Sustainable Consumption*, ed. Tim Jackson (London: Earthscan, 2006), pp. 357—66.

51 Allison J. Pugh, *Longing and Belonging: Parents, Children, and Consumer Culture* (Berkeley: University of California Press, 2009).

52 Jackson, *Prosperity without Growth*, p. 88.

53 Michaelson *et al.*, *National Accounts of Well-being*, p. 48.

54 Shane Gunster, "Self-Interest, Sacrifice, and Climate Change: (Re-)framing the British Columbia Carbon Tax", in *The Environmental Politics of Sacrifice*, ed. Michael F. Maniates and John M. Meyer (Cambridge, MA: MIT Press, 2010).

Chapter 3

Design activism confronting economic growth

INTRODUCTION

The four problems that concluded Chapter 2 offer some ideas about where designers might direct their activism. And although we don't delve all the way into methods of design activism until Chapter 5, in introducing this chapter we examine a few cases of design activism so that we can better consider design responses to consumerism and growth.

Some forms of activism are largely humanitarian in nature. They often work to change the physical conditions surrounding a group or issue of need. An

Humane Society of San Antonio Better design improved animal adoption rates. Photo courtesy of designer Alamo Architects.

example is the Humane Society of San Antonio, Texas which used design to combat the image of a typical animal shelter that tends to be impersonal, cold and smelly. Alamo Architects created an environment where people would be drawn into a prominent, light, attractive environment that better helped people picture the animals as future pets at home. When the shelter opened, adoption rates went up 95 percent and three times as many adult animals have been adopted than before.[1]

Other forms of design activism advocate for change by trying to influence broader patterns of practice through policies, guidelines or rating systems. An example is the Design for Reuse Primer by the nonprofit group Public Architecture. The primer profiles the key issues with reusing old building materials in new construction and illustrates the issues with 15 case study buildings.[2]

Although the above examples may be concerned with improving something we are already doing, a strand of design activism also concerns innovating what we do. An example here is San Francisco-based Rebar's "park(ing) day" project. Park(ing) day is a project to temporarily reclaim the street by using metered parking places to create mini, impromptu parks. At the level of a neighborhood or single street, the park(ing) project provides a simple mechanism for almost any community members to create temporary public spaces where there were none before. As the project evolved, Rebar created international park(ing) day, to get as many people as possible around the world to create parking spaces parks, all on the same day.[3]

This type of innovation also begins to suggest another way in which design activism calls for change, and that is by altering or opening social narratives. A number of projects do this by reinterpreting how we can use spaces, how we relate to each other, or how we use things. One narrative, for example, describes farms as rural, fixed-location entities. By contrast several recent projects have developed mobile, urban farms. In these cases designers have been involved with creating work spaces akin to very versatile garden sheds (for meetings, tools, seeds and related issues), site perimeters, compost facilities and transport mechanisms.[4]

Each of these projects aims at different targets for change. While some focus more closely on clients and users, others engage the wider public. Some projects target the design industry itself, for example, through guidelines. Similarly, they take different approaches to scale. While some try to be the change they are seeking perhaps personally or at a small project scale, others try to raise awareness at a much larger scale (such as national guidelines).

Park(ing) Day metered parking spaces become temporary parks. Photo Andrea Sher, courtesy of Rebar.

After this brief introduction we now turn to the question of how design activism confronts the four challenges identified in Chapter 2. The task is to clearly articulate the connection between project-level design activism and macro-economic issues of growth and consumerism. In this process we develop some generic terms of debate that are useful in connecting micro and macro.

Another key question in this chapter is—does it all add up? For example, how does Public Architecture, the organization that published the reuse primer, measure whether or not there were any actual social or environmental outcomes from their publication? Was that primer worth doing? And importantly, how does the result of this project add to the results of other projects to lead to cumulative change and sustainable outcomes? Although we cannot answer these questions definitively, there are some broad outlines emerging for ways to think about this measurement problem.

We examine the status of measuring social and environmental benefits at the project level using "social metrics." We also think about ways to determine whether or not the projects add up, in terms of achieving the societal or population-level change that is required.

LINKING THE MICRO (PROJECT) TO THE MACRO (GROWTH)

In Chapter 2's review of the economic system we noted that economic growth is the all-important metric in many contexts. But through the analysis of problems associated with growth we identified four areas that need change. In this section we look at how design activist projects address these four areas. To repeat the conclusion of the last chapter, broadly the issues and their implications are as follows:

1. Many important values don't have prices, so an important change is to get these values included, although not necessarily by putting a monetary price on them.
2. Consumerist society makes privately gained, instant rewards ever easier for individual consumers to access—the pace of instant gratification is speeding up. In this view an important change is to slow the pace of rewards in satisfying ways.
3. Traditional commitment strategies (that balance short-term rewards against investment in longer term gains) are being outmoded, although replacement commitment strategies aren't yet in place. This problem suggests that an important change is the improvement, invention or revival of relevant commitment strategies.
4. To a certain extent, private purchases form an element of our social language, turning some important aspects of societal meaning and purpose over to profit-seeking entities. This challenge suggests that a wider range of public, collaborative or shared rewards might lessen pressure upon consumer approaches to social position.

In the following analysis we treat the problem of the pace of reward (item two) and the problem of improving commitment strategies (item three) as two sides of the same coin. By combining them, we acknowledge that our ability to slow the pace of reward requires better commitment strategies.

VALUES WITHOUT PRICES

A common way for design efforts to express the fact that important values don't have prices is through the creation of issue-specific labels and other ways of rating or indicating the social performance of products, structures or processes. Examples of widely publicly known labels include "fair trade" and "organic."

Within architecture a well-known example is the US Green Building Council's LEED (Leadership in Energy and Environmental Design) rating system. LEED programs cover a range of building types such as commercial core and shell, healthcare facilities, schools, retail outlets and homes.[5] An offshoot from LEED is the Living Building Challenge, a certification program which takes green building to a higher level with its restorative paradigm. A more recent entry is the SEED (Social Economic Environmental Design) certification system that stems from a broader mission, "to advance the right of every person to live in a socially, economically and environmentally healthy community."[6] Example projects from SEED range wider than just buildings, including greenways, markets and farms, and neighborhood redevelopment.

For landscape design and maintenance, the SITES (Sustainable Sites Initiative) program is piloting a rating system that has outward similarities to LEED.[7] The Cradle to Cradle certification system covers a range of products, and was developed out of the work on Designtex fabric by McDonough and Braungart (described in Chapter 2).[8] Aside from SEED, most of these systems focus strongly on environmental values.

While these rating systems perhaps represent large-scale efforts to normalize the changes that these activists are seeking, there are a number of other types of rating or labeling systems that are more specialized or limited in scope. For example, the Rugmark label signifies that no child labor has been used in rug-making.[9] Planet Positive certification is for products that go beyond carbon neutral. After reducing carbon emissions as much as possible, product manufacturers buy vouchers for offsetting 110 percent of the remaining CO_2; the vouchers are passed on to end consumers who invest them in carbon-offset projects of their choosing.[10]

Certification The Hollygrove market and farm in New Orleans is certified by the SEED (Social Economic Environmental Design) rating system. Pavilion and photo by Tulane City Center.

Another way to view "rating" is through the ranking of important sites, buildings, or places. For example, the National Trust for Historic Preservation creates an annual list of America's 11 most endangered places. "Places" range from buildings (such as the John Coltrane House) to natural sites (Bear Butte in South Dakota) to neighborhoods (China Alley in Hanford, California), all from the 2011 list.[11] The World Monuments Fund biannually lists the 100 most endangered monuments. In 2006, for the first time, a whole country, Iraq, was included, along with Shackleton's Expedition Hut in Antarctica and several modernists buildings from the 1960s.[12] In a sense these "endangered" lists may be taken as ratings of social and environmental values and their degree of vulnerability.

Other indicator systems measure how we are doing with social values at a broader scale. An example here is the STAR Community Index program, a US effort to change the way local governments set priorities and improve their sustainability performance. STAR aims to create clear goals and performance measures (we might call them metrics) and a dynamic rating system that drives continuous improvement.[13] Although the STAR program is run by an association of cities and counties (ICLEI), it is a partnership effort of the US Green Building Council, National League of Cities and the Center for American Progress.

Endangered places Bear Butte, South Dakota is sacred to as many as 17 American Indian tribes but is threatened by proposed energy developments. Photo Jason Waskiewicz.

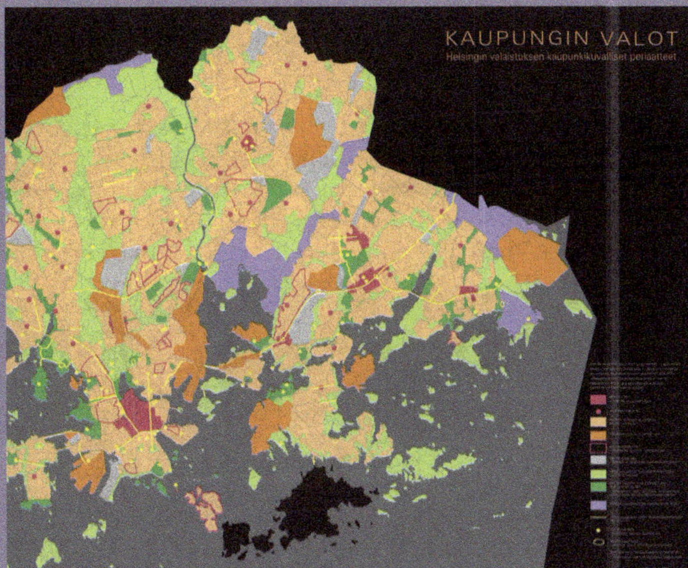

Night sky, Helsinki A lighting plan that embraces darkness. City of Helsinki Media Bank/Ari Leppä.

Many other projects may simply be involved in articulating lost values. For example, Helsinki's landmark lighting plan articulates the social value of connecting with night skies and the ecological value of respecting the fact that some urban ecological systems need darkness. As one Helsinki planner put it, "There is no need for more light but for more planning. ...If you look carefully, you will see there are also areas that are supposed to be dark ... we wanted people to be able to see the sky."[14]

SLOWING THE PACE OF REWARD/COMMITMENT STRATEGIES

Designers are addressing the twin problems of pace and commitment in a variety of ways. One approach arises from the slow design movement, another from durable and adaptable design strategies.

Cases of slow design often try to change modes of private consumption so that the meaning attached to it comes less from fast-paced novelty and more from deeper, long-term content. An example is Flock knitwear by designer Christien Meindertsma. The knitwear aims to put people back in touch with the source of their clothing; the fibers are traced back to specific animals (sheep and goats), and the clothing tag provides information about the animal and its location and breeding. It is a form of "slow" clothing, connecting people and environment to generate meaning.[15]

Another example is the Lunar-resonant street light (by design collective Civil Twilight).[16] Instead of simply making street lights more efficient, the proposal has street lights responding to the brightness of the moon, dimming when the moon is bright, possibly turning off completely. The aim is to save energy and reconnect people with the night sky and with lunar and tidal cycles. This

Connective fibers Wool fibers in each sweater are traced back to a single sheep. Sheep images courtesy of designer Christien Meindertsma.

Slow clothing can connect people and environment to generate meaning.

example ties novelty to (slower) natural cycles and to public goods (moonlight). The proposal also challenges current lighting standards, which call for bright light when studies show that even light is more important. The designers ask, "Do you need to be able to read a newspaper outside in the middle of the night?"

Architects and designers have done a reasonably good job of exploring aspects of durable design, linking durability to the notion of heirlooms and products or structures that tell a story.[17] They have linked durability to products with lifetime guarantees, alluring aging processes (patterned on the aging of leather and denim), or elements that the user can update or modify over time. Here notions of durability tie into "adaptable" products and structures, which are durable by virtue of their flexibility.

Some interesting examples have arisen from responses to the 2005 Hurricane Katrina. One is the grohome, originating with Austin's Center for Maximum Potential Building Systems. The home takes the form of a kit of parts that can be expanded as the homeowner can afford to, or needs to expand or change the structure. Architect Pliny Fisk has mapped out how a single unit can evolve over three generations and how materials can be sourced locally in most cases.[18]

Grohome Texas A&M University's interpretation of the grohome incorporates interchangeable rooms so that occupants adapt the home to changing needs. Photo Kaye Evans-Lutterodt/Solar Decathlon.

The Katrina cottage is another example of a kit (in this case do-it-yourself) developed by architect Marianne Cusato as an alternative to the more costly and sterile FEMA trailers. The cottage is faster to build than a FEMA trailer and it can eventually be converted or expanded to long-term use. The cottage became available to the public as a kit of parts through hardware chain Lowe's in the fall of 2006.[19]

Slow, durable and adaptable design goes some way toward giving us a longer term focus, toward changing our pattern of commitment. These forms of design may also perhaps be seen in terms of infrastructure. Related design approaches emphasize creating infrastructure that opens up potential for different kinds of behaviors and actions. Many of these approaches also work at the level of narrative, offering alternative narratives about what is important or valued.

In creating new infrastructures for commitment, design projects often tackle physical limitations to activities that address social and environmental values. For example, the development of green roofs and roof-top gardens expands urban green space, but also lowers energy consumption, reduces the heat from urban congestion, cleans the air, reduces storm-water run-off, and can enable urban agriculture. New York City's *Active Design Guidelines* suggest ways in which the design of buildings, streets and stores can make physical activity and exercise the norm.

Urban mobility jacket Making physical activity and material efficiency the easiest choice. Design by Kate Ludwig.

In product terms, infrastructure examples include the expandable urban mobility jacket, designed by Kate Ludwig, that provides a built-in alternative to plastic carrier bags. The jacket's normally hidden pocket-bag zips out and is supported by an interior shoulder strap.[20] In a similar vein, wind-up products such as radios and flashlights aim to make physical activity and alternative power sources the easiest choice.

The infrastructure approach also emerges in what designer Dan Lockton has termed "design with intent." Through a range of formal, affordance and material techniques, designers can guide what people choose to do. Lockton proposes 101 patterns for influencing behavior.[21] Although a number of the patterns concern virtual interfaces, many suggestions are material or spatial, such as:

- using the properties of different materials to make some actions more comfortable than others;
- designing an extra "confirmation" step before an action can be performed;
- setting people a challenge, or giving them a target to reach through what they're doing;
- using color, contrast or symmetry to suggest association or focus attention.

These types of guidance or methods of influence can then be applied to a range of choices and actions that people make in terms of transport, diet, education, household energy use, and many others.

The processes and outcomes of design can also contribute to alternative narratives that rebalance the short term and the long term. With the rise of "collaborative consumption", for example, the societal narrative about ownership and use is beginning to change.[22] Whereas a consumerist mantra has been, "Why rent when you can own?" or even "Mine, right now!", according to Simon Smith (on the blog *Shareable*) the collaborative consumption mantra is "Ownership is a last resort." Commenting on how the purpose of consumerism is ownership, he highlights the point that "No successful marketing campaign will promote the *risks*, *side-effects* and *negative repercussions* of ownership," even though ownership has some notorious downsides.[23]

Designers have begun exploring the idea of shared consumption. One example is MIT Media Lab's Smart Cities Group. This group developed the concept of a city car, a publicly shared car system that works in conjunction with mass transit for the "last mile" of local trips. The cars are small and stackable (like grocery carts—six to eight of them can fit into one parking space) and have an innovative design. The traditional engine and drive train are replaced by robotic wheels which each contain their own motor and steering and braking. When parked, the cars harvest and store solar energy.[24]

Design with intent Material properties, symmetries and other factors can guide what people do. Images from the *Design with Intent* toolkit by Dan Lockton.

Sharing Cars City cars are designed for sharing. Image courtesy of Franco Vairani/MIT.

This example shows that the conscious design of objects for the purpose of shared use can make them considerably smarter and more different than conventional models. Architects Jinhee Park and John Hong of SsD explored the design of a New York City apartment for the purpose of sharing among several families who are in the city at different times. A curtain wall system, among other features, allows users to customize the space in temporary ways.

In another approach, designers are involved in designing the process for sharing. An example comes from a design school in Paris (Ecole national superieure des Arts Décoratives) where three students, L. Bayon, M. Jaloux and V. Willerval, in conjunction with tutors Francois Jegou and Anna Bernagozzi, collaborated with the Logement Intergénérations (Intergenerational Lodging) association.[25] The idea was to create a way for students, who could rarely afford inner-city residences, to find rooms with elderly inner-city residents living alone. The process of creating these new "couples"—student with senior—requires that the intentions on both sides of the prospective pair are compatible, especially in terms of mutual aid. The design team created enabling cards that pictorially prompt prospective couples' discussions on a wide range of issues, including tidiness, smoking, overnight guests, birthdays and holidays, and so on.

Sharing residence HBNY curtain walls for temporary customization. Courtesy of SsD.

Sharing residence Cards as a tool to identify compatibility. Images courtesy of Ecole nationale superieure des Arts Décoratives, Design Object Department.

Kate Fletcher's Local Wisdom project takes a different tack by identifying where people are already sharing and extrapolating design implications from that. By exploring why people keep and share clothes over long periods, one finding concerned how users encounter overlock stitching as a barrier to modifying, adapting and reusing clothing and textiles, which then needlessly shortens the life of many garments.[26] The Local Wisdom project highlights and celebrates these stories of self-organized sharing through exhibits that include photographs and histories.

In these examples of collaborative or shared consumption, the emphasis shifts from the immediate rewards based on purchase and ownership—my car, my dress, my house—to a model where reward potentially comes from what Kate Fletcher calls "the craft of users."[27] Reward and stimulation in this model are paced by new patterns of access, such as planning ahead to reserve a car or negotiating with sharing partners. The quality of stimulation is also different, shifting from the acquisition and care of things, to the development of relationships within the system of use.

"Easiness" is a theme that emerges alongside "cheapness" in the fast pace of consumer reward. Easiness makes for even more instant rewards. "Ease of use," and especially "accessibility" are common in design criteria and there is no suggestion here that we abandon them. However, the idea that easy is always better becomes problematic under conditions of perpetual economic growth and affluence.

Designers are starting to address this issue particularly through processes such as co-design, hacking, and personal fabrication or self-assembly. In these cases designers, individuals or small groups of design practitioners conduct studio activities that provide communities with the tools and skills to make, change and repair items for themselves. MIT's fablabs, pioneered by Neil Gershenfeld, are one example. Fablabs bring not only tools, but also non-commercial spaces where communities often choose to make locally relevant objects. In one example a fablab located in a community center allows children to create their own toys and other objects. Gershenfeld comments, "personal fabrication is a new kind of literacy that can be brought to the community" which facilitates local, grass-roots invention.[28]

Fablabs and related activities also emphasize the craft of the user, but in this model it is the process of design and fabrication that paces reward and stimulation. In addition, the quality of stimulation is shifted from the thing to the process. This holds true not only for making new things, but also for hacking and remaking "old" things. Approaches that consider the craft of the user may have other benefits as well. The processes of collaborating, working together to fabricate, and sharing skills and knowledge each relate to the five points of well-being developed by the New Economics Foundation. These points echo the fact that the process of developing and applying skills to overcome challenges is an essential component of well-being. Yet truly developing a skill can take time and resources, and, like other social goods, it often may appear not to have a direct financial return.

Sharing clothes

Mother: *The people who lived next door gave me this dress from Antibes which they had worn there over many seasons and they said I could have it for our holiday. A great success. And, I can't think how many more years I wore it. ...*

Daughter 1: *I am one of three sisters and we were very keen to wear this dress and have shared it since we were old enough to have a grown-up figure ... a period of about 40 years. ...*

Daughter 2: *And now there's another generation coming up, our children, who have got their eye on that dress.*

Images courtesy of the Local Wisdom project. Photos Sean Michael.

Fabrication Laboratory Or Fablab. Image by Fablab Amersfoort, Netherlands, under Creative Commons Attribution.

HACKING

Hacking is a term that stems from the early days of computing, when hobbyists began tinkering with computer systems to see what they could make of them. The term today is more broadly used to describe a process for "overcoming the limitations of an existing object, service or system which was set for one purpose, and finding an access point, intellectually or physically, where its original function can be expanded, altered, or improved to serve a new purpose or solve a problem."[29] Hacking requires skill to open systems and master them.

Hacking also has a reputation for making things available, for sharing the results of a hack so that others can also use them. In this way hacking collectively and incrementally builds a common body of knowledge as well as a set of physical results.[30] Physical results stem from a focus on making rather than designing. There is a degree of invention and the aesthetic of the hack is often unfinished. Designers are increasingly interested in the concept of hacking for the way it offers new levels of engagement, both with material processes, and with the people involved. Informal, collaborative workshops have been springing up—about 500 worldwide—and they are typically not attached to any big "institutions" such as universities or businesses, the way past inventors may have been.[31]

OVER-RELIANCE ON PRIVATE PURCHASES AS A SOCIAL LANGUAGE

Consumerism provides a form of social language based on private consumption. Using this language we gain social status, avoid shame, even shape our identities. The challenge here is to lessen the pressure for positional consumption, for consumer approaches to social position. In a sense, this problem ties consumption to social capital. In response, design activists often pursue a wider range of public, collaborative or shared approaches to building social capital in and among people.

We reviewed Peter Victor's argument (see Chapter 2) that high-quality public goods and public spaces are a central component of "development" (as opposed to just "growth") in affluent countries where there are no shortages of goods, and "positional consumption" is the dominant form of consumption. Increasing the quality and availability of public, or social, goods and spaces begins to relieve the pressure on commercial pursuits; it opens up opportunities for different kinds of "productivity" and new social languages to emerge that are not so heavily reliant on profit-seeking entities. Here it may be useful to think of this arena of public or social goods as "the commons." A "commons" is a resource or place that is commonly held by a civic or public group (see box).

THE COMMONS

A "commons" is a resource or place that is commonly held by a civic or public group. An example of a resource might be a public forest or fish stocks in the ocean. An example of a place might be a public park. In similar terms, some products or other goods fall into the category of "public goods." Technically, these are goods that are available to everyone, and from which no one can be excluded. Light from a lighthouse is one example, the air we breathe is another.

Classically, most theories of the commons assumed that over-exploitation of a common resource is inevitable, an idea popularized as "the tragedy of the commons."[32] These theories were based in part on the flawed economic concept (see Chapter 2) that individuals act rationally to maximize their own profit, to the exclusion of all else. However, these theories have recently been challenged based on wide-ranging evidence that commons can be sustainably managed by the collective work of resource users themselves. Supporting these ideas is research on human altruism which suggests that cooperation and reciprocation are vital elements of human evolution and survival, in contrast to the idea that competition alone explains survival outcomes.[33] Related research, interestingly, suggests that money has an effect on people's attitudes about cooperation; it enhances individualism but diminishes communal motivations.[34]

Although any area of commons never really exists in an ideal form—as a "public good" from which no one can be excluded—we might think about a spectrum from private, individual ownership through cooperative or civic ownership, to public (government) ownership, to a "pure" commons. For example, Claudio de Magalhães highlights the distinguishing features of publicness in public space: the right of access and some degree of control, opportunity for meeting, and diversity of communication. He comments, "publicness should be seen as a relative quality; for any public space, there will be attributes that are more public than others."[35] In this section we first examine products in terms of the commons, then spaces.

Products in the commons

In terms of goods or products in the commons, urban street furniture and other urban "furnishings" provide some examples. An increasingly frequent way of thinking about products in terms of the commons revolves around the idea of open source. In this context, the product and the right to make it, change it or adapt it (as in hacking) should be available to all. This approach puts the "blueprint" for a given product in the commons, the public domain.

In terms of product design and development, the fablab example mentioned above is one avenue for producing goods in a way that contributes to the commons in various ways, and lessens the attachment to mainstream consumerism. More broadly, a recent review of digital fabrication suggests that "a transition from centralized production to a 'maker culture' of dispersed manufacturing innovation is underway today."[36] Collaborative, distributed communities that constitute "maker culture" perhaps offer further opportunities to put products and goods back into a commons, at least partially. At the same time the focus on developing and applying "maker" skills potentially offers a social language around making and doing, rather than owning and displaying.

What is the role of the designer in the context of distributed, collaborative making? Designer Ronen Kadushin offers one idea through his open designs; he creates products as "CAD information" that can be freely downloaded and produced by CNC machines anywhere.[37] Designer Otto von Busch suggests thinking of design in this context in terms of intensifying and hacking. The design role involves finding and intensifying local, or specific small-scale potential and then performing hacks that open up the bigger system to these potentials at the best spots. He also describes this as a designer who is not the "divine creator of the original and new" but rather one who negotiates, questions and works to develop design as a skill and a practical utility among people to help them become makers.[38] This is not so much about meeting people's needs with objects, but rather meeting people's needs through developing their skills and processes.

Spaces in the commons

With the contracting out of public space (discussed in Chapter 2), the public realm has shrunk. Edward Soja critiques the loss of public space from the perspective of property rights. He argues that private property rights are privileged over most other kinds of rights to the point that the right to own property is seen almost as the primary right of citizenship.[39] The issue of property control is central to many struggles over the use of space. Development of the commons enables a wider range of democratic rights such as the right to associate with others, the right to free speech and the right to political expression. These rights are often traded off against commercial needs (for idealized shopping environments) in privately controlled places.

The idea of providing alternative civic places picks up on Ray Oldenburg's "third place," a neutral meeting place in between first place (home) and second place (work).[40] Similarly, Soja proposes a "third space." His first space is that which can be physically measured and managed—the material reality of space. His second space is that which is imagined and interpreted—mental conceptions including utopian or idealized spaces. Third space is the dynamic result of the interaction between first and second space through human agency. The interaction manifests in a third, "lived space" which is alive with people acting on their own ideals for space and its possibilities.[41]

Third Place CAFÉ 524 Adaptive Reuse Project in the neighborhood of Homewood which responds to the community need for a third place. The Community Café and "Third Space" will be located on the first level of the building and the Business Incubator and Real Estate Investment Trust Offices on the upper level. Carnegie Mellon University Urban Design Build Studio (UDBS), Director: John Folan.

In addition to the fablab, or collaborative making spaces mentioned above, many kinds of public and social spaces currently offer alternatives to "consumer space." Design interventions are significant among these alternatives, including museums, memorials, open spaces, schools, libraries, and other places where commerce, or the profit-seeking agenda, is subdued, if not entirely absent. Many of these types of projects contain design activism where the role of design is to contribute directly to providing novelty and stimulation through public and community mechanisms.

Museums

Museums exist in traditional forms, such as art or natural history, but there are signs that the role and function of museums are evolving to take on a broader interpretive scope. For example, the idea of a "working museum" encompasses infrastructure facilities such as recycling stations or wastewater treatment as windows on to meaning, history or representation.

An example is architect Steven Holl Architects Lake Whitney Water Treatment Plant (landscape architecture by Michael Van Valkenburgh and Associates) in Connecticut, or architects Abalos & Herreros' material recycling facility near Madrid. In these cases the effort is on creating inspiring structures and spaces that open the "plant," or some aspects of its workings, to interactions with people. Although the facilities serve educational purposes, they also connect people with the flow of materials and resources in their communities.[42]

Whitney water treatment plant The landscape (a public park) is actually the green roof of the underground portion of the plant. The park contains six areas that mirror the six stages of water purification. Photo David J. Rodrigues.

Although museums have historically had a role in shaping citizens toward a social norm—an authorized societal narrative—recently more museums are providing opportunities to question authorized narratives.[43] Laurajane Smith describes how the notion of "heritage" itself is subject to dominant patterns of power that result in forms of authorized heritage. "Old" artifacts and monuments (e.g., Egyptian pyramids, Stonehenge) typify authorized heritage by which experts and authorities construct and regulate values and understanding.[44]

One example of breaking down a museum's traditional "authorized narrative" comes from The Red Location Museum by Noero Wolff Architects in South Africa. The museum is dedicated to the struggle against apartheid, but the space doesn't channel visitors through a single narrative history of apartheid because "most South Africans acknowledge there is no single truth about apartheid, only myriad perspectives."[45] Instead, inside the industrial and cavernish museum, a grid of "memory boxes" contain a range of stories that present a fragmented past.

However we read museums as public places, one of their central missions is to help people create meaning. Increasingly, as Lois Silverman points out, that meaning stems not only from interpreting history or places, but also from the relationships that museums help build by fostering contact among groups, building coalitions around important ideas, and using their spaces to catalyze

Red Location Museum Outside, a generous public space and inside, a series of tall memory boxes. Noero Wolff Architects. Photo Dave Southwood.

events.[46] Similarly "people's museums" and citizen involvement in museums is increasing; for example, people are getting involved in creating exhibits or setting up museums that address relevant interests and concerns.

Libraries

Libraries constitute an important and evolving public space that is no longer dedicated only to books and quiet contemplation. As the Salt Lake City's Public Library Director Nancy Tessman says, "A library is an institution that best embodies our society's values... Egalitarian, free, open to all – a place that prepares all who enter to participate in our democracy, and in our civic life."[47] A series of new US library designs are helping to redefine how libraries work, what they provide, and how they relate to the urban fabric.

The recent Salt Lake City central library by architect Moshe Safdie (with Valentiner Crane Brunjes Onyon Architects) incorporates a dynamic "urban room" that draws people in and leads into the library's diverse range of spaces, tailored to the sensibilities of different age groups and purposes, from young to old and from analog to digital. Seattle and Los Angeles have also recently undertaken new library construction—in 1998 Seattle passed the largest public library bond in US history. The design of the central Seattle public library also incorporates the idea of common social spaces, with a "living room," a "mixing chamber" and a children's area. The building's program balances the library's historic purpose of information with more contemporary social purposes.[48]

Salt Lake City Public Library The main urban room, library design by Moshe Safdie and Associates with Valentiner Crane Brunjes Onyon Architects. Photo BellaOra Studios, courtesy of the Salt Lake City Public Library.

Mind body dialogue at the Paolo Verde library and Maryvale community center, design firms Gould Evans and Wendell Burnette Architects. Photo Bill Timmerman

In an unusual collaboration between two city agencies in Phoenix, the library system and the parks department developed a joint complex containing both the library and the sports-leaning community center (with indoor gym, track and outdoor pool). The facilities have drawn people from both of the largest communities, African American and Hispanic, and library usage is up more than 65 percent.[49]

Schools and youth centers

Public schools represent another set of spaces that could support the commons. From a design perspective schools are accused of lagging behind most other learning institutions, with researcher Kelvin Sealy commenting that schools are "probably the last learning spaces to which intelligent thought has been applied."[50]

A number of recent design projects link schools to other community activities either through building wider programs into schools, or building schools into wider existing programs. For example, a proposed Perth Amboy high school in New Jersey by architect John Ronan is a hybrid facility that acts as a school and a civic cultural center. The school will serve as the center of the community for the town.[51] In a more extreme example, Ronan was also the architect of the Gary Comer Youth Center, a design departure from the typical concept of "youth center," which includes sports facilities, roof garden, recording studio, computer lab, tutorial rooms, cafeteria and dance studio. The facility is in constant use and "by night it's a warmly lit gathering place for a neighborhood that for decades has known only fear after dark."[52] The building, the first new construction in the neighborhood for years, is a major player in the revitalization of the area.

Parks and landscapes

Parks and other landscapes also serve as alternatives to consumer space. On one level a park can offer green spaces that facilitate outdoor play and physical activity. On another level recent examples of landscapes such as parks, plazas and squares show how they can also engage people in creating their own meaning.

One example is found in interactive installations that either provoke play or offer the opportunity to influence, even briefly, a bigger picture. J. Meejin Yoon (of Howeler + Yoon Architecture) describes her project "White Noise,

Play within the city Project "White Noise, White Light." Courtesy of Howler + Yoon Architects.

White Light" where instead of designing a set experience, designers created an interactive field of flexible, fiber-optic "stalks" that emitted sound and light as people passed near them. The designer comments:

> Collectively the units responded to the movement of pedestrians with an afterglow effect... Visitors attempted to decode the installation's responsive parameters by experimenting with their bodies in space: running, dodging, stamping, and tiptoeing. The field became an unpredictable aggregation of movement, light, and sound—a site of play within the city.[53]

A related project by architecture and design studio Electroland is a Los Angeles tiled walkway, "Enteractive," which responds to pedestrian motion on the ground, but also projects that motion onto the side of the adjacent building. The design's premise is that "there's a vast network of electronic information surrounding us, and we're navigating and participating in it all the time."[54]

In a relatively low-tech example, Chess Park, in Glendale, California by Rios Clementi Hale Studio, makes use of a derelict alley by converting it into a hardscape park frequently populated by members of the local chess club. Lighting in the park emphasizes the chess theme, and chess play typically continues until 2 or 3 a.m. But the infrastructure also facilitates performances and other activities in the space.[55]

Across the examples relating to our social languages, we can see a theme of relationships—relationships across time, relationships to nature and relationships to each other. These relationships in the context of the commons may help relieve pressure on positional consumption as a prominent aspect of our social language. Relationships fostered in these less commercial spaces correspond to the

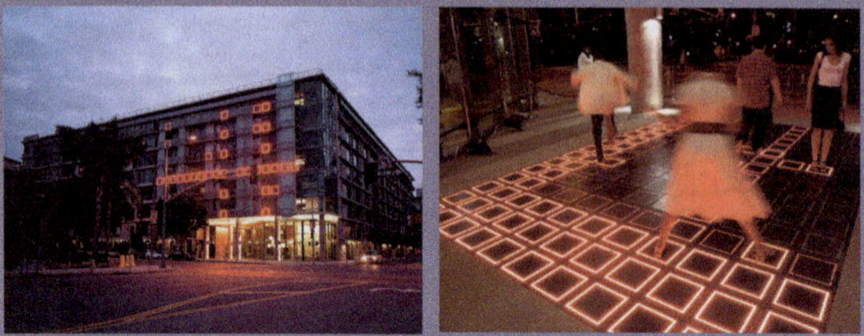

Enteractive Movements on the walkway are projected onto the side of a building. Photos: Electroland LLC

New Economic Foundation's first point of well-being, "connect" (highlighted in the previous chapter, see p. 66). Arguably these spaces also make various forms of giving and receiving (the fifth point "give") more likely.

The discussion above highlights four key concepts: the absence of prices, the fast pace of novelty and stimulation, the loss of longer term commitment strategies, and the commercial nature of some aspects of our "social language." Keeping in mind that design is necessary but not sufficient in most efforts for change, we can summarize what design brings to these examples in Table 3.1.

Chess Park Brand Boulevard, Glendale, CA, designed by Rios Clementi Hale Studios. Photo Tom Bonner.

Table 3.1 Summarizing design's responses to consumerism

Issues	Design strategy	Example cases
Absence of prices	Rating systems	Such as LEED, SEE, SITES or Cradle to Cradle
	Labels	Such as Rugmark or Planet Positive
	Ranking	Endangered sites
	Reveal social values	Lighting plan and night skies
Slowing the pace/commitment strategies	Slow design Durability:	Heirloom, narrative products, material aging
	Adaptability:	Kit of parts and modular architecture, hacking
	Infrastructure that enables	Wind-up products, opening up spaces for alternate uses and activities, design with intent
	Alternative choices and rebalance of narratives	Sharing and using vs. owning, short term vs. long term, hacking (skill and process) vs. acquisition
Over reliance on private purchases as a social language	Re-energizing the commons: public and social spaces as alternatives to consumer space	Libraries, parks, museums, schools, and emerging types of spaces
	Shifting emphasis toward "making" in a collaborative (commons) context	Sharing product blueprints and patterns online, meet needs through skills and abilities (e.g. use of digital fabrication) rather than objects

These four concepts amount to consumerist challenges and help us articulate the fact that although individual design projects themselves might aim to remedy a situation for a specific group or location, the social and environmental values in play are typically linked to much bigger economic issues. These concepts help link activists' specific cases to large-scale ideas and problems that can otherwise seem abstract or overwhelming. They also begin to lay out some broad criteria for how we measure the success of these projects, and we discuss this idea of "metrics" below.

The small set of examples above can only be suggestive of the ways in which design activism addresses our four consumerist challenges. Clearly some examples address more than one challenge, and there are many more examples that could be included here. The aim of this section is to use these preliminary examples to develop terms of discussion and debate, perhaps to propose an agenda for linking project-level work to the changes needed in the broader economic system.

DOES IT ALL ADD UP?

Design activism is confronting consumerism and growth on a variety of levels, but do all these individual projects amount to a big enough change? To examine this question we need to consider what we are measuring and whether it is "big enough." Below we first consider the issue of social metrics—what to measure if we are not measuring money and growth. Then we consider how it adds up ecologically and socially.

Social metrics

Growth leaves out social and environmental values, and social metrics try to capture and represent those values in some meaningful way. In a sense, the consumerist challenges highlighted earlier and social metrics are two sides of the same coin. In this discussion "social value" generally refers to "wider non-financial impacts of programs, organizations and interventions, including the well-being of individuals and communities, social capital and the environment."[56]

Money and profits are an easy way to measure businesses' success, but what are the right metrics for social value that activists, social enterprises, and even some conventional businesses pursue? In particular, when we decide to invest in projects, programs or policies that counteract the problems of consumerism and economic growth, how do we decide when they've been successful, and how do we make decisions between different kinds of investments if we don't have dollar figures that we can easily attach to the benefits? For example, if our goal is to strengthen social networks through mobile urban farms, how do we measure the results?

The practice of measuring social value is still too young to offer any uniformly accepted approach.[57] However, this is an important area that ultimately ties our social behavior to our ability to make use of infrastructure or technologies of reduced consumption. For example, social commitment strategies and social languages that move us away from dependence on short-term consumerism also reduce resource use and environmental impact. In that sense the four consumerist challenges from above can perhaps serve as broad targets.

The point of this section is not to investigate or even debate the nuances of the different methods available for measuring social value. Rather, the purpose here is to look broadly at the concept of social metrics and briefly consider their use in design. In the following paragraphs we first look at several key questions underlying social metrics. We then consider how some of these terms arise within design activist discussions.

What to measure?

The first question is what we should measure. Putting aside ecological costs and benefits (discussed above), we can consider, for example, the case of Chicago's mobile urban farm. Should we measure community cohesion, or accessibility, or both? The question points out the obvious underlying issue of what we are trying to accomplish.

One example of what to measure comes from the case of public footpaths in Britain. Claudia Wood and Daniel Leighton report that intuitively we know that these footpaths provide community benefits, but "local authorities have

Footpaths Characteristics might include fences, surfaces, amenities, views and more.

found it hard to justify how much to invest in footpath creation and upkeep."[58] In response, the National Environmental Agency created a tool to evaluate the social and environmental impact of public footpaths. The impact was measured by a set of outcomes, including:

- community cohesion
- community safety
- culture and leisure
- well-being
- transport and access
- economic well-being
- environmental quality.

These outcomes were then linked to the attributes of the paths (such as physical characteristics, relevance and facilities) and to user groups (such as transport users versus leisure users). The tool then calculates incremental benefits from investments in individual variables, such as the surface quality of the footpath. Like any method of calculating social impact, the tool has limitations. For example, the variables are pre-set and cannot easily be adapted to local circumstances, such as unusual types of path surfaces, or path access to unusual locations such as caves.

Outcomes compared to outputs

Once we decide what to measure, say, community cohesion, a second question follows on—how can we measure an outcome of "improved community cohesion"? For many projects, such as the material reuse publication mentioned above, it is easier to measure the project "output," or what the project produced, than it is to measure "outcomes," or those changes that occurred because of what the project produced. Even if Public Architecture's report were downloaded hundreds of times (an output), what happens (outcomes) after people download the report? The mobile urban farm may have generated a high quantity of produce (outputs) but what resulted (outcomes) from the cultivation, distribution and consumption of the produce?

In architecture and design where we tend to focus on objects and structures, the question about what to measure may be further complicated. For example, it is tempting to catalog the outputs (reduction in material use) tied to an artifact without examining the processes—why is the artifact justified at all? How was it made? And related questions.

Representing value

A third question then arises in terms of how to represent the value. Should we attempt to convert social values into dollar figures? This conversion, sometimes called "monetization", underpins the method known as "social return on investment," which the UK government is championing.[59] In a hypothetical example, what if the mobile urban farm project were able to show that by bringing people together in cultivating agricultural produce, several new social groups had formed in the community, such as a knitting group, a babysitting exchange, and a book club?[60] Clearly there is an argument that community cohesion has been improved, that social capital has been built, but what's the dollar value of a knitting group?

Whether or not we choose to monetize social value, a more pressing issue for many activists is how to afford the monitoring and measurement of outcomes, a cost not usually built into funding arrangements. For example, in terms of the knitting group example, "connecting people" is not often measured by funding groups. Even if it is formally counted, it may take years for the real outcomes to become apparent, and it often takes a great deal of research to determine how much any one activist output may have contributed to outcomes, compared to other factors. For example, improved childhood education may result from better school design, but nutrition and family life are also big contributors. What share of better outcomes should be attributed to innovative school design, for example?

Social metrics within design

In interviews with design activists themselves, there seemed to be a potential tension between predefined metrics and the experimentation and iteration often found in innovative design. For example, Blaine Merker of Rebar, which initiated park(ing) day among other projects, said that their studio often takes the commons as the primary site for design. Rather than solving a specific design problem, the studio looks for opportunities to intervene in the commons such that, he says, "people have a new way of thinking about the commons as a result of seeing something that we do." The metric here is "a new way of thinking about the commons."[61]

Rebar's work isn't co-design or participatory design, but rather experimental, based on the studio's sense of where social and cultural needs resonate with what the commons can offer. In the case of park(ing) day, which started as a one-off, two-hour experiment, the result was an autonomous community that now has a new language for talking about public space. In addition, San Francisco and other cities have developed pavement-to-parks programs spurred on by park(ing) day activists. As Merker admits, in experimentations like these, some things take off and others don't.

Architect Liz Ogbu, who worked at the nonprofit Public Architecture, comments that many times designers rely on anecdotes rather than metrics. She relates a story of the nonprofit organization Homeless Prenatal that got a facility redesign through pro bono architecture services (at Peterson Architects two architects gave about 425 hours of time). After touring the new space, a long-time funder invited the organization to increase their funding application ten-fold. The story has it that the funding agency saw the redesign as a sign of the organization's commitment and capability. It was a "statement" that the architecture and the space could make.[62]

In the same way, she argues, when working on the Day Labor Station, a portable "base" station for migrant and immigrant day laborers, Public Architecture built the case that quality design brings dignity to often excluded populations. Jane Kolleeny echoes the idea of the design "statement" noting that "quality design elevates the profile of the client's cause in the eyes of the public."[63]

The Winterhouse Education Symposium on Design Education and Social Change also captured a sense of tension as described in the final report. [64] In that report Kriss Deiglmeier noted that there may be more uncertainty in social *design* than in other social projects because it's "about piloting and prototyping and uncertainty." Further, as far as many designers are concerned, in cases where projects are client driven then accountability for social values falls to the client. Still, designers seeking funds for social-change work "need to be better prepared to demonstrate positive outcomes."

Whether or not we use the term "metric," we typically do have some idea about what we are trying to do with each project or process. This idea might be general, such as Rebar's "giving people a new way to think about the commons" or it might be much more specific, such as the aim of San Antonio's Humane Society to improve animal adoption rates.

Melinda Tuan reports that several program officers at grant-making foundations clearly recognize that estimating social value is an exercise fraught with problems. Many assumptions can never be scientifically justified, real data don't exist, timeframes are too short to capture actual outcomes, and it is often hard to attribute an outcome entirely to one intervention. Yet, these program officers argue that going through the motions of estimating social value sharpens one's awareness of all these limitations. Tuan reports, "Weinstein of Robin Hood Foundation acknowledges that 'there's no way to get around the ugly problem. The virtue of our metrics is that they are brutally clear about the assumptions we're making along the way, some of them embarrassing.'"[65]

For designers, a key message from this section on social metrics is that metrics provide a way to link projects to broader issues of consumerism and growth. Developed with thought, metrics offer a way of expressing not only a project's benefits to clients and immediate users, but also to the broader challenge of overcoming consumerism and the negative aspects of economic growth. For example, durable products that age well reduce material use and waste, but they also affect the pace and quality of novelty and stimulation. These are two ways to frame the same project.

Ecological consumption

In ecological terms there is a scientific basis for understanding sustainable levels of consumption, in terms of resource use, emissions and the earth's ability to absorb other impacts (such as habitat loss or species extinction).

Estimates are that the world population will level off at around 9 billion people: about 30 per cent more than today's nearly 7 billion people. But if affluent countries continue on roughly the same path of consumption on which we are now, and if developing countries follow a path of "catching up" with affluent countries, then there will be a tripling of global annual resource extraction and consumption by 2050. That's an amount equivalent to a world population of 18 billion people consuming at today's levels.[66]

By contrast, a United Nations Environment Program (UNEP) group estimates that in a scenario that is compatible with relative climate stability, affluent countries would need to reduce resource use and consumption by a factor of 3 to 5. Even some developing countries would need to make 10 to 20 percent reductions in consumption. Although some of this reduction will come from drastic improvements in the efficiency with which we use resources, some will come from simply consuming less. In Chapter 1 we reviewed evidence that although efficiencies are improving, they are nowhere near offsetting increases in resource use from annual economic growth. Sometimes increased efficiency even "rebounds", causing individuals to use savings from efficiency on even more environmentally damaging activities.

Regarding the factor 3 to 5 reduction scenario, the UNEP group comments, "Taken as a whole, this would be a scenario of tough restraint that would require unprecedented levels of innovation."[67] The group also comments that even if a political consensus could emerge around the need for absolute reductions in resource use, these reductions can only be achieved as fast as the investment in innovation is made—innovation across technical, institutional and social solutions. This idea recalls the urging, in Chapter 1, of a bigger and almost entirely "green" stimulus package in response to the current global economic slump.

The needed reductions in resource consumption are not uniform across all aspects of production. For example, food consumption ultimately can only be reduced by a much smaller amount than other areas. Similarly there are complexities around the relationship between resource use and impact. Taking metal ore extraction as an example, the UNEP group highlights the fact that although metal extraction may be conducted more carefully now than decades ago, impacts are actually likely to increase, for several reasons.

First, since much metal has already been extracted, "Today, depending on the metal concerned, about three times as much material needs to be moved for the same ore extraction as a century ago, with concomitant increases in land disruption, groundwater implications and energy use."[68] In addition, most of this extraction is likely to take place in developing countries where environmental regulations are more lax, so environmental impact per unit of metal extracted may become more severe.

Given these complexities, however, it is useful to think about how we understand these targets at the project level, as well as at the societal level. At the societal level we can convert these targets into legal policy requirements (which become regulations) over time. Although many governments have carbon emission reduction goals, few are legal requirements and there is no international framework to ensure that together we reach a planetary target. Short of legal requirements, a number of groups such as Architecture 2030 or the more broad-based group 350 (standing for the safe level of 350ppm of carbon in the atmosphere) are advocating for organizations, businesses and individuals to implement and lobby for legal adoption of these target levels. This advocacy begins to formulate new norms that work their way into standards and policy over time.

We can also think about meeting these targets on a case-by-case basis. Here each project attempts to meet these broader targets for reduced consumption within the terms of the project, for example, with a carbon-neutral building or a zero waste production line for a given product. An example of a net zero energy building is the Aldo Leopold Foundation's Leopold Center in Wisconsin by The Kubala Washatko Architects. It meets all of its energy needs onsite. Another example is Lloyd Crossing Sustainable Design Plan, by Mithun Architects + Designers + Planners, for an area of Portland, Oregon. For this plan the team "began its work by conceptually recreating the native ecosystem of the site's 54 acres to determine exactly how much CO_2 would be absorbed and emitted annually if no human development had ever occurred."[69] The plan then had to at least match, if not outperform, this environmental footprint. For example, the plan had to absorb as much water and carbon as a forest.

The footprint idea of the last example is based on the idea that every activity has an "ecological footprint" in terms of the surface area or land on earth required to provide the resources and absorb impacts (such as waste).[70] The available surface area is known, and will not increase, so we can only meet growing needs (for example, of a growing population) by each consuming less and/or consuming more efficiently.

In the long run one can almost envision a system of accounting based entirely on resource consumption and environmental impact. Where, instead of seeing a chair that costs $20, we see a chair that used 10 units of metal resource with 5 units of water impact, 5 units of chemical impact and 10 units of energy impact. In this scenario our budget is not money but resource and impact. We can only spend as much as we have in our individual budgets, which are connected to globally sustainable levels of consumption.

Currently, although some environmental targets seem established, such as "safe" levels of CO_2 in the atmosphere or factor 3 to 5 reduction in overall consumption in affluent countries, there is less certainty about how the reductions roll out across different areas of consumption, such as buildings, products, metals, food or consumables. Data aren't always available to help us calculate resource use or impacts associated with a given project. As the UNEP groups suggests, however you look at it, the reductions in consumption or improvements in efficiency must be dramatic, and this challenge ultimately filters down to the project level.

Social consumption

A further step in social metrics is perhaps to consider how social change "adds up" to a result that meets criteria for long-term sustainability. Here we don't have a number, such as keeping carbon dioxide below 350ppm in the atmosphere. Instead we have the challenge of linking our social behavior to our ability to make use of infrastructure or technologies of reduced consumption. At the same time, the five points for real well-being, introduced in Chapter 2 (see box on p. 66) (connect, be active, keep learning, take notice, give), can guide us toward activities that provide more substantive well-being that doesn't have to be materially based.

In social terms, the past few chapters have begun to suggest some initial criteria for linking social sustainability to environmental sustainability. For example, improved income equality seems to be linked to reduced positional consumption. Social networks and the degree of social capital (or positive connections among people) also play a major role in our social behavior. These social networks are tied to commitment strategies that help us balance short-term reward against investment in longer term, and often much bigger gains. The social languages we use to gain status or create identity are also centered in social networks and affected by their dependence on consumerism. Finally, social networks are closely related to human health, which again connects directly to environmental health (a topic to which we will return in our future scenarios of Chapter 7).

CONCLUSION

But a larger question remains. How do we get from here to there? "Here" is our current economic system where nearly every activity is directed, pressured or compromised by the societal goal of economic growth fueled by consumerism. "There" is a transformed system that prioritizes real well-being and uses a variety of metrics to assess it. Quite probably "there" we have low growth in poor countries and a steady state or even de-growth economy in affluent countries. "There" is a system that stays within one planet or ecological footprint limits, a system that Tim Jackson has called "prosperity without growth." In this system social and environmental "wealth" has a much bigger role to play than financial and material wealth.

NOTES

1 "A Communal Feel Delights Inhabitants, Clients, and Staff", *Architectural Record* (November 2004).
2 Liz Ogbu (ed.), *Design for Reuse Primer* (San Francisco, CA: Public Architecture, 2010).
3 Sources on the park(ing) project include Rebar's own publications as well as an interview with the author: Rebar, *PARK(ing)* (San Francisco, CA: Rebar, 2005); and Rebar, *The PARK(ing) Day Manual* (San Francisco, CA: Rebar, 2005).
4 See, for example, Ned Cramer, "Crop Circles: Chicago's Mobile City Farmstead Breeds a New Strain of Sustainable Design", *ID* (June 2004); Jonathan Solomon, "What's The Problem", La Biennale di Venezia: 12th International Architecture Exhibition, "Workshopping: An American Model of Architectural Practice" (Venice, 2010); and "The Farm Proper" Set & Drift (San Diego, 2010). Available at http://setanddrift.org/projects/projects-current/the-farm-proper/ (accessed 29 September 2011).
5 "Rating Systems", US Green Building Council, Washington, DC (n.d.). Available at http://www.usgbc.org/DisplayPage.aspx?CMSPageID=222 (accessed 8 September 2011).
6 "SEED Certification: Guided by Ethics, Framed by Community Values", The SEED Network (n.d.). Available at http://www.seednetwork.org/certification/ (accessed 8 September 2011).

7 "The Sustainable Sites Initiative", American Society of Landscape Architects, Lady Bird Johnson Wildflower Center, and the US Botanic Garden (n.d.). Available at http://www.sustainablesites.org/report/ (accessed 8 September 2011).
8 "Certification Overview", Charlottesville, MBDC Cradle to Cradle (n.d.). Available at http://www.mbdc.com/detail.aspx?linkid=2&sublink=8 (accessed 8 September 2011).
9 Laurie Manfra, "The Ethics of Rugs", *Metropolis* (February 2006).
10 Joann Gonchar, "On the Greenhouse Gas Trail, One Engineer Aims beyond Carbon Neutral", *Architectural Record* (March 2007).
11 "America's 11 Most Endangered Historic Places", National Trust for Historic Preservation. Available at http://www.preservationnation.org/issues/11-most-endangered/ (accessed 8 September 2011).
12 Thomas De Monchaux, "WMF Watch List Includes Ancient and Modern", *Architectural Record* (August 2005).
13 *STAR Community Index: Sustainability Goals & Guiding Principles* (Seattle: ICLEI, 2010).
14 Kristi Cameron, "Bright Lights, Big City", *Metropolis* (April 2005).
15 Nancy Nowacek, "From Farm to Closet", *Metropolis* (December 2006).
16 Karen E. Steen, "Lunar Light", *Metropolis* (May 2007).
17 See, for example, Jonathan Chapman, *Emotionally Durable Design: Objects, Experiences & Empathy* (London: Earthscan, 2005); Stewart Brand, *How Buildings Learn: What Happens After They're Built* (New York: Penguin, 1994); Ed van Hinte and Liesbeth Bonekamp (eds), *Eternally Yours* (Rotterdam: 010 Publishers, 1997); and Tim Cooper (ed.), *Longer Lasting Products: Alternatives to the Throwaway Society* (Farnham: Gower, 2010).
18 Sam Martin, "Pliny Fisk III, Gail Vittori Architecture", *Metropolis* (January 2006).
19 Sam Lubell, "Lowe's Makes Katrina Cottages Available for Purchase", *Architectural Record* (November 2006); and Angelle Bergeron, "Designers Hope Katrina Cottages Will Replace FEMA Trailers", *Architectural Record* (April 2006).
20 "Expandable Urban Mobility Jacket/Kate Ludwig", *ID* (September/October 2005).
21 Dan Lockton with David Harrison and Neville Stanton, *Design with Intent: 101 Patterns for Influencing Behavior Through Design* (Windsor: Equifine, 2010).
22 Rachel Botsman and Roo Rogers, *What's Mine is Yours: The Rise of Collaborative Consumption* (New York: HarperCollins, 2010).
23 Simon Smith, *A Transumer Manifesto*, Shareable (San Francisco: CommonSource, 30 June 2010). Available at http://shareable.net/blog/a-transumer-manifesto (accessed 1 July 2011).
24 William J. Mitchell, "Going the Extra Mile to Make Mass Transit More Personal", *Architectural Record* (August 2007).
25 Francois Jegou, Joelle Liberman, Sara Girardi and Anna Bernagozzi, "Design for Social Innovation: Enabling Replication of Promising Initiatives for Sustainable Living in Brussels and Paris", in *Changing the Change* (Turin: Umberto Allemandi & Co., 2008).
26 Kate Fletcher, interview by author, digital audio file, London, 1 March 2011.
27 Kate Fletcher, "Post Growth Fashion and the Craft of Users", in *Shaping Sustainable Fashion*, ed. A. Gwilt and T. Rissannen (London: Earthscan, 2011), pp. 165–75.
28 Ernest Beck, "Customize This", *ID*, Vol. 6 (June 2005), pp. 56–9, 58.

29 Scott Burnham, *Finding the Truth in Systems: In Praise of Design-hacking* (London: Royal Society for the Encouragement of Arts, Manufactures and Commerce (RSA) 2009), p. 4.
30 Otto von Busch, *Fashion-able: Hacktivism and Engaged Fashion Design* (Gothenburg: Camino Forlag 2009), p. 59.
31 Tom Igoe and Catarina Mota, "A Strategist's Guide to Digital Fabrication", *Strategy + Business*, no. 63 (August 2011).
32 Claudio de Magalhães, "Public Space and the Contracting-out of Publicness: A Framework for Analysis", *Journal of Urban Design*, Vol. 15, no. 4 (2010), pp. 559-74.
33 Amy R. Poteete, Marco A. Janssen and Elinor Ostrom, *Working Together: Collective Action, the Commons, and Multiple Methods in Practice* (Princeton, NJ: Princeton University Press, 2010), p. 31.
34 See, for example, Ernst Fehr and Urs Fischbacker, "The Nature of Human Altruism", *Nature* Vol. 425, no. 23 (October 2003), pp. 785-91; Martin A. Nowak, "Five Rules for the Evolution of Cooperation", *Science*, Vol. 314 (2006), p. 1560.
35 Kathleen D. Vohs, Nicole L. Mead and Miranda R. Goode, "The Psychological Consequences of Money", *Science*, Vol. 314 (2006), p. 1154.
36 Igoe and Mota, "A Strategist's Guide to Digital Fabrication".
37 Ronen Kadushin, *Open Design Manifesto* (Berlin, 2010).
38 von Busch, *Fashion-able*, p. 50.
39 Edward W. Soja, *Seeking Spatial Justice* (Minneapolis: University of Minnesota Press, 2010), p. 45.
40 Ray Oldenburg, *The Great Good Place: Cafes, Coffee Shops, Bookstores, Bars, Hair Salons, and Other Hangouts at the Heart of a Community* (New York: Marlowe & Company, 1989).
41 This explanation of Soja's trialectics of space is simplified from Edward W. Soja, *Third Space: Journeys to Los Angeles and Other Real-and-imagined Places* (Oxford: Blackwell, 1996), pp. 68–79.
42 Sara Hart, "Steven Holl Creates a Prototype with Connecticut Water Purification Facility and Park that Establishes Public Works as Works of Art", *Architectural Record* (October 2005); and Eric Demby, "Waste Not", *Metropolis* (July 2003).
43 See, for example, Fiona Cameron, "Moral Lessons and Reforming Agendas: History Museums, Science Museums, Contentious Topics and Contemporary Societies", in *Museum Revolutions: How Museums Change and Are Changed*, ed. Simon J. Knell, Suzanne MacLeod and Sheila Watson (London: Routledge, 2007), pp. 330–42.
44 The concept of authorized heritage is developed well by Laurajane Smith, *The Uses of Heritage* (New York: Routledge, 2006) p. 11.
45 Lisa Findley, "Noero Wolff Architects Commemorates the Struggle against Apartheid at the Red Location Museum in South Africa", *Architectural Record* (March 2006).
46 Lois H. Silverman, *The Social Work of Museums* (London: Routledge, 2010), p. 148.
47 Ken Shulman, "Urban Renewal: Salt Lake City's New Public Library", *Metropolis* (June 2004).
48 Sheri Olson, "Thanks to OMA's Blending of Cool Information Technology and Warm Public Spaces, Seattle's Central Library Kindles Book Lust", *Architectural*

Record (July 2004); Karen E. Steen, "The Seattle Public Library: The Making of a Library", *Metropolis* (October 2004).

49 Clifford Pearson, "Gould Evans and Wendell Burnette Make Urban and Social Connections at the Palo Verde Library and Maryvale Community Center in Phoenix", *Architectural Record* (October 2006).

50 Thomas De Monchaux, "A is for Adaptable: Today's Most Progressive School Designs Put the Stress on Flexibility", *ID* (May 2007).

51 Sam Lubell, "Ronan's Design Will Alter a Town, not Just a School", *Architectural Record* (November 2004).

52 John Hockenberry, "Miracle on 72nd Street", *Metropolis* (December 2006).

53 J. Meejin Yoon, "Public Works: Projects at Play", *Journal of Architectural Education*, Vol. 61, no. 4 (2008), pp. 59–68, 61.

54 David Sokol, "Electroland Turns an Apartment-building Facade into a Billboard for Pedestrian Movement", *Architectural Record* (August 2007).

55 Ruth Altchek, "Chess Nuts Playing in an Open Park: A Recreation Space Opens in Glandale", *ID* (November 2004), p. 30.

56 Claudia Wood and Daniel Leighton, *Measuring Social Value: The Gap Between Policy and Practice* (London: Demos, 2010), p. 20.

57 Melinda T. Tuan, *Measuring and/or Estimating Social Value Creation: Insights into Eight Integrated Cost Approaches* (Seattle: Bill & Melinda Gates Foundation: 2008).

58 Wood and Leighton, *Measuring Social Value*, pp. 43–44.

59 Office for the Third Sector, *A Guide to Social Return on Investment* (London: Cabinet Office, 2009), p. 45.

60 Cramer, "Crop Circles".

61 Blaine Merker, telephone interview with the author (22 August 2011).

62 Liz Ogbu, telephone interview with the author (18 August 2011).

63 Jane F. Kolleeny, "Practice Matters: Giving Versus Getting: Altruism is Alive and Well in Architecture", *Architectural Record* (September 2003).

64 William Drenttel and Julie Lasky, "Winterhouse Education Symposium on Design Education and Social Change: Final Report", *Change Observer*, posted 11 November 2010. Available at http://changeobserver.designobserver.com/feature/winterhouse-symposium-on-design-education-and-social-change-final-report/22578/ (accessed 28 August 2011).

65 Tuan, *Measuring and/or Estimating Social Value Creation*, p. 15.

66 M. Fischer-Kowalski, M. Swilling, E.U. von Weizsäcker, Y. Ren, Y. Moriguchi, W. Crane, F. Krausmann, N. Eisenmenger, S. Giljum, P. Hennicke, P. Romero Lankao and A. Siriban Manalang, "Decoupling Natural Resource Use and Environmental Impacts from Economic Growth, A Report of the Working Group on Decoupling to the International Resource Panel" (United Nations Environment Program, 2011).

67 Fischer-Kowalski *et al.*, "Decoupling Natural Resource Use and Environmental Impacts from Economic Growth", p. 30.

68 Ibid., p. 25.

69 Russell Fortmeyer, "Zero Effect", *Architectural Record* (March 2007).

70 Duncan Pollard (ed.), *Living Planet Report 2010: Biodiversity, Biocapacity, and Development* (Gland, Switzerland: WWF-World Wide Fund for Nature in conjunction with Zoological Society of London and Global Footprint Network, 2010).

Chapter 4

From here to there, sketching a sustainable economy

In Chapter 3 we looked at the question of social metrics (which represent social and environmental values) mainly with respect to design projects. In this chapter we examine the bigger picture. What are some of the models being proposed for transitioning from the current economy to a more sustainable economy? A key question is how we formally include social metrics alongside financial values. One idea is to reform markets and capitalism, but to retain them as the central mechanism for change. A more radical idea suggests introducing other sectors, alongside the market, to create a sustainable economy. Although these are all speculative ideas and we don't have a definitive answer about transition, we conclude the chapter by reviewing how design practitioners are currently financing activist practice.

REFORMING MARKETS

The idea that the financially driven markets are the key to a sustainable economy is a popular one. One notable example is the Social Capital Markets Group (SOCAP) which aims to "direct the power and efficiency of market systems toward social impact, leading to a more balanced set of 'returns'."[1] In a SOCAP model businesses should have a bigger and more accountable nonprofit agenda. A parallel idea, "philanthrocapitalism," suggests that nonprofit organizations should act more like businesses and think of their work in terms of creating new markets for goods and services.[2] Philanthrocapitalism emerges as many successful entrepreneurs, such as Bill and Melinda Gates, move into philanthropic territory by forming foundations and nonprofit groups.

The idea of reforming markets extends to the redesign of corporations so that they are legally allowed to pursue goals that are broader than simply maximizing profits.[3] One example is the B-corporation. In addition, a number of other models for business ownership and control already exist such as employee ownership, cooperatives, mutuals and public interest companies. But, argues William Davies, these other models of business have wilted in the monoculture of corporate structures prioritizing shareholder value. Davies argues that the recent banking crisis is "the most explosive example of how the shareholder value model failed, both as a mechanism for accountability and for value creation."[4]

Since architects and designers are trained and practice largely in the context of commerce and the private sector, it is perhaps not surprising that they lean toward the SOCAP model of widening business agendas to include nonprofit elements. For example, a recent SOCAP conference track features design for social innovation. Among architects working in social or public design, it is common to hear discussions of "market creation." The US Green Building Council and STAR Community Index view their work in market terms as well, with a recent STAR report noting, "For every successful standard, framework, or certification, there are scores of examples that have simply not achieved significant market penetration."[5]

Some design education programs pioneering social or public interest design also lean toward the model of reforming markets, perhaps along SOCAP lines. For example, the Austin Center for Design is a new independent one-year design program that aims to develop and direct design knowledge toward humanitarian and social problems. Director Jon Kolko comments:

> I'm adamant that this movement cannot be successful if students are taught to pursue nonprofit or pro-bono work. They need to learn how to produce operationally self-sufficient organizations, and if they take grant money or venture money, it needs to be to bootstrap the organization—finite and small. So, the most important 'tools' my students need to learn are those related to entrepreneurship.[6]

There is also a trend to marry up design education with business education programs, not least for purposes of social innovation, as illustrated by Stanford's "D-school" and the management programs at Parsons The New School For Design.[7]

However, as long as prices don't include social and environmental values, it is very difficult to be operationally self-sufficient in the arena of humanitarian and social problems. As long as the infrastructure and social norms all around us scream for short-term, individualized consumerism and growth, it is very hard to embed social innovations that address long-term commitment and the pace of stimulation and novelty.

QUESTIONING MARKET REFORM

Jonathan Porritt argues that markets will be able to include social metrics when governments reform capitalism by setting prices correctly (for example, by levying higher taxes on carbon and other natural resources) so that true social and environmental costs are paid. In this view we can retain capitalism but add new forms of capital such as environmental and social capital.[8] Still, even if it were technically possible to reform market pricing, there is no evidence to suggest that such reforms will address problems of individualism, income inequality, the pace of novelty and stimulation, the loss of commitment strategies, or the reliance on private consumption as a social language.

The problem of infrastructure shows another obvious limitation of the marketplace. Evidence clearly shows that free markets alone won't ever make the investments needed for large-scale infrastructure changes that can convert us to a sustainable economy in areas such as transportation, energy and water. We also know that historically many technologies (particularly infrastructural ones) only survived and then thrived due to massive public investment. One example is nuclear power; another is automobile transport and the current highway/road networks. Cars and roads are further subsidized with military interventions in oil-producing countries. Together, these make driving a car appear "cost-effective" or even "the only choice" for most people in North America.

Philanthrocapitalism suffers some of the same critiques as the proposals to simply make businesses more socially accountable. Michael Edwards argues that ultimately, phlianthrocapitalism itself is "a symptom of a disordered and profoundly unequal world," and he notes that "the increasing concentration of wealth and power among philanthrocapitalists is unhealthy for democracy."[9] He suggests that it is dangerous to begin melding together—even confusing—business practices and business agendas with civil society practices and agendas. Civil society holds a place for democracy, citizen action, human rights and other agendas that are lost in translation to business contexts.

Obviously markets and businesses have an important role to play in transforming the economy, and a large literature is available on that topic. There is nothing wrong with adopting a business framework within which to work for change, and as David Hess suggested in Chapter 1, "alternative pathways" are made up of a complex mix of motives and actors, which include profit and business. However, limitations of the marketplace have created a large body of evidence that businesses and individual consumerism simply cannot overcome many of the problems we need to solve. The argument here is not that business and market models have nothing to contribute to social change, but rather that we should also start considering other models of social change, alongside what business can do.

Figure 4.1 The traditional way of conveying the economy

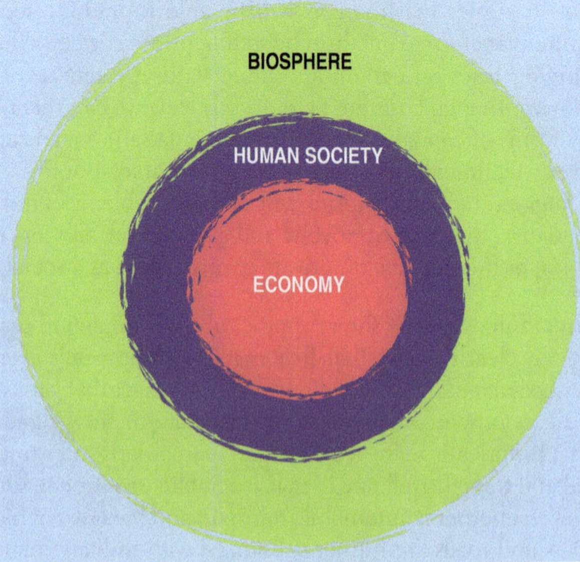

Part of the challenge stems from an earlier observation, that the market and its terminology are the ocean in which we swim. It is as though we have no other language to talk about social design work—or that no other language is acceptable or credible. Even diagrams that attempt to show how the market is entirely reliant on the planet's natural ecosystem have the effect of putting the market at the center, and nature at the periphery.

Figure 4.1 shows the traditional way to convey the economy sitting within, and depending on, the biosphere. However, the diagram has the effect of centering the economy—and financial markets—putting them at the heart of society rather than emphasizing their dependence.

DIVERSIFYING BEYOND MARKETS

Rather than trying to take a market structure and impose it onto the biosphere, by creating social and environmental forms of "capital", we can also consider an increasingly prevalent argument for compartmentalizing the market and its purpose, while acknowledging parallel and equally important "economies," such as social and ecological economies. The idea here is to balance the market's role (anonymized competition through monetized consumption) against other mechanisms that recognize contributions from a "gift" economy.

Political scientist Karen Litfin suggests that gift and market economies already exist alongside one another and each play particular roles: "Gift systems and market systems foster two distinct yet necessary social values. Without gifts, community is lost; without the individuality and anonymity of the market, freedom can be lost."[10] The gift economy plays an important but neglected role in optimizing social economies (reputation, trust, sharing, reciprocation and cooperation) and ecological economies (natural resources, ecosystem services, spiritual and intrinsic value of nature). An example of how these economies might work alongside each other comes from sharing systems.

In the market economy, sharing is usually anonymous and sequential, and the previous user leaves no trace. We find this pattern in commercial rental cars or hotel rooms, where we don't expect to find someone else's stuff stored on the car's back seat or in the hotel closet. In these cases sharing is expedient, perhaps in locations away from home, and the social, interpersonal aspects of sharing are not sought. By contrast, sharing in a gift economy occurs in real time, or "in company," so that sharing is social and its social aspects are seen as beneficial. In a neighborhood lending scheme, you might borrow a neighbor's car for an unexpected journey. You don't expect every trace of the owner's life (such as a baby seat) to be removed from the car. An example of this type of sharing might be a neighborhood tool-sharing scheme, where the process of arranging to share builds social capital and leads to other productive outcomes, for example, getting help with a home repair project.

Another emerging model that incorporates the gift economy is "social enterprise" and social entrepreneurship. These entities are distinct from regular, profit-maximizing businesses in that they aim to maximize social good without losing money. This is not so much about broadening the traditional business agenda as it is about turning that agenda on its head. For example, some view social enterprise as a "non-loss" business, in contrast to a "for-profit" business. Earnings aren't distributed to shareholders; rather they are plowed back into the social agenda. Social enterprise is also different from nonprofits. Although both nonprofits and social enterprises plow their resources into social good, social enterprises attempt to do this through earnings rather than grants or member donations.

An example of a social enterprise is the Greyston Bakery ("We don't hire people to bake brownies, we bake brownies to hire people") or the Swiss toy company Momoll which operates similarly, making dolls' houses and other wooden toys.[11] The social enterprise terrain is still wide and ill-defined, and some people seem to interpret a social enterprise as a normal business that simply tries to do more good alongside its money-making aspirations.[12]

Indeed, some proponents of widening business agendas suggest that ultimately we should aim to convert social values into dollar figures that can be compared in the same way that people compare the financial return-on-investment in companies. Melinda Tuan comments that expectations for this type of conversion, or "monetization," are unreasonable because "the infrastructure necessary to calculate social value creation for social programs is virtually non-existent."[13] She notes that it has taken centuries just to develop the infrastructure to calculate financial return-on-investment, an infrastructure that includes financial accounting, brokers, financial analysts, financial reporting and so forth.

Mohammad Yunus, discussing social enterprises (or social businesses), suggests that the social value sector requires its own normative arena, away from the regular financially driven stock market and its for-profit indicators. He comments:

> Along with the creation of the Social Stock Market we'll need to create rating agencies, appropriate impact assessment tools, indices to understand which social business enterprise is doing more and/or better than others—so that social investors are correctly guided. This industry will need its Social Wall Street Journal and Social Financial Times to bring out all the exciting, as well as the terrible, news stories and analyses to keep the social entrepreneurs and investors properly informed and forewarned.[14]

It seems likely that alongside a formal financial "market" a sustainable economy will need to introduce several new formal sectors. One might be a social enterprise sector that follows the trajectory Yunnus describes above with a "social stock market." Still another might be a sector that recognizes, supports and protects distributed peer networks engaged in forms of social production and social innovation. These networks are increasingly responsible for socially productive work among individuals and informal groups who trade, donate and share resources through real and digital network interactions. Examples include Freecycle or schemes such as the one that facilitates connections between would-be gardeners, and people who have space available for gardening.

The potential benefit of this type of citizen "work" is very large. It is estimated that there are now about a billion people in societies where affluence affords ubiquitous computers and internet access, which serves as a key tool for a great deal of peer networking.[15] Further, Yochai Benkler suggests, "A billion people in advanced economies may have between two and six billion spare hours between them *every day*."[16] The implication is that productive citizens in their spare time, and partly through a gift economy, could provide in a single day the output that would result from several hundred full-time employees working for about five years.

John Quiggin similarly argues that, "There has been a huge shift in the location of innovation, with much of it either deriving from, or dependent on, public goods produced outside the market and government sectors, which may be referred to as social production."[17] Further, he notes that in many cases there are little or no monetary returns for this type of social production, making it unlikely that financially driven markets will allocate resources to support social innovation and production.

Instead, in a market-dominated context, the tendency would be for socially productive networks to either be brought into the for-profit market (along the lines of eBay) or to be left on their own, often struggling without any infrastructure of support and then withering away, taking their social and environmental benefits with them. Bringing socially productive peer networks into the market skews their development toward only the types of activities, such as online selling, that are financially profitable while neglecting valuable social and environmental outcomes that might arise from them. As we have seen, in many cases if these positive outcomes aren't captured, they end up requiring even more resources to fix, clean up, heal and restore later. This is not to say that some peer networks cannot be financially profitable, only to recognize that many others may create value in other ways.

Although we have seen that design activist projects confront problems of growth, they struggle to do this in a system that has no infrastructure for handling social value, as Tuan and Yunus describe. Designers are doing this work, however, and we look at how they currently operate in the closing section of this chapter.

Similarly, other analysts assembled by the United Nations Environment Program (UNEP) who have assessed the transition to a green economy suggest that two other key elements are eco-efficiency and alternative indicators.[18] Eco-efficiency requires an intensive increase in resource efficiency and impact efficiency (reduced environmental impact per unit of resource used). In addition, a green economy requires new sets of indicators that measure and prioritize factors related to sustainability rather than resource extraction and use. We touched on this in the previous chapter, in terms of a scenario where our budget is not money but environmental resource use and impact.

Eco-efficiency stems from innovation, and although we tend to think of this in terms of technology, UNEP's analysts characterize three kinds of innovation. The first is technological innovation, based on equipment and technical processes. The second is institutional innovation that organizes people's activities on a society-wide basis. These may include social enterprises and distributed peer networks as new institutional sectors, for example. The third is relational innovation, which may be thought of as "social innovation." This innovation changes the way we share, cooperate or manage social benefits and social learning. In terms of the discussion in Chapter 3, these last two types of innovation might also affect how we slow down the pace of stimulation and novelty while also building new commitment strategies.[19]

Another central feature of a sustainable economy is likely to be shorter, possibly much shorter, work weeks. For example, the New Economics Foundation proposes a 21-hour work week.[20] Here, "leisure" takes on broader meanings and its social and environmental productivity is formally recognized. As we saw in Chapter 2, the need for continued economic growth is largely driven by the need for employment; the argument is that reducing work hours could reduce the need for growth. Although growth is a way to employ more people, ultimately the efficiency and productivity incentives associated with growth have as much potential to replace workers with technology as they do to create new jobs.

Economist Juliet Schor notes that historically, in the century from 1870 to 1970, employment rates improved not only through growth but also through steady decreases in work hours.[21] She suggests that during this period productivity was not only used to increase the size of the economy, it was also used to reduce hours worked. After 1970, work hours began to climb again as nations began to pin employment exclusively to growth, without consideration of hours worked. Shorter work time is a central component of reducing the pressure for economic growth, and evidence suggests that it also reduces environmental impact. Economist Peter Victor included shorter work weeks in his model of a steady state economy for Canada (see Chapter 1, p. 24).

Clearly a sustainable economy requires substantial changes. Table 4.1 summarizes the factors that we have speculated on here for a sustainable economy. Admittedly no one knows exactly how this will work. Tim Jackson comments:

> Currently environmental and social investments appear to "soak up" income without increasing economic output. In a conventional growth-based economy this is problematic. In a sustainable economy this kind of investment needs to be seen as an essential component of macroeconomic structure. And yet, at the moment, the tools to analyze this dynamic properly don't exist, even if the political will to implement such a strategy were in place.[22]

Jackson believes that this new sustainable economy will involve rebalancing of almost every kind, between debt and savings, public sector and private sector, consumption and investment, and productivity and employment. Further, Jackson suggests, "The truth is that there is as yet no credible, socially just, ecologically sustainable scenario of continually growing incomes for a world of nine billion people."[23] A sustainable economy requires new systems and perhaps also a way to visualize them that doesn't feature the market, or financial economy, as the center. Figure 4.2 takes ideas from Table 4.1 to suggest a possible way to represent a new system where the ecological foundation is emphasized as the center.

These facets of a sustainable economy also respond to the four issues discussed in Chapter 3. For example, accepted and included social and environmental metrics address the pricing problem. Shorter work hours, combined with a

Table 4.1 Facets of a sustainable economy

- Accepted social and environmental metrics, but not necessarily boiled down to monetary terms.
- Formal inclusion of social and environmental metrics, possibly through "new sectors" that run alongside market/financial economies, such as peer networks and social enterprise, that utilize aspects of gift economies.
- Shorter work hours.
- Eco-efficiency driven by technical, institutional and social innovation.

Figure 4.2 Putting the biosphere at the center of the economy

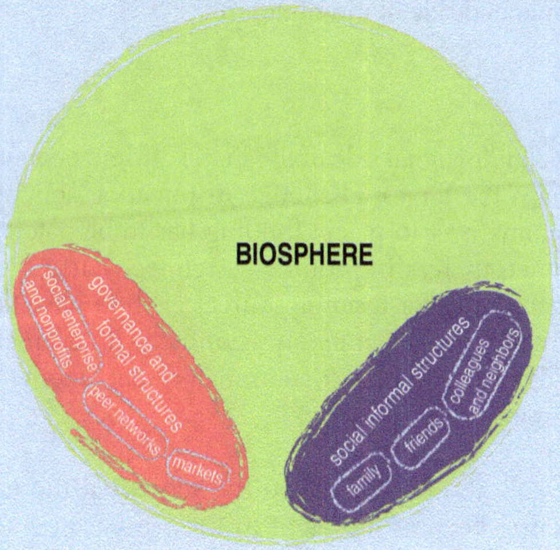

bigger role for gift economies and social production, could support new, less consumerist forms of novelty and stimulation, as well as develop new commitment strategies. By taking the emphasis off financial markets we open up opportunities for new, less consumerist forms of social language. These facets are important to a sustainable economy because it seems likely that they will help us avoid the rebound effect, in which efficiency gains (savings) simply become absorbed by new and expanded forms of consumption.

We cannot deny the fact that life has a financial side, and quite obviously financial resources are a part of supporting ourselves and our work. Indeed, a steady state economy does not equate to an economy without financial transactions. The argument that economists such as Tim Jackson, Juliet Schor, Peter Victor and Richard Norgaard are making, rather, is that the pursuit of continuous economic growth is not a suitable goal for society. Many aspects of well-being don't come from material wealth or high incomes, but rather from the quality of our social relationships, our daily surroundings and meaningful activities (recall the box on p. 66 on well-being). The market simply does not make all the right decisions for population-level well-being.

It is beyond the scope of this book (and probably the readers' interest) to investigate in detail the economistic issues of public sector investment, consumer debt and savings, and so forth. The point here is that as yet there is no simple blueprint for a sustainable economy. There are instead a number of struggles across disciplines that converge on the consumerist challenges we have identified. The notion of struggle, and particularly the politics of this struggle, is the topic of Chapter 5. Below, we look at the practical issues of how to fund and professionalize design activism in the conditions of the "here and now", looking at the financial side of the situation.

FINANCING ACTIVIST PRACTICE

Turning back to that financial side of life in the current economy, we find that funding is perhaps the largest challenge in pursuing activist work. Since a sustainable economy isn't in place, funding has to be patched together and can involve numerous funding sources. Architect Larry Scarpa comments that it is not uncommon for funding sources each to have their own design guidelines; "in most cases the guidelines conflict with each other" and it can be difficult finding a common denominator that doesn't compromise a design's ability to inspire.[24]

Architect Liz Ogbu also comments on the sense that the use of design for social benefit hasn't been as prevalent in the US because a number of US foundations are focused on overcoming poverty in the developing world, and use social design mainly in that context.[25] For many design activists there is also a financial trade-off between consulting work (such as publications, expert advice or plans) that provides income and capital projects that require large-scale investment and full-time project management. In addition, architects have found that many foundations won't fund capital projects such as buildings.

And yet, the work is happening. Activist clients are bringing designers on board. Activist designers are bringing clients on board. Activist designers are working as their own clients, and activist governments are creating policies and projects that facilitate design solutions. The following section profiles five approaches that designers are using to find their financial way through activist territory.

Articulate lost social values and harvest them

An overarching theme concerns how activist projects speak up for lost social and environmental values. One approach is to become more adept at harvesting cost savings from social and environmental benefits. For example, the developers of the mixed-use BedZed (Beddington Zero Energy Development) in south London argued that social and environmental values emerging from the project through reduced car travel, better land use, lower energy use and so forth meant that although they did not bid the highest for the land that they bought from the council, their bid constituted the best whole value to the council.[26] In this case designers call upon "subsidy" from outside the project itself, based on wider values that the project provides.

Values may also link one design practice to another. This sometimes leads designers to develop networks that serve as shadow, values-based teams that can be called upon quickly and easily to develop cost-effective, compelling bids on social change projects. Although this may happen organically from actual project experience, it can also be planned through a conscious effort to develop networks.

As Rebar's Blaine Merker commented, another path involves taking activist concerns into your "day job," speaking up for those issues that are left out by norms of cost and profit. He says, "Whenever we talk to students we try to talk about … the opportunities you have as a designer to be an activist on the inside, that there're a lot of different ways to be an activist. Sometimes just being in a meeting and really pushing hard for an idea that might be unpopular, you're being an activist." He also points out that Rebar's work has relied on people "inside" city agencies, who see value in the work and push for it in enabling ways. In a sense these city-employed design enthusiasts are also design activists.

Design's unique aspects

Design's visual nature, hands-on materiality and sometimes playful experimentation can make its activism particularly exciting and inspiring, often to stakeholders who may never have thought about "space" or the design of processes before, or in the context to hand.

In a number of cases, one or two exciting design activist projects build a reputation that then leads to commissions for further work. Perhaps this amounts to "spectacular design" in social and environmental terms. Design groups such as Fantastic Norway, Rebar, Public Architecture, Electroland, The Living and a number of other firms have experienced this phenomenon.

In one example where an outsider picked up on design's unique aspects, UK Baroness Lola Young saw design as a way to open a discussion; she set up a project on fashion and ethics partly as a way to attract young people to discussions of political issues. In a related case, activists have consciously manipulated fashion sensibilities in an effort to reduce cooling requirements in office settings. In a Japanese program designed to encourage more informal and "cooler" dressing during summer, the tool was a fashion show. During the show, "dozens of CEOs and other senior executives strutted about in casual business wear with open necks and lightweight materials."[27] Japanese Prime Minister Junichiro Koizumi was also featured in the press wearing a short-sleeved shirt without a tie.

Rebalance

Another approach to activist work takes the "rebalancing" of the economy down to the level of an individual design practice. One common approach to practice concerns offsetting lower paid, values-based work with higher paid commercial work, making the design firm somewhat like a social enterprise. For example, Pyatok Associates, specialists in affordable housing, cross-subsidize lower paid housing work with higher paid design for student accommodations.[28] In another case, one architect formally connects individual commercial projects with pro bono or reduced fee work, so that commercial clients are aware of the contribution they make.[29]

Some designers rebalance by taking up part-time academic posts as a base for experimental, activist work that might be viewed as academic research or might occur collaboratively through teaching projects.

Of course, we also subsidize this work with plain old volunteerism and individual contribution. According to the five points of well-being (see Chapter 2 p. 66), which highlights "giving," this is probably a healthy choice.

New organizational forms

Other design activists delve into new organizational types. Nonprofit advocacy organizations, membership networks, certification agencies and independent educational institutions are springing up to promote and implement design activism. This blossoming of organizational formats probably also speaks to the real lack of infrastructure in the social sector. And although the rise of these "new" organizational formats suggests that the old professional service design studio isn't always suited to design activism, this old format arguably still has plenty of life in it.

Architect John Peterson formed Public Architecture, a nonprofit group separate from his professional practice, to pursue "activist" projects. He now writes that he wouldn't recommend this approach to others. He comments, "One thing I would like to make clear is that forming a nonprofit organization is probably one of the *least* efficient ways for mainstream firms and professionals to do public interest work."[30] He points out that even for projects that require nonprofit status, firms can partner with fiscal sponsors. He emphasizes the need for better public interest projects, not different kinds of design organizations to work on them.

Peterson's point may be well taken for building projects, but looking across the range of project types and scopes and the diverse partnerships involved, one does get the sense that new formats are useful. Architecture for Humanity or Architecture 2030 wouldn't function in a professional services format. Design rating systems, such as LEED or SEED, that develop through inclusive and collaborative processes benefit from having an active membership. Even so, some prominent design firms are still forming nonprofits for service design efforts. For example, product design industry leader IDEO launched a nonprofit arm, IDEO.org.

Policy formulation and interpretation

Architects and designers have the scope to create policy as well as interpret policy through a design lens. One example is a Canadian National Architecture Policy proposed by the Royal Architectural Institute of Canada. The policy would guide how the federal government invests in infrastructure and explicitly links the quality of public design to social health.[31] Lucia Athens outlines another example where designers within public agencies have championed green building policies that guide the design and construction of all new public buildings.[32] The author's own experience of working with a county solid waste agency suggests another approach. During three years of interpreting policy to create programs on solid waste and recycling, few policies ever mentioned "design." Yet in the hands of the author and colleagues, the resulting programs had distinct design dimensions, particularly emphasizing the transformative power of design with respect to "waste."

Some forms of city hacking also make use of creative interpretation of the spatial and material potential within policy. For example, Rebar's park(ing) day makes use of parking policies that allow time-based access to land. Other efforts involve getting permits for things that are allowed, and then converting them to things that are desired—often in keeping with the policy goals of public agencies, such as creating more urban green space, improving urban environments for children or encouraging alternatives to car travel.[33]

A national design council, if you have one, can also serve as a place for reinterpreting the value of design, beyond a simple contribution to economic growth. The UK Design Council recently held a summit on design's role in stimulating economic growth. But at the same time, the Council has also recently taken on an agenda to address social policy problems, such as national healthcare and aging. This agenda usually engages a diverse range of participants and gives designers opportunities to network on topics of social design.

A national design council The UK's Design Council, London, now merged with the Commission for Architecture and the Built Environment (CABE).

Table 4.2 Financing for design activism

Technique	Description	Areas of knowledge
Articulate lost social values and, where possible, harvest them	Articulate social and environmental values to justify choices, build values based networks	Familiarity with social metrics or ways of estimating social and environmental values, knowledge of stakeholders (often members of a social movement) who might serve as a network around different social and environmental issues
Leverage design's unique elements	Aim for "spectacular" in social and environmental terms	Ability to frame social and environmental issues through design in compelling ways that resonate within a broader system (a form of spatially or visually compelling "social" innovation)
Rebalance economic issues within a single firm or group	Offset lower paid activist work with higher paid commercial work	An understanding of the potential for rebalancing in different contexts: academic, commercial, government
Use new organizational forms	Alongside professional services studios, consider a range of other organization formats	Working knowledge of possible organizational forms: nonprofits, co-ops, social enterprise, membership networks, independent educational groups, certification agencies, etc.
Interpret or reinterpret policy	Propose design-related policies at various scales (cities, states, nations), interpret existing social and environmental policies through a design lens	Knowledge of policy access points—the people, ideas, and techniques behind policies

Whereas commercial models of practice typically focus on knowledge about business benefits and costs, financing activist practice takes designers into new territory. Table 4.2 summarizes the five approaches discussed above, but also highlights how these approaches suggest relatively new areas of knowledge for design.

CONCLUSION

This chapter, together with Chapter 3, has outlined the problems with consumerism and economic growth, arguing that many activist projects aim to articulate and often counteract exactly those problems that the financial system ignores or causes. We now turn to the topic of social movement activism, to look at these same issues through the lens of political methods for change and shifting patterns of power.

Above, we saw rating systems such as LEED in market terms, influencing consumer "demand" for socially improved products. But LEED and other rating systems may also be seen as collective action ultimately aimed at political change—changing policy and the norms of practice. The US Green Building Council mobilized (large numbers of rated buildings), advocated (encouraged and cajoled the use of the rating to improve the environment), and organized (through LEED professional certification). Similarly, public, nonprofit and educational institutions—activist clients—built many of LEED's "firsts," the most aspirational buildings. Whether or not it is useful to publicly discuss LEED in activist terms, there can be little argument against the usefulness of understanding it in these terms.

NOTES

1 "About SOCAP," (n.d.). Available at http://socialcapitalmarkets.net/about-socap/ (accessed 9 September 2011).
2 Michael Edwards, *Just Another Emperor? The Myths and Realities of Philanthrocapitalism* (London: The Young Foundation and Demos, 2008), pp. 7–9.
3 Marjorie Kelly and Allen White, *Corporate Design: The Missing Business and Public Policy Issue of Our Time* (Boston, MA: Tellus Institute, 2007).
4 William Davies, *Reinventing the Firm* (London: Demos, 2009), p. 14.
5 "STAR Community Index: Sustainability Goals & Guiding Principles," ICLEI, Local Governments for Sustainability USA (October 2010).
6 Jon Kolko, email interview by the author, 6 September 2011.
7 Bruce Nussbaum, "Let's Give an 'F' to the FT List of Best Business Schools", ChangeObserver: News about Design and Social Innovation, 10 March 2011. Available at http://changeobserver.designobserver.com/feature/lets-give-an-f-to-the-ft-list-of-best-business-schools/25528/ (accessed 12 September 2011).
8 Jonathan Porritt, *Capitalism as if the World Matters* (London: Earthscan, 2007).
9 Edwards, *Just Another Emperor?*, p. 8.
10 Karen Litfin, "The Sacred and the Profane in the Ecological Politics of Sacrifice", in *The Enironmental Politics of Sacrifice*, ed. Michael F. Maniates and John M. Meyer (Cambridge, MA: MIT Press, 2010), p. 130.
11 Eve Kahn, "Play: Toys by Momoll", *ID* (December 2006).
12 Edwards, *Just Another Emperor?*, p. 12.
13 Melina T. Tuan, *Measuring and/or Estimating Social Value Creation: Insights into Eight Integrated Cost Approaches* (Seattle: Bill & Melinda Gates Foundation, 2008), p. 6.
14 Muhammad Yunus (n.d.) "Social Business Entrepreneurs are the Solution". Available at http://www.grameen-info.org/index.php?option=com_content&task=view&id=217&Itemid=172&limit=1&limitstart=0 (accessed 10 May 2008).

15 Yochai Benkler, *The Wealth of Networks: How Social Production Transforms Markets and Freedom* (London: Yale University Press, 2006); and David Rejeski, "Anticipations", in *Sustainability at the Speed of Light*, ed. Dennis Pamlin (Solna: WWF Sweden, 2002).

16 Benkler, *The Wealth of Networks*, p. 55 (emphasis added). Benkler estimates that if you used a workforce to try to capture an amount of time equivalent to that theoretically available time on a single day, you would need 350,000 people working 40-hour weeks without vacation for between three and eight years.

17 John Quiggin, "The End of the Cash Nexus" *Crooked Timber* (March 2009). Available at http://crookedtimber.org/2009/03/05/the-end-of-the-cash-nexus/ (accessed 15 September 2011).

18 M. Fischer-Kowalski, M. Swilling, E.U. von Weizsäcker, Y. Ren, Y. Moriguchi, W. Crane, F. Krausmann, N. Eisenmenger, S. Giljum, P. Hennicke, P. Romero Lankao and A. Siriban Manalang, "Decoupling Natural Resource Use and Environmental Impacts from Economic Growth, A Report of the Working Group on Decoupling to the International Resource Panel" (United Nations Environment Program 2011).

19 Ibid., p. 38.

20 Anna Coote, Jane Franklin and Andrew Simms, *21 Hours* (London: New Economics Foundation, 2010).

21 Juliet Schor, "Time for a Change: The Role of Working Hours in the Transition to Sustainability". Keynote speech at RESOLVE Conference of Surrey University, "Living Sustainability: Values, Policies and Practices", London, 15 June 2011.

22 Tim Jackson, "Prosperity Without Growth? A Transition to a Sustainable Economy" (Sustainable Development Commission, 2009), p. 82.

23 Ibid., p. 8.

24 Jane F. Kolleeny, "Practice Matters: Giving Versus Getting: Altruism is Alive and Well in Architecture", *Architectural Record* (September 2003).

25 Liz Ogbu, telephone interview by the author, 18 August 2011.

26 Pooran Desai, *One Planet Communities: A Real Life Guide to Sustainable Living* (Hoboken: John Wiley & Sons, 2009); and Pooran Desai, interview, 10 March 2011.

27 Tim Brown, *Change By Design* (New York: HarperCollins, 2009), p. 131.

28 Jane F. Kolleeny, "Practice Matters".

29 Liz Ogbu, interview.

30 John Peterson, "Mobilizing Mainstream Professionals to Work for the Public Good", in *Expanding Architecture*, ed. Bryan Bell and Katie Wakeford (New York: Metropolis Books, 2009), p. 102.

31 Andrew Blum, "Canadians Propose National Architectural Policy", *Architectural Record* (April 2003).

32 Lucia Athens, *Building an Emerald City: A Guide to Creating Green Building Policies and Programs* (Washington, DC: Island Press, 2010).

33 Some examples are found in Scott Burnham, *Finding the Truth in Systems: in Praise of Design-hacking* (London: Royal Society for the Encouragement of Arts, Manufactures and Commerce (RSA), 2009).

Chapter 5

Picking up moves from social movements

Within design disciplines, design activism is often seen as "social" or "public interest" rather than political. It is viewed as a good deed rather than as a political struggle. By contrast, social movement campaigns start with the premise of political struggle for change. For this reason we can see design activism's political side more clearly when we view it in social movement terms. In particular, the framework shows methods for trying to bring about change in arenas where the issues are typically cash poor and value rich.

The introductory chapter showed evidence that there is a spectrum of views among designers on the issue of politics. Some designers have particular reasons for avoiding explicit political connotations—even when they themselves may see the work as political—whereas others feel that architects and other designers are typically politically naïve, neutral, or even irresponsible.[1] But to be fair, where would architects or designers learn about political struggle within a typical design curriculum? Even in courses that discuss politics, how often would design processes or artifacts be viewed in terms of political methods for change?

That is what we attempt in this chapter: to view architecture and design in terms of political methods for change. We start by considering how activism has been framed in design terms, before moving on to the task of framing design in movement activist terms.

ACTIVISM FRAMED IN DESIGN TERMS

We can describe several broad categories starting to emerge within design for describing what constitutes design as activism. It is useful to review them here to get a sense of the breadth of this work.

Unique cases defying classification

Several recent book treatments of design as activism have emphasized the uniqueness of each case. In architecture, for example, Bryan Bell and Katie Wakeford's *Expanding Architecture: Design as Activism* is a collection of essays centered largely on affordable housing. Strikingly, reviewing this book, Fred Bernstein suggests that there isn't a single rubric with which to compare the projects presented; there is no way to generalize what architects should do as activists.[2]

Another Book, Lisa Findley's *Building Change: Architecture, Politics and Cultural Agency*, examines four recent architectural projects that aim to represent previously marginalized peoples or causes, primarily through the design and construction of cultural centers. Findley writes, "projects that explicitly take on the issues of cultural and political power, that are an overt reassertion of cultural agency and dignity, that seek to symbolically represent a formerly invisible people, or that have overt agendas for social change are, by their very definition, *unique* in almost every way."[3] In terms of products, Fuad-Luke's *Design Activism: Beautiful Strangeness for a Sustainable World* includes such a broad landscape for design activism that the reader is again left feeling that design activism defies classification—each case is unique.

Conventional activism by designers

Design activism also includes cases where designers take up conventional activist approaches. For example, The Designers Accord uses the conventional format of pledging or formally signing on to a set of positions, as in a conventional petition signing.[4] Jody Boehnert in the UK recently conducted a design teach-in under the name "2012 Imperative," to educate designers on ecological literacy. These and other examples show that designers do use conventional activist formats, but this categorization leaves out a more explicit role in activism for design processes, structures and objects.

Design elements of protest

A related theme in the literature concerns designed elements as features of protest, including the nature of places for public protest, symbolic artifacts used in protest, and tools of protest. For example, Tali Hatuka and Rachel Kallus profile Yitzhak Rabin Square in Tel Aviv and note that the "architectural placemaking in the square has shaped public discourse by reinforcing certain formal patterns of congregating."[5] The square, site of the 1995 assassination of Prime Minister Rabin, is highly controlled through barricades and surveillance. The authors document how the architecture of the site makes it powerful for both authorities who control it and crowds (as large as 400,000) who use it as a site of protest. Authors quote one political protester saying, "It is perceived as a place of power due to its size. Pictures of the crowd taken from the roofs convey that power."[6]

Lance Hosey offers the example of the shanty towns built on US college campuses to protest university investment in apartheid South Africa. He notes, "The shanties' aesthetic dissonance with their site expressed the moral irony that the protestors saw in the university's investments."[7] He calls these "protest constructions" which reduce architecture to its most rudimentary form that still has social meaning. Cowan reports on another protest construction, the Aboriginal Tent Embassy located adjacent to Australia's Federal Parliament. The structure symbolically reclaims land for the Aboriginal people, and the author calls this "a rich architecture of land rights activism" and suggests that activists are "deploying the architectural structure and symbol of the tent to reclaim the freedom to dwell nomadically across the Australian continent."[8]

Other examples show design more explicitly as a tool for activism. For instance, architects have created tree houses for protestors occupying threatened forests, and designed protest housing (temporary housing erected illegally) to raise awareness of housing shortages.[9] Jody Boehnart describes how designers for the UK's climate camp created shields emblazoned with large photographs of faces representing the diversity of the world's population.[10] The camp itself is an example of a "protest construction" such as the shanty towns mentioned above. These examples show that design does have a role in conventional protest, but this categorization leaves it bound to these conventional forms.

Collections of cause-oriented case studies

One of the most common ways that the field of design has characterized activism is as groups of cause-specific cases, such as green buildings or humanitarian design services. Chapter 3 highlighted the Design for Reuse Primer. Other collections of case studies feature pro bono projects, eco-products, participatory design or emergency shelter. A variation on this approach is a collection of work on social issues from one designer or one organization, such as the work by Rural Studio. These sets of cases are often collected to demonstrate principles for best practice related to the cause. While these are useful and productive, they offer specialized definitions for specific kinds of design activism.

Catalogs of case studies *The Eco-Design Handbook* catalogs eco-products.

Critical design and critical architecture

Another common way that design has taken up activism is through the notion of criticism and criticality. Critical architecture arose partly in response to early consumerist society. For example, George Baird suggests that critical architecture resists the commoditization of culture.[11] K. Michael Hays sees critical architecture as resisting "conciliatory representation of external forces," and at its best producing new cultural knowledge.[12] An example might be Maya Lin's Vietnam Veterans Memorial in Washington, DC.

Simon Bowen cites "critical artifacts" as those that examine ideologies embedded in products, often providing a proposition against which audience members balance their own values.[13] Further, Benjamin Millen suggests that critical design engages with cultural experimentation and criticism by presenting singular, radical or confrontational objects, sometimes characterized as "fictional products."[14] An example is Stuart Walker's roughly hewn, exposed designs that critique the "perfect" aesthetics of mass-produced goods. He argues that these perfect products seduce and trick consumers by using many different slick exteriors to present essentially the same innards.[15] Critical design projects often operate in an abstract or indirect way.

Wall phone This critiques the perfect aesthetic of mass production.
Photo courtesy of Stuart Walker.

The protest of bad design

It is worth noting that some researchers within sociology and political science, upon hearing of design activism, assumed that it meant "protesting against bad design." Although design literature describes cases of protest against design proposals (often on the basis of historic preservation, aesthetics or contextual suitability), this is typically not what designers have in mind when they discuss design activism.

Architects and designers have sometimes struggled to make sense of this wide spectrum of work, with people at one end of the spectrum often critical of those at the other end. One useful aspect of social movement concepts is how they gracefully explain this diversity within one meaningful framework for activist methods.

METHODS AND TACTICS

Activist Rinku Sen offers a useful way to characterize methods when she describes five main types of what she calls "change work": community organizing, service provision, advocacy, mobilization and solidarity.[16] Sen's work focuses specifically on organizing, so the following interpretation is derived from her skeletal list.

Community organizing involves people working on their own behalf—people suffering from an abuse or injustice taking action themselves, for example, to fight for civil rights or for access to decent housing. Organizing often leads to new organizations being formed. Community organizing involves long-term engagement and cultivating leadership among those who suffer most in current conditions. In design terms this might take the form of self-build or community design.

Service provision often fills gaps in basic services to those in need such as legal advice, health clinics or homeless shelters. Services also include education such as job training or access to resources such as tools or financing. Common in architecture, service provision might take the form of a university design-build project for a nonprofit client.

Advocacy involves lobbying for and acting on behalf of a group in need, without much involvement from that group. An extreme case would be advocating for "nature" where it has no means to advocate for itself. But degrees of advocacy exist for many different groups and issues in society. In architecture or design terms, advocacy often occurs through cause-specific trainings, rating systems or demonstration buildings.

Mobilization describes a large-scale show of concern, traditionally in forms such as petition signing or marches, but without expectation of repeat or continued involvement of the participants. In design terms there are several ways to think about this, but an example might be a design competition. Solidarity involves expressing common concerns with social movements, often through efforts to influence popular culture's language and concepts, for example, through opinion pieces or artworks. In design terms, critical design, especially visually radical design, could be an example of solidarity, as might be expressed in the design of a memorial or other symbolic feature.

Sen notes that these are all legitimate approaches to social change, even though they have their own tactics. She suggests that each has weaknesses. For example, community organizers sometimes build locally powerful organizations that are too narrowly focused; mobilization and solidarity efforts sometimes don't build permanent power.[17] At the close of this chapter we examine these methods more thoroughly through design examples.

Situating methods in between campaigns and tactics

A social movement framework is useful to architecture and design in the way it focuses on the process of bringing about social change—change solutions as opposed to design problems to be solved. Here we examine the social movement framework in more detail. While a social movement provides a broad narrative, actors within a movement propose specific strategies, better alternatives to what exist now. For example, the environmental movement proposes that we need social change to "save and protect" the environment. Individual organizations propose diverse strategies such as species conservation, urban forestry or cleaning up toxic sites. To implement any one strategy, an organization develops a particular campaign.

For urban forestry a strategy might be to expand the acreage of urban forest. To form a campaign, or set of campaigns, to "expand urban forests" we must identify the changes needed and determine who can make those changes. Is the problem availability of land? Poor survival of seedlings? Protection of existing trees? Once we diagnose the problems, we propose better alternatives and a way to motivate action toward these alternatives. For example, using mobilization, we might hold a mass event. An alternative method would be community organizing. Each method contains a variety of possible tactics. For example, a mass event could use the tactic of a tree planting, a petition signing or a tree festival. For organizing, our tactics might be to teach school children how to map existing urban forests, or to train community tree wardens. This nesting of movements, organizations, campaigns, methods and tactics is shown in Figure 5.1.

Urban forestry What's the problem and how do we solve it?

Figure 5.1 Movement, method, tactic

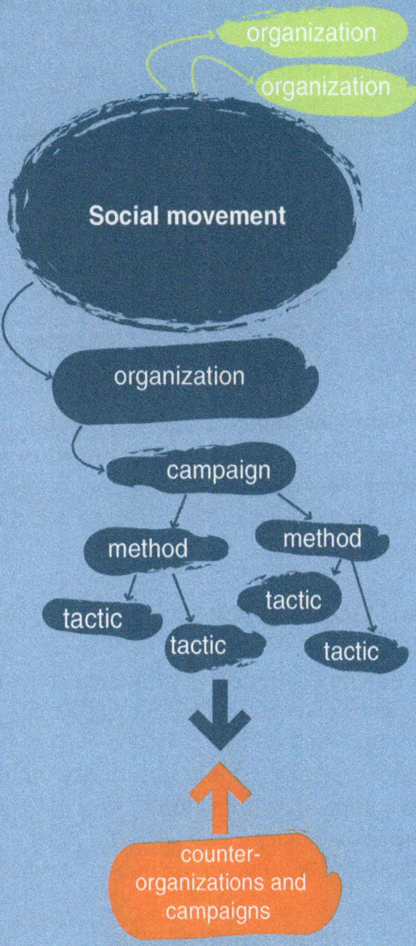

Chapter 1 mentioned that social movement dynamics are complex and even contradictory, and typically, actual campaigns are never so straightforward as shown in Figure 5.1. In addition, no campaign exists in a vacuum and every campaign message meets with counter-messages. For example, a campaign message to expand urban forests might meet with a counter-message in favor of cutting public spending or moving money from parks and forestry to urban transportation. In that sense social movements can be in competition with each other. Nevertheless, the sequence in Figure 5.1 presents a useful mental model for design activists, whether for their own campaigns (within design), or for thinking about how to support or complement the campaigns of others.

The urban forestry movement, like any other, has a wide range of actors. Some are located in nonprofit advocacy and organizing groups, others are located in local government (such as environmental or parks agencies). Businesses offering the tools and technologies of urban forestry also play a role, as do individual citizen volunteers—possibly even celebrity advocates. In addition, university-based researchers and scholars may be involved, examining everything from carbon sequestration by urban trees, to social meaning derived from urban nature. It is useful to have a sense of this broader movement because it may suggest relevant partner organizations, reveal related campaigns that are already ongoing, show lessons learned from past campaigns, and clarify where design approaches, projects and tactics might make the most difference relative to other campaigns.

Tactics

The above sections have touched upon tactics, but we examine them here in more detail. Conventional activist tactics include a range of approaches such as sit-ins, petitions or strikes. The list below is adapted from two studies of tactics where a large number of events (more than 5000 in each) were studied.[18] The tactics include:

- petitions and public letters, leafleting;
- press conferences;
- teach-ins and other "alternative" or contrasting formats and mechanisms;
- silent protests (such as a candle-light vigil);
- demonstrations and marches;
- public/outdoor assemblies/rallies/inside assemblies;
- procedural complaints—litigation;
- defamation, verbal attacks;
- physical blockades, sit-ins, occupations and other hindrances;
- strikes;
- theft/burglary/physical property damage;
- violence/bodily harm.

Studies show that many of these tactics are durable and long-standing. For example, the tactic of barricades has been used for at least five centuries in France.[19] This set of commonly known tactics forms a public "repertoire" of actions. To use a term more familiar in design, they form a set of types. Tactics occur in familiar types for several reasons. First, they represent a stable body of knowledge about what to do in struggles for change. Stability is important for gaining wider participation—activism is often constrained by what people know how to do.[20] Second, tactics are modular and flexible. Consider the classic tactic of a sit-in and its flexibility to become a teach-in, or even a die-in (in the case of AIDS activists). Third, the tactics often communicate key attributes of an issue and its supporters, such as an issue's worthiness, as well as the unity, number and commitment of supporters. Indeed, Charles Tilly and Sydney Tarrow characterize these four aspects as the acronym WUNC.[21]

An extensive review of more than a thousand cases of design-related activism suggests that there is also a set of activist tactics found in architecture and design.[22] These tactics take spatial and material form, or occur in design processes. The tactics represent what people involved in design commonly know how to do in efforts to bring about change. Some of these tactics have come up in previous sections, such as competitions, demonstration buildings or visualizing information (for example, in maps). The range of tactics is shown in Table 5.1.

Although designers do make use of conventional tactics, such as the Designer's Accord pledge, mentioned above, there are some themes that make design-related tactics different. First is the theme of generation instead of resistance. Although many conventional tactics shown in the above list stem from a protest stance that is oppositional or resistant, by contrast many design tactics are generative—rather than "opposing" they "propose," or generate better alternative solutions. David Hess, writing about technology-oriented movements, argues that social movements "not only oppose certain types of new technologies and products but they develop and diffuse alternatives."[23]

A second key difference between conventional tactics and design-related tactics is their duration. Many conventional tactics involve temporary events. Indeed, the social movement literature includes a strand that researches "protest events" as a way of understanding the progress of social movements.[24] But design-related tactics such as demonstration buildings, mapping projects or landscape connections are often not temporary events, although they may comprise a number of event-like moments. Both of these differences suggest that design-related tactics may be working in different ways from conventional tactics, a subject that we investigate in more detail in Chapter 6.

What happens after the campaign?

Some campaigns are successful, and others fail. When a campaign is successful, typically the change sought by activists becomes a new norm. For example, disability rights campaigners succeeded in getting the Americans with Disabilities Act passed. The new norm raises the bar for social or environmental performance. Yet movements typically carry on beyond any one campaign and efforts continue to raise the bar further. For this reason we see continuing activism to improve access for disabled people, for example, through improving regulation or demonstrating how to integrate new technologies.

Table 5.1 Design activist tactics

Tactic	Description
Protest artifact	Protest structure, product, space, place, plan or graphic: often opposed, offensive or confrontational artifacts that make a cutting, critical statement prompting reflection on the morality of the status quo. May also be a specific tool of protest.
Service artifact	Service structure, system, product, space, place, plan or graphic: humanitarian aid to victims, for example, of war, disaster or poverty. Some groups are victims of their environments, for example, disabled people.
Demonstration artifact	Demonstration structure, system, product, space, place, plan or graphic: a better alternative to the status quo, typically seen as a positive, if imperfect effort, a model that others can use.
Communication	Make information visual or tactile, create symbols: an effort to make information visual or tactile (or both) or to create, preserve or extend symbols, where a symbol is something that represents something else by association, resemblance or convention.
Connection	Linkages such as doorways, gateways, borders, bridges or view corridors: attempts to make physical or visual links that often repair, restore, signify or enrich social and environmental conditions.
Rating system	Criteria, guidelines, rating schemes: includes formally structured rating systems or labeling systems, but also guidelines and criteria that typically set out metrics by which we can measure performance: Where the guidelines adhered to? Did the project meet the criteria?
Competition	Competitions that call for proposals or that call for already complete work, award schemes.
Exhibitions	Exhibits, gallery and museum shows, site-specific installations.
Research and critique	Design research, critiques, polemics, manifestos: the process of using research results or critical thinking as evidence or basis for change, often takes the form of written arguments.
Event	Conferences, lectures, seminars, workshops.
Conventional	Testimony, policy drafts, fundraising, books, publications, TV shows, films.
Social exchange	Links among people, consultation/stakeholder input, self build, co-design: efforts to make social connections, and weave social fabric, hinging on specific relationships (as opposed to general ideas of "community").

Accessibility The passage of laws or regulations, such as ADA (Americans with Disabilities Act), doesn't end activism, but rather raises the bar. Photo Catherine Parsons Stokley.

Another case is the US Green Building Council's LEED rating system, which has become a norm to the extent that a number of cities and states use the silver rating, for example, as their own building standard.[25] Yet the green building movement has continued to raise this bar, for example, with Architecture 2030's tackling of carbon-neutral buildings or The Living Building Challenge's "restorative" paradigm for green building.

PORTFOLIO OF DESIGN METHODS

At this stage we return to the idea that the portfolio of five activist methods, such as organizing or mobilization, applies fairly well to design activism. Below we look at the design relevance of each method in turn.

Organizing

Background

At its core, organizing involves working with people so that they develop a capacity to solve their own problems across a range of issues such as neighborhood renewal, education, employment and social networks. Community organizing is a long-standing professional practice of community development, through which an organizer gets to know a community, helps the community to identify and cultivate its own leaders, and contributes to strategic plans for making positive changes for the community through the community's own actions organized by its leaders.

Traditionally organizing is a very local process, often targeted at neighborhoods in extreme poverty or other disadvantage. Community organizers, community workers, and community development groups employ a wide range of approaches all aimed at developing community skills, awareness, competency and confidence. Some strands of organizing are more political than others, with a focus that sees community development as a process of building more powerful local organizations that can gradually shift the balance of power and resources within society toward more just and sustainable ends.[26] In some cases community organizing is aligned with collective action or protest, through which community members confront institutions or elected officials directly with demands for change.

Designers partnering with organizers Clarifying street vending rules for all concerned. © The Center for Urban Pedagogy, 2009 "Vendor Power" is an issue of Making Policy Public produced by CUP in collaboration with the Street Vendor Project and Candy Chang.

How designers engage with this method

Designers have engaged with community organizing in various forms, sometimes in partnership with organizers, sometimes initiating projects that communities then take forward. Although not all of the examples listed below fit the community organizing model precisely, they do suggest how designers are moving in a direction that takes them beyond simply "designing for" or even "designing with" to a point of empowering others to design.

The CUP (Center for Urban Pedagogy, based in New York City) is an example of a design-aware group that partners with organizers. The CUP's "making policy public" program aims to visualize complex policy issues for specific constituencies, such as immigrants. Example projects have concerned clarifying the legal rules for street vendors and examining access to banks. Through clarifying how cities work, these projects enable people to more effectively understand and participate in the processes that affect them.[27] In terms of the tactics introduced above, the CUP often makes use of visual and material realization of information.

An example from the UK is The Glass-House, a nonprofit group that supports community-led design in other organizations. The Glass-House specifically emphasizes building design skills within organizations, as well as developing community leadership of the design process. An example is St. Paul's Park in Bristol, where a citizen group initiated and led the design of a new park. The design training that citizens received from The Glass-House helped them gain not only skill to lead the design process (working with Play by Design) but also confidence to defend their aspirations with the city council and deliver on their vision.[28]

In the case of both the CUP and The Glass-House, the organizing group serves as a client. The CUP example shows the development of an enabling tool as an outcome—a tool that may serve as a starting point for community organizing processes. The Glass-House acts more like an organizer in terms of building design-related capacities within a local community. Other groups that follow this model include community design centers and university-based design studios that work with organizing groups.

Otto von Busch provides a range of examples of design-led hacking experiments in fashion. For example, Giana González leads participants in decoding well-known fashion brands. The "code" is made up of finishing details, fabrics, colors, silhouettes, patterns or material combinations. After decoding (or reverse engineering) the brand, participants then remake old clothes using the code revealed. He comments:

St. Paul's Park The community model helped to defend the design ambition for the final project. Photos courtesy of The Glass-House Community Led Design.

> [T]hey mimic the original brand, but they do not make copies. Instead they analyze their resources to see how these old components best become new code, but a code performing the same visual or material function as the original brand. They remake something new, something unique, an experimental "program" out of an existing and branded code.[29]

Different than hacking, but arguably related to organizing is the approach of making design processes and approaches "open." An example is Architecture for Humanity's Open Architecture Network, which serves as a platform for freely sharing design solutions and concepts. The prospect behind such "open" efforts, which make them somewhat parallel to or suitable for organizing, is their aim to move the passive consumer into a role of active production. They are a step removed, perhaps, for not having a physical place from which to catalyze neighborhoods or other groups.

Previous examples such as Fablabs and the park(ing) project also contain aspects of organizing. At the level of a neighborhood or single street, the park(ing) project provides a simple mechanism for everyday community members to organize themselves through urban hacking.

On the face of it, decoding couture fashion labels or making your own toys (as in the Fablab example) may not seem at all activist, unless we revisit the question of who activism is for. In a previous chapter we defined activism as being carried out on behalf of an excluded or neglected group. We noted that the effects of consumerism and economic growth in our capitalist system mean that we are all struggling with the way in which that system suppresses real values, such as local economic self-determination or healthy environments. In this sense we are all excluded from meeting our real needs, those that are embedded in social and environmental systems.

Yet the view is that many people experience this reality, this suppression of social and environmental values, as a vague or abstract sense of dissatisfaction, depression or stress. In community organizers' terms, many people fail to see the connection between their own vague or abstract personal feelings and the wider social, economic and political circumstances that make these personal feelings widely shared. For this reason, some activists have begun to address issues of consumerism and consumption through community organizing that frames consumers as the neglected and excluded group. Examples are behavior change initiatives such as the global action plan and transition towns.

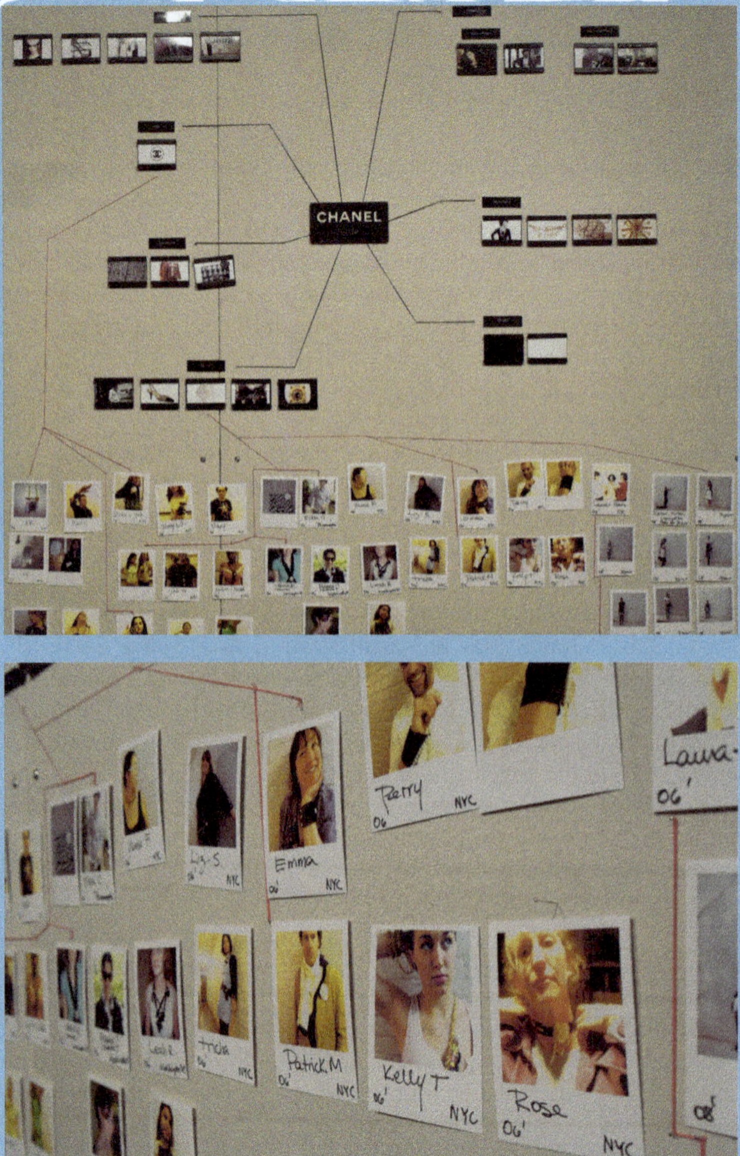

Fashion experiments The top image shows a mapping of the visual and material Chanel code. The bottom image shows how people used the code to remake old items. Photo Maria Mayer Feng.

TRANSITION TOWNS

The transition town concept was initiated by Rob Hopkins with the idea that local community members can take on the task of adapting their own towns to a scenario when cheap oil is no longer available. The approach emphasizes localization and resilience and, in addition to helping people form and work in action groups, it encourages groups to get out and try things, to find things that work.

Transition towns try to plug leaks in their local economies through inventive community initiatives. Examples include community-owned bakeries (interest is paid in bread) and shops, as well as food initiatives that improve the resilience and breadth of local agriculture. The approach is also asset-based, starting from what is possible and moving on from there. For example, in moving toward self-sufficiency in food, one town declared that it could at least be self sufficient in garlic. Small projects then build social capital and empower groups to take on bigger tasks.[30]

Services

Background

Service provision has typically revolved around facilities, training and specialist or technical advice, typically for people in relatively extreme need. Beneficiaries for service provision may include homeless people, victims of natural disasters or wars, members of an impoverished community, or people who are excluded by disabilities. Examples of conventional services might include community centers, transportation services or legal aid.

Service provision crosses a spectrum from difficult to dire circumstances. Job training for inner-city youths is perhaps a less dire need than emergency shelter after a natural disaster, or refugee shelter in a military conflict. Still, service provision articulates the fact that society hasn't addressed a certain problem area well enough. Service providers both make the claim that something needs to change and act on that claim.

How designers have used this method

Designers have a fairly well-established role in service provision, particularly for facilities such as housing or equipment.

For example, readers may be familiar with the work of groups such as Architecture for Humanity, Design Corps, Design that Matters, Rural Studios or Project H. Each of these groups has concentrated on responding to

Pennsylvania apple pickers' migrant unit A housing unit aimed at helping growers improve the housing supplied to migrant farmworkers. Design by Design Corps: Bryan Bell, Kindra Welch, Melissa Tello Poole, Lesli Stinger, Andrea Dietz, Justin Staley, Mathew Heckendorn, Anne Thomas, local farmworkers, advocates and farmers.

Florida hurricane-resistant migrant housing Design Corps' migrant farmworker housing in response to active hurricane seasons in Florida that adversely affected many of the 300,000 migrant farm workers and their families. Client: Florida Legal Services, Design: Shaun Patchell, Laura Shipman, Bryan Bell, Rob Williams, local farmworkers, advocates and farmers.

emergencies, providing much-needed devices to poverty-stricken communities, or bringing design services to excluded groups such as migrant workers. In many instances design activists have used the tactic of designing buildings or products, such as immigrant housing, emergency shelter or equipment (e.g., low-cost or portable medical equipment) to help low-income communities or communities in developing countries.

Not all service design work occurs through organized groups such as these, however. Many architecture firms regularly provide "pro bono" or low-cost services to organizations in need. Recent efforts by The 1% attempted to coordinate pro bono efforts by setting up a national register for architects and prospective pro bono clients.[31] Under a Robin Hood Foundation program, a number of New York city architects volunteered their time to redesign libraries for inner-city schools, including Public Schools 42 and 101, with new libraries by Weiss/Manfredi and Tod Williams and Billie Tsien, respectively.[32]

The Raynes Rail A component of the Braille and audio information system at Charles de Gaulle Airport, Paris. Design and photo by Coco Raynes.

Individuals, students, and design companies also act on projects that improve the quality of life for disabled people, the elderly, the homeless, and others who are often disadvantaged by their material and spatial environments. For example, students from the Southern California Institute of Architecture created a shaded place serving both the street population and the Los Angeles Men's Project, a program for mentally ill homeless men.[33] Other examples include the Danish-designed Cheetah wheelchair for children and the Raynes tactile rail for the visually impaired.[34] In these cases the tactic tends to be a service structure or artifact.

Architects are also increasingly putting their skills to less conventional use. For example, following Hurricane Katrina at least one architecture group turned its skills to map-making. Architect David Perkes of the Gulf Coast Community Design Studio (GCCDS) relates that in the immediate aftermath of Hurricane Katrina he saw a local city councilor using a hand-drawn, sticky-noted map to direct volunteer efforts. Perkes tells us, "I said, 'We can make maps,' and a few days later delivered a stack of maps that were used for many months by dozens of volunteer team leaders to organize the cleanup and relief efforts of the area."[35] The GCCDS produced many additional maps to communicate information about complex issues including flood zones, land uses and rebuilding progress. Similarly, another university architecture design studio at the University of Kansas found itself designing not only structures but also notice boards.[36] In these cases visualizing and materializing information was the central tactic.

"We can make maps" So said architect David Perkes. Maps of East Biloxi produced by the Gulf Coast Community Design Studio.

The service provision method is often intrinsically tied into ongoing campaigns oriented toward helping the beneficiary group. For example, a number of campaigns and legislation address disability access in various forms. Emergency preparedness, emergency response and recovery, refugee services and related efforts form the work of many types of organizations such as the Red Cross and the United Nations. The same is true of movements combating homelessness.

Recently there has been a move to link emergency preparedness and disaster relief to efforts for adaptation to climate change, particularly in cities.[37] Many no longer view natural disasters as merely acts of god. A recent United Nations report noted:

> Over the last few decades, thinking has begun to change. Information on climate change is building a new perception of disasters as *of our own making*. The increase in storms, droughts and other hazards expected to arise from the accumulation of greenhouse gases in the atmosphere as a result of industrialization and deforestation is clearly not natural.[38]

In a sense the message is that natural disasters, particularly storms, floods and other weather extremes, are going to increase, and so gradually disaster preparedness must simply become adaptation. This puts the role of service provision in an interesting light.

In design terms the idea of adaptation has resulted in ideas for housing or emergency shelter, for example, that can float as needed on flood waters. One concept by students Kiduck Kim and Christian Stayner is "truckable," a two-level emergency module with pontoons that float on rising waters but stay tethered by utility service umbilical cords.[39] Another example is the tsunami design initiative, the result of a partnership between the Harvard Graduate School of Design and the MIT's SENSEable City Lab, which led to a house design that can structurally withstand tsunamis and tropical storms.[40]

Design strategist Tony Fry has also explored the issue of massive migration that might be associated with disruptive climate change, and examined (through the tactic of a competition entry) the process of adapting the inland Australian town of Boonah. He comments that the town was chosen "because it is exactly the kind of place that would be deemed appropriate for 'resettlement' by people abandoning areas exposed to the coming climate [changes]" including coastal storms and increasing drought in the western interior.[41] He calls this adaptive redesign "future proofing."

Tsunami Safe(r) House By carlorattiassociati | walter nicolino and carlo ratti (MIT SENSEable City Lab) with Luis Berrios and the Tsunami design initiative, Harvard GDS. For full credits visit http://senseable.mit.edu/tsunami-prajnopaya/.

Advocacy

Background

Advocacy involves working on behalf of others, typically without their direct involvement, or with limited, occasional involvement. A classic form of advocacy is environmentalism, where advocates speak up for ecosystems because they cannot speak up for themselves. But advocates act across a wide range of issues such as housing, justice, public health, safety and security, cultural diversity, human rights, democracy, regeneration and renewal, education, women's issue, peace, animal rights, and so forth. Indeed, research for this book found cases of design activism on each of these issues.

How designers have used this method

Designers commonly take up advocacy and tend to advocate by generating positive alternatives to the status quo. Advocacy may come from designers themselves, but is often driven by activist clients, or clients that have within their project at least one activist agenda, such as environmentalism, equality or access. In particular, designers often use the tactic of creating demonstration structures or products. Demonstrations range across green buildings, improved landscapes, humanized security features, higher performing recycling systems or better public libraries. But there are other approaches too, as indicated by a range of projects (discussed below) by theme, advocating for the environment, rights and affordability, education, and cultural diversity.

Theme: environmentalism

There are probably more cases of environmental advocacy among design activists than any other theme.[42] Many cases involve demonstrating green building. But taking green building down a notch in size, Sustainable San Mateo County, along with the American Institute of Architects and the US Green Building Council, sponsored a "green" dolls house competition. Criteria included energy and water conservation, reused or salvaged materials, and healthy indoor environments.[43] The event sought to raise wider awareness about environmental issues, particularly among parents and children.

Within the advocacy method we also find the tactic of design research. For example, the state of California and the nonprofit Collaborative for High Performance Schools joined forces to test building materials for the emission

Silvercup Studios Green roof by Balmori Associates after research indicated neighborhood-wide potential for Long Island City. Photo Mark Dye courtesy of Balmori Associates.

of chemicals into indoor air, the results of which enabled design decisions that can be made on the basis of health risks.[44]

In another case that used research, landscape architect Diana Balmori initiated a study in New York City to identify the areas of the city most suitable for green roof-tops on a neighborhood-wide scale. Her study revealed that Long Island City had the most potential, which led to a demonstration project at Silver Cup Studios.[45]

Theme: rights and affordability

Colorado Court in Santa Monica, by Pugh + Scarpa architects, is unusual for combining affordable housing (single-room occupancy for low-income earners) with extreme energy efficiency and features such as rainwater collection. It was the first affordable housing project in the US to generate its own energy.[46]

Colorado Court Combines single-room occupancy with high-level ecodesign strategies. Pugh + Scarpa Architects, Photo Ali Adair.

The tactic of exhibition can also serve as a platform for advocacy, such as the National Building Museum's exhibit "Affordable Housing: Designing an American Asset." The exhibition demonstrated that low cost does not have to mean low quality and that well-designed affordability has potentially far-reaching community benefits. Similarly, the Cooper Hewitt National Design Museum held "Design for the Other 90%" advocating the use of design to improve life for the world's poor by showcasing 30 socially responsible products such as the Lifestraw.

Theme: education

At a time when research suggests that public education is in trouble and that public education facilities aren't keeping pace, the American Architectural Foundation ran the program "Great Schools by Design" to investigate the role of design in improving learning and contributing to communities.[47] Similarly, a collaborative project called "The Third Teacher" explores ways in which design can transform teaching and learning.[48] These projects run parallel to exhibitions and individual school projects that all advocate for improvements in teaching and learning, particularly in public school settings.

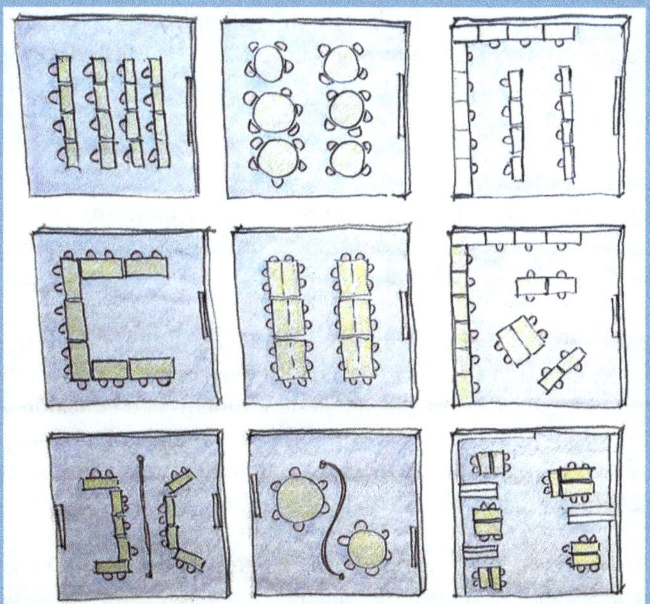

Learning spaces Nine variations created during a school design institute. Illustration courtesy of the American Architectural Foundation.

Theme: cultural diversity

The Merrima Aboriginal Design Unit in Sydney, Australia's Department of Public Works, offers design services to aboriginal communities across Australia by aboriginal architects, "breaking their historic reliance on Caucasian architects coming in and interpreting their culture."[49] In this sense the service advocates for aboriginal community interests. The exhibit Harlemworld profiled how 18 black architects imagine possibilities for Harlem (a historically black neighborhood in New York City), in an attempt to address the feeling that Harlem's future is out of the control of the local population.[50]

Mobilization

Background

The method of mobilization brings together large numbers of participants for a particular purpose, without expectation of their further, day-to-day involvement. Usually mobilization efforts are aimed at showing that a particular issue has salience for a large number of people who might have power in terms of voting, purchasing choices or volunteering their time. The classic form of mobilization is a public march, boycott or petition signing. In recent years, following events such as "earth day," mobilization has also taken the form of other designated days ("buy nothing day" or "bike to work day") as well as festival-like events (dubbed "protestivals").[51] The UK's climate camp is an example of a protestival.

How design has used this method

Architects and designers have used mobilization methods that adopt conventional activists' approaches, although some of design's other approaches can also usefully be seen in mobilization terms.

Architecture 2030 organized an emergency "teach-in" aimed at bringing design education into the environmental movement. The global event was webcast in February 2007 to 250,000 design students and educators across 48 countries.[52] Rebar's international park(ing) day, already mentioned, encourages a form of mass urban hacking—although distributed—through a designated day format.

In another example, the San Francisco chapter of Architects, Designers and Planners for Social Responsibility organized a boycott on the design, construction and renovation of American prisons. Three hundred participants signed on in an effort to voice disapproval "of the prison system's treatment of inmates, and its inherent racial and social inequalities" as well as to challenge the rampant growth in new prisons.[53]

Competitions Three entries addressing Uganda for the 2009 Open Architecture Challenge: Classroom

Cool Uganda Architect Céderic Choné.

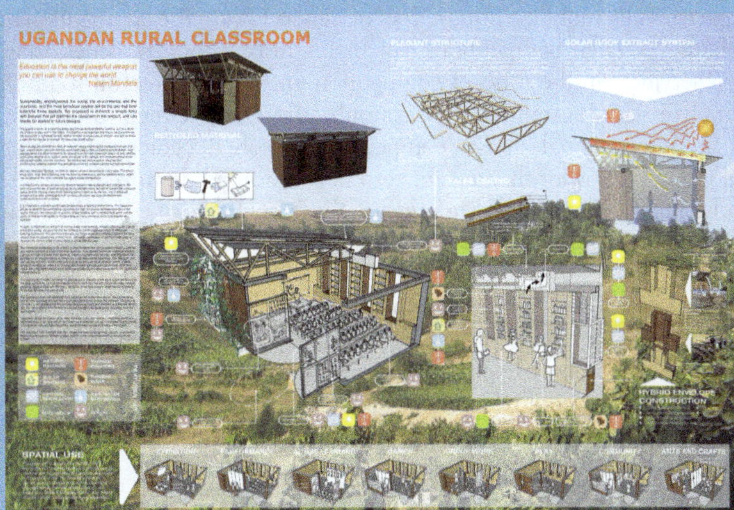

Ugandan rural classroom For Bunyonyi Community School, Kabale, Uganda. Architects Gifford LLC.

Adaptable hillside classrooms © Feilden Clegg Bradley Studios.

Design competitions and award schemes aimed at social and environmental change typically mobilize hundreds of designers toward the competition's call for change. Design competitions can highlight or publicize issues, draw in design services (in the form of competition entries), and recruit sponsors to materialize winning entries. For example, the group Green Ground Zero held an international design competition to solicit ecologically sensitive development plans for the ground zero neighborhood destroyed by the 9/11 terrorist attacks. The aim was to pressure those in charge of redevelopment to more closely consider sustainability.[54]

The tactic of competition was also used by the organization Global Green, founded by actor Brad Pitt, which solicited entries for, and then built, replacement housing in the wake of Hurricane Katrina.[55] Although the competition process mobilizes people around an issue, individual competition entries that are locally driven may serve as catalysts for organizing, and the competition as a whole may also serve as advocacy.

Design exhibitions, often in conjunction with festival-like events, are another way that designers mobilize large numbers of people around an issue. An example comes from the UK's regional Design of the Time (DOTT) program which engaged the community in design-driven solutions

DESIGN COMPETITIONS

When faced with the question of how to make their own practice more meaningful, some architects and designers turn to socially related design competitions. But are design competitions worth the time and effort they take? John Peterson rejected this idea, noting:

> More than anything, I couldn't stop thinking about the hundreds upon hundreds of proposals, representing countless ideas and thousands of hours of work that go into each competition. So much of this work ends up on storage room shelves or in rarely seen portfolios. Is this the most effective use of our collective time and energy?"[56]

By contrast, T. Luke Young and Alix Ogilvie, of Architecture for Humanity, argue that although competition entries may not be built, the process of a design competition leads to change in several important ways.[57] First, competitions raise awareness of the spatiality of an issue, not only within the design community but also in other disciplines such as education (school design), sports and health (football facilities as health clinics) and the military (repurposing former military sites). Second, the process of peer review and the diversity of entries serve to develop a knowledge base about design's potential in a given challenge area, while also highlighting potential tensions or trade-offs in approaches that may not be as apparent in a single design response.

Third, a competition's real results may not be felt until much later. Luke Young comments that Architecture for Humanity grew out of a single competition. Anecdotal evidence suggests that although a competition doesn't require long-term engagement with the issue, individuals and groups who participate in "social change" competitions do sometimes carry the issue forward in their own work.

Fourth, and finally, the design of a competition matters. Luke Young and Ogilvie suggest that competitions are more meaningful when they prefer a community-driven agenda and design teams that formally collaborate with local partners. This makes it more likely that entries will take on a life of their own, whether or not the entry wins. Similarly, competitions can be more revealing when they encourage diverse design teams that include other disciplines along with designers, and competitions can have greater relevance when there is a way to ensure that all competition entries end up in the public domain (the commons) such as Architecture for Humanity's own Open Architecture Network.

Exhibitions Contains mobilized visitors around the social and environmental issues of products. Visitors got a credit-card-sized takeaway on how to buy better. Photo courtesy of www.redesigndesign.org.

to local issues.[58] DOTT hosted the Contains exhibition, curated by [Re] design, that explored social and environmental issues associated with product design and the use of products. The venue was a series of shipping containers put down in Newcastle's retail district where an estimated 40,000 shoppers engaged with the exhibit over 10 days.[59]

In some senses, any major structure that attempts to seriously address social or environmental issues through design could arguably be seen as a mobilization, although the people working on a structure don't all come together physically at one point in time. The design and construction of a significant demonstration building (for example, the California Academy of Sciences' recent building by Renzo Piano Building Workshop) requires that many participants, including people up and down the supply chain, mobilize around the project. The centerpiece of the California building is a rolling green roof, complete with hills sloping up to 60 degrees punctuated by skylights.[60]

California Academy of Sciences A significant demonstration building by Renzo Piano Building Workshop, Stantec Architecture and SWA group. Photo Rebeca Stovall.

Solidarity

Background

The idea of solidarity is to show, often in general terms, alignment or unity with a given issue or need for change. Solidarity activities often occur at the level of cultural discourse and popular culture. Areas for solidarity work might include influencing the language and terms of debate in popular culture, introducing new concepts or critiquing the status quo.

How designers have used this method

One way in which architecture and design use solidarity methods is through the practice of "critical" architecture and design, as mentioned at the start of this chapter. Many of these approaches make use of the tactic of protest artifacts such as Cleanup soap by Hideaki Matsui.[61] The soap puts a full-scale replica of a landmine into the hands of those who donate to the cause of landmine removal. The use of the soap symbolizes how contributors help to wash away the landmines through their actions.

Another common way in which design uses solidarity is through symbols that express unity around a given issue, for instance, memorials that commemorate victims of war, disaster, terrorism or disease. An example is the FAM Studio's memorial to the victims of 2004's Madrid train bombings. The inside cylinder wall of the memorial is covered with messages taken from the original condolence cards placed at a makeshift memorial. Architect Mauro Gil-Fournier Esquerra said, "We want to speak to the light and the future: the spirit of the monument is to take all of the messages of these days, the feelings of the people, and create an eternal meaning for them."[62]

Cleanup soap Supporting landmine removal. Designer Hideaki Matsui, Photo Shigenobu Matsui.

Atocha station memorial To the victims of terrorist train bombings in Madrid, 2004. Studio FAM architects, Photo Barry Hoggard.

Designers also engage with solidarity by lending design resources to causes that are not directly related to design. For example, in 2003 architect Maya Lin solicited cake designs (renderings) from well-known architects to raise money at auction for the Greyston Foundation's bakery (designed by Lin) that trains and employs formerly homeless people.[63] In another example, architects participate regularly in "canstruction" events where they build structures out of canned food that is later donated to local food banks.

REFLECTION ON METHODS

It is clear that methods are sometimes blurred and one event, such as park(ing) day, may be seen in terms of either organizing or mobilization, depending on how we think about it. Similarly, some competitions held by Architecture for Humanity may be seen as both mobilization of many designers, but also service provision, in that the winning design is built for deserving beneficiaries. An exhibition might advocate and mobilize.

Scale is one way of reflecting on these boundaries. An international competition or international "day" mobilizes many participants, but on the ground, the winning entry or the actual park might do something more like organizing. We can also see these cases as sequences of modular tactics. A competition might be the first tactic, and a demonstration building created from the winning entry is the second tactic.

Canstruction Photo Jerome Strauss.

Table 5.2 Summarising methods of change work

Type of Work	Common form in design	Example cases
Organizing: developing the community's ability to bring about change	Co-design and other participatory, self-design, or design-enabling processes	City hacking for parks, fablabs, fashion hacking, community design training
Services: providing facilities, training, professional services	Humanitarian design services and structures	Emergency/recovery shelter by groups like Architecture for Humanity
Advocacy: working on behalf of others, often without their direct involvement	Advocacy for nature when natural systems cannot advocate for themselves, or response to ideas competition for a distant location	Green building, affordable housing, design for education
Mobilization: bringing together large numbers of participants for an event, without expectation of their further involvement	Design use of conventional activist methods, design elements of conventional protest, competitions, large-scale structures, designated days	Architecture 2030 teach-in, Designers Accord pledge, Green ground zero competition
Solidarity: engaging with cultural discourse to express unity or change the terms of debate	Critical design and critical architecture, fundraising	Cleanup soap, canstruction, memorials

One may argue that there are better or worse cases to illustrate the methods and tactics described above, and that in some examples the fit might feel forced. Yet recall that our purpose here is not to suggest that a social movement framework is the only way to view design activism, but rather to explore what we can learn from a whole body of work that exists around social movements and conventional activism. The methods are summarized in Table 5.2.

The important thing about methods and tactics is to recognize them as conceptual tools for bringing about change. There are several benefits to these tools. Thinking about methods and tactics stretches designers to think about campaigns for change that lie beyond the boundaries of any one project. In addition, using concepts and terms borrowed from social movements gives designers a common language to use with other activists.

In Chapter 4 (Table 4.2) we considered how some emerging forms of activist design practice had implications for developing particular areas of knowledge. The activist methods profiled here highlight that knowledge of the social movement arena might also usefully inform design activism. For example, for any given issue, designers might research the relevant social movement, and the movement's campaigns, methods and tactics. This context holds opportunities to learn from, partner with and build power across a bigger network than the design "project" scope normally allows.

Designers may also be able to make more sense of the wide spectrum of design activism described at the opening of this chapter, when they consider how the methods span from hands-on community action to abstract solidarity symbolism. It is typically not the case that there is one right method, no one right "place" to locate activist work, such as at the bottom (organizing) or at the top (solidarity) or in the middle (advocacy or mobilization). In fact, social movements are derived from a wide range of actors working through different methods and scales.

Methods and tactics also suggest different ways of thinking about social or public design. In a sense, the concepts ask designers to think less about specific design solutions and more about change solutions. For example, instead of thinking about design activism as the process of solving a specific design problem, awareness of different methods and tactics enables designers to evaluate a wider range of ways to try to bring about change.

This introduction to political methods also offers the prospect for architecture and design to build on, expand and innovate these methods through careful thought about spatial and material influences in power relations.

CONCLUSION

The methods described above offer a range of approaches to calling and acting for change in areas of life that are compromised by priorities for economic growth. The process of highlighting these lost values, and struggling to create better ways to address them, is a key step toward changing the way the economy works. In a sense, the methods connect political arguments to "economic" arguments; instead of making decisions based on profit or cost, these methods connect decisions to real values, such as ecology or social capital, that are lost in consumerism and the financially driven market economy. These are the same issues that social metrics are trying to capture.

These methods ultimately involve efforts to shift existing patterns of power, and this makes the methods overtly political. Simply by understanding design approaches in these terms and thinking about power relationships, we can begin to show how design may strategically "be more political." This is the subject of Chapter 6.

NOTES

1 Randolph Hester, "Design Activism ... For Whom?" *Frameworks*, Vol. 1, no. 1 (spring 2005), pp. 8–15.
2 Fred Bernstein, "Books: Architecture that Makes a Difference", *Architectural Record* (October 2008).
3 Lisa Findley, *Building Change: Architecture, Politics and Cultural Agency* (London: Routledge, 2005), p. 38, emphasis added.
4 Tim Brown, Aaron Sklar, Sany Speicher, Doug Solomon and Jocelyn Wyatt, *Design For Social Impact* (New York: The Rockefeller Foundation, 2009), pp. 80–81.
5 Tali Hatuka and Rachel Kallus, "The Architecture of Repeated Rituals: Tel Aviv's Rabin Square", *Journal of Architectural Education*, Vol. 61, no. 4 (2008).
6 Ibid., p. 91.
7 Lance Hosey, "Slumming in Utopia: Protest Construction and the Iconography of Urban America", *Journal of Architectural Education*, Vol. 53, no. 3 (June 2000), pp. 146-58, 149.
8 Greg Cowan, "Street Protest Architecture", *Bad Subjects* (January 2004).
9 Randy Greenberg, "Discovering Designs from Down Under", *Architectural Record* (November 2004); and Kevin Lerner, "Looking for a New Way in Norway", *Architectural Record* (May 2003).
10 Jody Boehnert, "In the Front Line", *Creative Review* (October 2008).
11 George Baird, "'Criticality' and its Discontents", *Harvard Design Magazine* (fall/winter 2004), no. 21, pp. 1–6.
12 K. Michael Hays, "Critical Architecture: Between Culture and Form", *Perspecta*, Vol. 21 (1984), pp. 15–29, 17.
13 Simon Bowen, *A Critical Artefact Methodology: Using Provocative Conceptual Designs to Foster Human-centered Innovation* (Sheffield: Sheffield Hallam University, 2009).
14 Benjamin Millen, *Critical Wayfinding, or, A Psycho-spatial Model for Critical Design*, Faculty of Environmental Design, University of Calgary, 2009.
15 Stuart Walker, *Sustainable by Design* (London: Earthscan, 2006), pp. 90–1.
16 Rinku Sen, *Stir It Up: Lessons in Community Organizing and Advocacy* (San Francisco, CA: Jossey-Bass, 2003), p. 25. Sen's work goes on to explore organizing specifically, so this is the author's own interpretation of her five main methods.
17 Ibid., p. 22.
18 Susan Olzak and S.C. Noah Uhrig, "The Ecology of Tactical Overlap", *American Sociological Review*, Vol. 66, no. 5 (2001), p. 701; and Sidney Tarrow, "Cycles of Collective Action: Between Moments of Madness and the Repertoire of

Contention", in *Repertoires and Cycles of Collective Action*, ed. Mark Traugott (Durham, NC: Duke University Press, 1995), pp. 89–115.

19 Mark Traugott, "Barricades as Repertoire: Continuities and Discontinuities in the History of French Contention", in *Repertoires and Cycles of Collective Action*, ed. Mark Traugott (Durham, NC: Duke University Press, 1995), pp. 43–56.

20 Sidney Tarrow, "Cycles of Collective Action: Between Moments of Madness and the Repertoire of Contention", in *Repertoires and Cycles of Collective Action*, ed. Mark Traugott (Durham, NC: Duke University Press, 1995), p. 91.

21 Charles Tilly and Sidney Tarrow, *Contentious Politics* (Boulder, CO: Paradigm Publishers, 2007), p. 120.

22 Ann Thorpe, *Design and Political Resistance: Tactics, Power and Transformation* (Milton Keynes: Open University, 2010).

23 David J. Hess, *Alternative Pathways in Science and Industry: Activism, Innovation, and the Environment in an Era of Globalization* (Cambridge, MA: MIT Press, 2007), p. 85.

24 See, for example, Ruud Koopmans and Dieter Rucht, "Protest Event Analysis", in *Methods of Social Movement Research*, ed. Bert Klandermans and Suzanne Staggenborg (Minneapolis: University of Minnesota Press, 2002), pp. 62–91; and S. Olzak, "Analysis of Events in the Study of Collective Action", *Annual Review of Sociology*, Vol. 15, no. 1 (1989), p. 119.

25 Lucia Athens, *Building an Emerald City: A Guide to Creating Green Building Policies and Programs* (Washington, DC: Island Press, 2010).

26 Alison Gilchrist, *The Well-connected Community: A Networking Approach to Community Development* (Bristol: Policy Press, 2004), pp. 13–24.

27 Christine Gaspar, telephone interview by the author, 21 February 2011.

28 "St Paul's Park" (n.d.). Available at http://www.theglasshouse.org.uk/projectshowcase/st-pauls-park/ (accessed 22 August 2011).

29 Otto von Busch, *Fashion-able: Hacktivism and Engaged Fashion Design* (Gothenburg: Camino Forlag, 2009), p. 86.

30 Rob Hopkins, "Transition as Cookery: Assembling the Ingredients of Community Resilience", keynote at RESOLVE Conference 2011 – Living Sustainably: Values, Policies and Practices, London, 15 June 2011, Surrey University.

31 Casius Pealer, "Professionalizing Pro Bono", *Architectural Record* (October 2008).

32 Jane F. Kolleeny, "The Library Goes Back to School", *Architectural Record* (September 2005), pp. 87–92.

33 Jade Chang, "Good Shelter", *Metropolis* (April 2005), p. 40.

34 Mireille Hyde, "Joy Ride: 3Part's Cheetah Wheelchair for R82", *Metropolis* (February 2006).

35 David Perkes, "A Useful Practice", *Journal of Architectural Education*, Vol. 62, no. 4 (May 2009), pp. 64–71, 66.

36 Robert Corser and Nils Gore, "Insurgent Architecture: An Alternative Approach to Design-build", *Journal of Architectural Education*, Vol. 62, no. 4 (May 2009), pp. 32-9.

37 World Bank, *Climate Change, Disaster Risk, and the Urban Poor, Summary* (Washington, DC: The International Bank for Reconstruction and Development/The World Bank, 2011).

38 Commission on Climate Change and Development, *Links between Disaster Risk Reduction, Development and Climate Change* (Geneva: United Nations International Strategy for Disaster Reduction, 2008), p. 1, emphasis added.
39 James S. Russell, "New Orleans Prototype House Competition", *Architectural Record* (June 2006), p. 124.
40 Maria Finn, "Shelter from the Storm", *Metropolis* (February 2006).
41 Tony Fry, *Design Futuring* (Oxford: Berg, 2009) pp. 59–62.
42 Thorpe, "Design and Political Resistance" (2010), pp. 152–3.
43 Colin Berry, "Barbie's Green House", *ID* (October 2005).
44 Ted Smalley Bowen, "California Tests Conventional and 'Green' Products for Emissions", *Architectural Record* (June 2004).
45 Lisa Chamberlain, "View from the Bridge", *Metropolis* (September 2006).
46 Ken Coupland, "Livable L.A.: A New Nonprofit Brings Green Building and Affordable Housing Together for Angelenos", *Metropolis* (March 2003).
47 American Architectural Foundation and Knowledgeworks Foundation, *Report from the National Summit on School Design: A Resource for Educators and Designers* (Washington, DC: 2005).
48 OWP/P Architects, VS Furniture and Bruce Mau Design, *The Third Teacher: 79 Ways You Can Use Design to Transform Teaching and Learning* (New York: Abrams, 2010).
49 Davina Jackson, "Merrima Mines the Riches of Australia's Aboriginal heritage and Points to its Future", *Architectural Record* (December 2003).
50 Lyle Rexer, "Reimagining Harlem", *Metropolis* (May 2004).
51 Graham St John, "Protestival: Global Days of Action and Carnivalized Politics in the Present", *Social Movement Studies*, Vol. 7, no. 2 (2008), pp. 167–90.
52 Susan S. Szenasy, "Calling All Designers", *Metropolis* (June 2007), p. 28.
53 Sam Lubell, "Prison Design Boycott Aims to Slow Growth of Correctional Facilities', *Architectural Record* (June 2005).
54 Deborah Snoonian, "Contest Hopes to Spur Green Development Around Ground Zero", *Architectural Record* (October 2003).
55 David Sokol, "High-profile New Orleans Competition Names Winner", *Architectural Record* (October 2006), p. 30.
56 John Peterson, *Founder's Vision* (San Francisco, CA: Public Architecture, 2011). Available at http://www.publicarchitecture.org/about/Founders_Vision.htm (accessed 25 September 2011).
57 T. Luke Young and Alix Ogilvie of Architecture for Humanity, email interview, 16 August 2011.
58 John Thackara, *Wouldn't It Be Great If…* (London: Design Council, 2007).
59 Sarah Johnson, *[re]design likes you: Annual Report 2007–2008* (London: [re] design, 2008).
60 Martin C. Pedersen, "California Academy of Sciences, San Francisco", *Metropolis* (September 2006).
61 Cleanup. Available at http://www.cleanupsoap.com/ (accessed 20 October 2010).
62 Stephen Zacks, "The Eternal Glow", *Metropolis* (June 2007), p. 37; and C. J. Hughes, "Victims of Terrorist Attacks Memorialized", *Architectural Record* (July 2007).
63 Jane F. Kolleeny, "Cakes for a Cause", *Architectural Record* (May 2003).

Chapter 6

Political power on a budget

INTRODUCTION

Chapter 5 examined methods activists typically use to try to bring about change and showed that architecture and design may also be understood in terms of these methods. Although that chapter hinted at the political nature of these methods, this chapter examines politics more explicitly, particularly the idea of building power to bring about change, even on a low budget.

The process of considering power is important for several reasons. Just as previous chapters have shown how wealth is increasingly concentrated in society, power is also concentrated. Creative Commons founder Lawrence Lessig comments:

> There has never been a time in our history when more of our "culture" was as "owned" as it is now. And yet there has never been a time when the concentration of power to control the uses of culture has been as unquestioningly accepted as it is now.[1]

Another reason for considering power stems explicitly from one critique of activism in general: that it tends to over-focus on what *should be*, and under-focus on building power to make changes. In focusing on what should be, it is as though once we "raise awareness," perhaps forcefully, by pointing out wrongs and injustices, then existing political actors such as mayors, city councils or cultural leaders will simply begin taking action to fix things. As practicing organizer and activist Michael Gecan says, "You can't get near what *should be*, not even close, unless you build and use power, unless you manipulate that power so that you can slog through the mud of the world as it *is*."[2]

The task of this chapter is to explore how we might interpret Gecan's message in terms of architecture and design. Our exploration goes through several steps. First, we look at the concept of power, considering various forms and patterns of power and examining their relevance to architecture and design. Second, we consider the capacities that conventional activists, typically working on low budgets, have to build power. These capacities include disruption, framing and targeting. We argue that these capacities also help us describe design activism's capacities to build power. At the same time, these capacities operate in different ways for architecture and design than for conventional activists.

PATTERNS OF POWER AND POWER STRUGGLES

For our purposes, politics is the distribution and patterns of power in society (first explored in the box in Chapter 1, "Patterns of Power"). Further, we use economist Kenneth Boulding's perception that power is only meaningful in terms of making choices and influencing decision making that affects us. He comments, "In this human sense, power is a concept without meaning in the absence of human valuations and human decision. Decision is a choice among a range or set of images of the future that we think are feasible."[3] Power is not an end in itself, but rather has meaning in terms of human goals and aspirations.

The term "patterns of power" is apt because broadly speaking, society is made up of institutions and systems that typically maintain things as they are. These are stable patterns of power based on past sets of decisions. Of course, stability is not a bad thing. Sociologist John Scott describes how "stable and enduring social relations" are necessary to create large-scale social structures.[4] In other words, we need some form of status quo, a sort of establishment, within which civilization can operate.

We make decisions and act on the basis of being able to rely on stability from, for example, laws and traditions. Yet the fact that elements of the status quo are unfair or destructive is cause for many people to want change for the better. Sociologists Neil Fligstein and Doug McAdam argue that broader patterns of stability actually contain continuous change and negotiation, although most of this change amounts to minor reform. Only more rarely do transformational changes come along.[5]

The constant tension between stability and change represents the essence of many power struggles. How much should things stay the same to maintain stability and certainty, and how much should things change in attempts to improve on the weaknesses and problems of the status quo?

Figure 6.1 Tensions in patterns of power

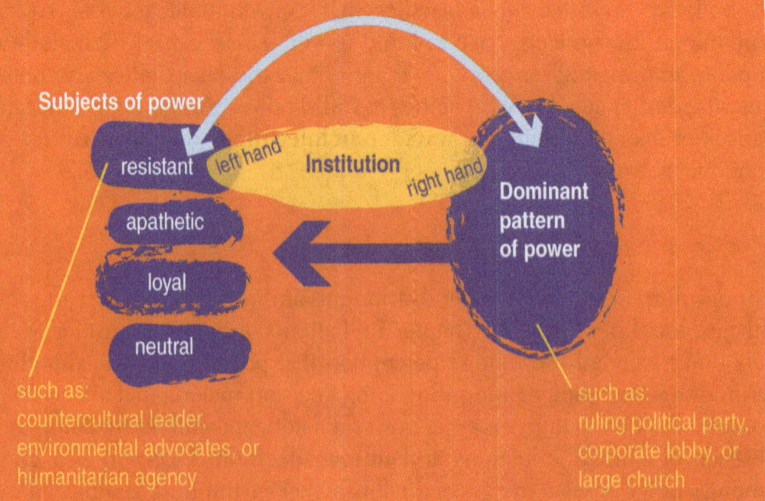

Michael Gecan echoes this idea of tension, noting that for many individuals there is a challenge in "maintaining a conservative's belief in the value and necessity of stable institutions, along with a radical's understanding of the need for persistent agitation and reorganization. We are called to love, engage and uphold our most cherished institutions, while watching them, questioning them, and pressing them to change, all at the same time."[6] Similarly, David Hess notes that most organizations have a right hand (conservative of the norms) and a left hand (attempting to keep up with changes and "progress" with current societal concerns).[7] These ideas are captured in Figure 6.1.

In simple terms, power struggles are usually enacted through several means (often combined), particularly organized money, organized people, and to a certain degree, organized representations, materials and spaces.[8] Further, based on these means of power, there are different forms of power in play, which Boulding usefully summarizes as the *stick*, the *carrot* and the *hug*. Where, perhaps obviously, the stick consists of influence through force or punishment, the carrot consists of influence by reward or incentive, and the hug consists of influence by love, loyalty or other forms of social bonding. Boulding's view aligns with other views on power such that we can consider power as described in Table 6.1, using the terms of force (stick), exchange (stick/carrot) and persuasion (hug).[9]

Table 6.1 Forms of power

	Force	Exchange	Persuasion
	Maintain power through destructive physical measures (restrictions, violence, imprisonment, use of weapons, etc.)	Maintain power through bargaining and exchange, whether "political and social exchanges" such as votes or favors, or economic exchanges such as costs and payments	Maintain power by retaining subscribers to your beliefs/knowledge and acquire new subscribers through conversion (acknowledges that power can be effected without being exercised)
How A has power over B	**A** must have control over some physically destructive power against persons or structures that **B** values	**A** and **B** must have something to exchange; includes commodities, but also votes, favors, policies, attendance, or informal reciprocity (e.g., conversation)—unless there is production, there is nothing to exchange	**B** does something for **A** because he/she respects (loves) **A**. The form of power slips back to exchange (bargaining) if **B** doesn't love/respect **A** enough to do what **A** wants
Aim	To control **B** by force of will	To get **B** to do what **A** wants through deal-making	To convert **B** to the identity or belief that **A** holds which might involve the following: emotions of suffering, sympathy, empathy and shame; compelling visions for the future; expertise, obligation, or other social or intellectual bonds

Table 6.1 does not address the possibility that power struggles might occur by means of organized representations, materials and spaces, but the literature on design and power suggests that the types of power in Table 6.1 also describe spatial and material aspects of power. For example, in terms of architecture and the built environment, architects Kim Dovey and Thomas Markus both highlight sticks, carrots and hugs in material terms. For example, prisons and fortresses "strip the subject of any choice of non-compliance" such that they align with destructive force.[10]

In terms of exchange or bargaining power, most spaces constitute a sort of "spatial offer" concerning how a space may be seen, used or accessed. A public plaza makes a different spatial offer than an office building or a private residence, yet these "offers" serve as constant points of bargaining or negotiation. In addition, in terms of persuasion, spaces often work in terms of seduction or authority in order to uphold conventions, as in formal or classic architectural forms reinforcing a sense of authority.

Working more in the area of product design, Dan Lockton and Tracy Bhamra, and their respective teams, uncover these same forms of power in terms of material objects.[11] For example, material objects may require compliance through forcing functions that require one condition to be met (such as the electricity being switched off) before a function is enabled (the opening of the maintenance panel).

Rationing on the part of material objects is an example of exchange power. Rationing may occur in terms of portioning, where only a certain amount of time, material, or energy is enabled. Washing powder tablets create an ideal "portion." Rationing may also occur in terms of limits on the total amount allowed at any one time or a maximum allowable amount. A limit of one can-full of garbage collected per week may affect recycling patterns, depending on the size of the can. The idea of rationing is tied to product or structural affordances; that is, the functions or actions that the user perceives. For example, a dial with 10 temperature settings has a different affordance than an on/off button.

In terms of persuasion, material objects make use of the seduction and authority mentioned earlier, but also often include forms of guidance. For example, a kettle marked with cup measurements informs users how much water to use, or a car dashboard offers real-time information about fuel use. A warning light informs users of inadvisable behavior (such as a camera being out of focus).

Table 6.2 puts these material and spatial elements into the stick/carrot/hug framework shown in Table 6.1. Although it may go without saying, market/monetary exchange value is arguably one of the largest elements of influence that architecture and design have on power relations. This describes the added value perceived from good design, the cost savings derived from cheaply designed goods or structures, and the increased sales from the expanded offerings created through the design process.

Any of these forms of power may be used either in efforts to maintain the stability of the status quo, or in efforts to change the status quo. What differs between these two types of efforts, between stability and change, is the capacity different groups or individuals have to organize money, people, or symbols and spaces.

Table 6.2 Forms of power, design

Force	Exchange	Persuasion
Incarceration or exclusion: strips the subject of "any choice of non-compliance," forcing functions	Manipulation and coercion: involves exchanges often around a "spatial" offer, such as what can be seen or accessed, how places can be used Affordances, rationing, some aspects of "forcing functions," the division or distribution of resources, financial exchange power	Seduction by creation of desire, and authority by legitimation through the symbols or by professional expertise/license Guidance: attempts to persuade people to use objects in certain ways

In a society that privileges economic growth, monetary forms of exchange dominate many power relations. Society is currently organized largely around exchange power underpinned by money and wealth. Those who have wealth and financial resources apply them directly and indirectly across all the dimensions of politics in ways that heavily influence decisions about our future.[12] Many if not most of these decisions favor the current system that accepts economic growth as a central goal, and assumes that increases in material wealth mean improved well-being.

By contrast, those people working to question these central assumptions – who challenge the system of economic growth and consumerism– typically have to work on a very low budget. These activists are working to different metrics, namely the various social and environmental metrics outlined in Chapter 3. What becomes clear in this discussion is that power exists in relations between individuals and groups. The ideas we have about these relations are evolving, not only in terms of interconnected issues areas, such as suburban sprawl and health or climate change and diet, but also in terms of digital networks and the role of space and material (see box, p. 174, "Power relations").

The way resources are organized and distributed is one determinant of the capacity for building power. For example, the leader of a country has the capacity to draw upon organized people in the form of military armed forces, participation in which may be required through a draft or conscription. By contrast, citizen groups may organize people by recruiting volunteers to participate in a protest march or petition signing. Physical space may organize

POWER RELATIONS: WHO'S ON TOP? WHO'S ON THE INSIDE?

A classic concept of power relations concerns a dominant institution of power, such as a government, and its subjects, "the people." An extreme example would be a dictatorial leader. This pattern of power, a focus of recent "Arab spring" uprisings, describes the ability of one person or group to influence or bend the will of others—how one has "power over" others.[13]

However, in Western democracies we see other institutions (alongside governments) symbolizing dominant patterns of power, such as global corporations, churches and universities.[14] In addition, rather than government vs. people, we see the emergence of a wide range of social movements challenging dominant patterns of power across a range of institution types, for example, animal rights and university research, gay rights and church laws, labor rights and multinational corporations, and so forth. This view argues for an understanding of power as diffused throughout society.

In this view, cultural norms (such as consumerism), institutions (such as museums) and understandings (such as the importance of family) also generate a range of power relations that are widely distributed and intertwined. Some perspectives on culturally diffuse power view it as the basis for cooperation by ordinary people, the root of collective action.[15] Diffuse power then offers the "power to" influence—"empowerment" that gives people the ability to shape their lives—as opposed to a ruler's "power over" others.

These views underpin the growing sense that change doesn't come either solely from the top or solely from the bottom of society. Robin Murray, Julie Caulier-Grice and Geoff Mulgan of the Young Foundation suggest:

> most social change is neither purely top-down nor bottom-up. It involves alliances between the top and the bottom, or between what we call the "bees" (the creative individuals with ideas and energy) and the "trees" (the big institutions with the power and money to make things happen to scale).[16]

Given globalism and digital networks, some also argue that there is no longer an "outside" from which to launch challenges to existing patterns of power "inside."[17] Hyper-connectivity in the context of industrialized societies puts almost everyone "inside" to at least some degree.

The relatively spatial concept of inside and outside directs our attention to the emerging idea that buildings, material objects, landscapes, technologies or spaces play a distinct role in power relations.[18] This thinking, particularly in the fields of geography and the sociology of technology, rests on the idea that material objects and spaces both constitute and are constituted by social relations. Markus suggests that there exists no asocial space or place, just as there is no aspatial or amaterial social relation. Social relations always take place some*where.*[19] Since power emerges in social relations, materiality and spatiality have a role in extending, reproducing or even shifting the balance of power.

Bruno Latour, among others, has explored the role of structures and objects in power relations and proposes that we view agency, or intentional action, as distributed across networks of human and non-human actors.[20] Building on this idea, Linda Nash uses landscape as an example of how structures and objects not only constrain human actions, but also shape intention.[21] For example, we don't decide where to farm or where to build purely through mental contemplation, but rather through practical interaction with the physical world.

These three strands of power relation—sovereign, diffused, and spatial and material—obviously work together in real-life situations.

people by allowing or preventing large gatherings—recall the large gatherings in Rabin Square.[22] Other determinants in the capacity to build power include the creation and use of meaning and the navigation of societal structures and institutions. We examine some of these common social movement capacities for building power, and the design implications, below.

GARNERING POWER ON A LOW BUDGET

Considering the range of activist methods profiled earlier, we perhaps have an intuitive sense of their forms of power, particularly persuasion and bargaining power. But here we examine more closely the particular capacities which activists use to build power, particularly when few resources are available.

Conventional activists have largely been identified by the creative uses of the limited resources they do have, which often leads them to "use unconventional methods of political participation" in efforts to persuade authorities or decision makers to make changes.[23] The methods profiled in Chapter 5 have grown out of the necessity of limited resources. The key, low-budget capacities behind these methods include disruption, framing and targeting.[24] In this section the argument is that we can understand design activism in terms of these same capacities, although the capacities operate in somewhat different terms due to their visual, spatial and material nature.

Conventional protest Known for unconventional methods of political participation. Climate action event in Australia. Photo © Erland Howden 2011, all rights reserved.

Disruption

One view of social movements sees them in terms of their capacity to access resources.[25] In this view, an important, even central resource is collective action and its ability to disrupt routines.[26] As Doug McAdam and Yang Su note, "The idea is simple: Through extreme disruptions of public order, otherwise powerless groups are able to compel favorable state action motivated by the need to restore 'business as usual'."[27] This is the type of bodies-on-the-line activism that we see in sit-ins, blockades or strikes, often using methods such mobilization, solidarity or organizing. And the description "extreme" captures the notion of civil disobedience, where activists create disruptions by refusing to comply with laws and other norms of civic behavior.

Disruptive activism displays both negative and positive forms of exchange power. With negative disruptions, activists typically create undesirable obstructions, then agree to remove obstructions in exchange for getting concessions to their position. Using positive disruptions, activists create alternative "offers" that are more appealing than the status quo. An example might be an alternative school or "teach-in" that proposes alternative models for curricula. Both forms represent exchange power through deal-making.

Although maximum disruption is often seen to have more influence, there is evidence that persuasive disruption, which aims to signal the importance of the issue (rather than maximize disruption), is also effective.[28] In industrialized societies, large pre-planned marches are often highly orchestrated, permitted events, where efforts are actually taken to minimize any disruptions. In this case the effect is not so much to disrupt as to indicate that an issue holds a great deal of public support or concern, and could affect voters and public opinion.[29] Such an event might attempt to persuade key decision makers, converting them to the view that the issue is too important to avoid or oppose, for example. In addition most participants in a large march represent a vote, which also creates bargaining power.

There is also a precedent for disruptions to emerge from protocols, such as legal proceedings, from cultural performances, and from spaces and artifacts. For example, the disability access movement often centers on structures and products.[30] Next we examine this design-relevant aspect of disruption.

Disruption in design terms

Disruptions stemming from design activism may arise within protocols, visualizations or social narratives, but they are often material and spatial; they concern the way form configures space, the way materials are sourced and assembled, and the way users can operate spaces and forms. Most often these design disruptions are creating positive alternative "offers."

Given the way in which design projects unfold over time, it is useful to consider how disruptions are located in different places through the design life cycle—anywhere along the line from commissioning, design, fabrication, use, to end-of-life (see Figure 6.2). It is apparent that some disruptions live only in one or two phases, and are not carried through the whole life cycle. For example, a dress that results from fashion hacking disrupts the fabrication process, but in use the dress could be worn and seen in the same way as any other dress. In the case of an "ideas" competition, which may be conceptually disruptive, nothing is ever fabricated or used. Below we investigate disruption through the stages of the life cycle (shown in Figure 6.2).

Figure 6.2 Points of disruption throughout an artifact's life cycle

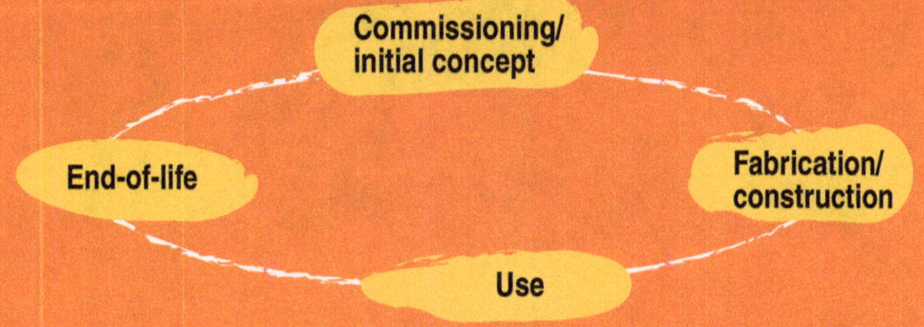

Commissioning or initial concept

The concept development phase of design typically involves a range of activities such as setting the brief, research, idea generation and prototyping, among other things. In the concept development phase, before anything is fabricated or used, design activities disrupt norms through protocols (such as regulations and guidelines) and narratives.

Narratives might concern user groups and clients, or places and things. For example, when Dutch schools required Muslim girls to remove their headscarves in gym class for safety reasons, designer Cindy van den Bremen disrupted this pro/anti headscarf debate by redesigning the headscarf itself, making an athletic version that complies with hijab. The design disrupted the all-or-nothing headscarf debate by conceptualizing a previously unconsidered middle ground.[31]

In another example, when design collective Release1 conceptualized the McDonald's project, the aim was to explore McDonald's as the "everycorporation" and its symbolism of American values. In thinking about this societal narrative, individual entries such as the peel-off, french fry voting ballot disrupt the audiences' sense of trade-off between efficiency and democracy embodied in global corporations.[32]

Tennis capster A disruption to the all-or-nothing headscarf debate. Design by Cindy van den Bremen. Photo copyright by Peter Stigter.

Mark your ballot Fry box voting ballot from the MacDonald's project by Release1. Courtesy of Stefane Barbeau.

Guidelines and rating systems typically aim to disrupt by presenting alternatives to existing good practice. The US Green Building Council did this through its LEED rating system, and similarly labeling and certification schemes, such as Cradle to Cradle or the Living Building Challenge, aim to disrupt at the conceptual stage of design. These rating systems give people a way to ask for—to bargain for— something different than the norm.

Architect Teddy Cruz has also sought to disrupt regulatory frameworks by proposing projects that meet a client's or city's broader objectives but in ways that challenge existing limitations in the regulations. Cruz comments that an affordable housing project built on a marginal site "became a political instrument to change code."[33]

It is at the stage of commissioning/conceptualization that defining the issues takes place, making some disruptions definitional. For example, David Hess notes that in the case of organic food, a persistent struggle has been over the definition of "organic"—what qualifies and what does not. The normal definition of a park might be a piece of land, but Ann Buttenwieser of the Neptune

Foundation and architect Jonathan Kirchenfeld conceptualized it as a barge-mounted floating swimming pool.[34] These types of definitional struggles also surround norms for housing, transportation, and public space, among others.

In terms of disrupting narratives, several interesting examples arise from designers' development of card decks as a means of exploring narrative. We heard about the set of enabling cards for intergenerational lodging in Chapter 3. By contrast, landscape architect Jane Wolff's Delta Primer playing cards examine the Sacramento River delta and enable players to deconstruct the narrative of the place to increase its accessibility. Each "suit" (toy, machine, garden, wilderness) represents a set of ideas about the landscape, and each card contains an artifact or practice that details the suit's ideas. The cards may be played in a game that "deals out an endless series of contradictory, yet systemically intertwined, surprises."[35] Although card decks may be familiar for their use in prompting designers through sets of creative tools (for example, IDEO's method cards), designers are also developing and using card decks in a variety of contexts to disrupt existing social narratives.

Floating park The Neptune Foundation's floating swimming pool. Design by Jonathan Kirschenfeld. Photo Timothy Schenck.

Hovering above individual projects but still concerning the conceptualization of design, a range of disruptions concern what design should do. Examples arise where designers adopt conventional activist methods, such as the previously mentioned prison boycott, Architecture 2030's, call for carbon emission reductions from architecture, or eco-literacy teach-ins. Although these are not tied to the life cycle of a given artifact or project, they are tied to the idea of change enacted through an activity of design—such as deselecting prison clients, or embracing low- carbon architecture. They disrupt routine knowledge and practice.

In all of these cases, the disruptions caused by design activism tend to build exchange power because they put alternative "offers" into play, such as protocols for green building or alternative definitions and narratives. But at the same time, a compelling alternative to the status quo is also persuasive, showing convincingly how well an alternative could work, how good it might look, or how numerous the benefits are.

Fabrication and construction

Disruptions in the fabrication stage of the life cycle often involve "resources" such as skills, expertise, siting and specification. In these cases the redistribution of resources often shifts the balance of power.

Temporary appropriations The nomadic prayer space is lightweight and self-assembled. Photo courtesy of designer Michael Herrman.

One approach to disrupting typical patterns of power involves shifting the skills or capability for assembly and fabrication from the hands of experts to the hands of regular people. An example is architect Michael Herrman's Nomadic Prayer Space.[36] When he observed displaced populations of Romanians in Rome worshiping informally at various locations around the city, his response was a portable, lightweight, self-assembled structure that enabled these communities to "temporarily 'construct' their own culturally specific spaces."[37] The structure can be disassembled and put in the back of a compact car, and beyond prayer, the spaces may be used in other temporary appropriations of the city. Other examples of shifting skills to laypeople include projects like fablabs or fashion hacking.

In another example, when architect Frederic Levrat was helping to rebuild the city of Kabul, Afghanistan, he wanted to employ Afghan labor, but there was little local construction skill, leaving the construction market to powerful Turkish firms. The architect worked with partner Abdullah Rafiq to identify an interlocking brick system that enabled unskilled Afghan workers to make bricks on site and stack them in straight walls reinforced by threaded rebar. Within a couple of years the system had created 12 schools and 25 clinics.[38]

Enabling construction Brick-making and assembly by local Afghan labor. Photo courtesy of Frederic Levrat.

The specification process can also serve as a site for disruption, particularly when materials are linked to wider social issues. For example, New York architect Max Bond, designing Harlem's Schomburg Center for Research in Black Culture, implemented "material justice" by specifying a brick building. Research showed that masonry unions had relatively high percentages of minorities from Harlem. The architect commented that he wanted to "make it as likely as possible that people of color would work on the construction of our buildings."[39]

Design activists use siting as a point of disruption when they arrange a "misuse" or unexpected use of a site. For example, landscape architects Herbert Dreiseitl and Greenworks put "wilderness" in an urban park, in an attempt to protect nature from within the city.[40] Toronto architects Reigo & Bauer build starter houses on sites that were formally considered too small and deemed worthless.[41] Designers at UrbanRock proposed parks on sidewalk strips in neighborhoods that lack other space, not unlike the way Rebar's park(ing) project reassigns car spaces as people spaces.[42] These approaches challenge the legitimacy of official designations or restrictions, offering viable alternatives of use that begin to form new social narratives about sites.

In the fabrication stage of the life cycle, some power is built through disruptions that redistribute skills. Other points of disruption, such as siting and specification, also serve to redistribute resources in the form of land uses or opportunities for work.

Schomberg Center for Research in Black Culture Materials linked to wider social issues. Photo Cia Bernales.

Use

During the use phase, design activism disrupts routines in a variety of ways. Aesthetic messages and symbolism that remind us of shame or aspiration can disrupt our levels of emotional comfort. Spatial programming can disrupt norms of use, and material or technical systems can disrupt routines of resource use. By contrast other projects aim to disrupt narratives about places, people or lifestyles.

Arguably many design-related symbols and aesthetic messages serve commercial purposes, often feeding consumer aspiration. However we can all relate to shame and aspiration that is connected to issues beyond our individual situation. Examples that disrupt commercial norms include cases where persuasive aesthetic approaches resonate with past and future shame or aspiration. For example, the Michigan Holocaust Memorial Center-Zekelman Family Campus has prompted "consternation for its brutal and difficult imagery" such as using steel cable-wrapped brick to evoke a Nazi concentration camp.[43]

In another example, South Africa's Constitutional Court opened in the Old Fort Prison Complex (now preserved as a living museum) that had housed many key anti-apartheid campaigners such as Nelson Mandela and Mohandas Gandhi. The building (designed by Urban Solutions and OMM Design Workshop) contains a number of interior and exterior features that represent

Evoking feelings Holocaust Memorial Center Zekelman Family Campus. The brick wrapped in steel cable and the "guard" towers evoke the past shame of Nazi concentration camps. Design by Neumann/Smith & Associates. Photo courtesy of Joshua Nowicki.

notions of justice and echoes of the past where elements of the prison have been preserved. Transparency in the design, through visual connection, is a key part of the court operation. This case encompasses both past shame and future aspiration.[44]

Issues of justice and its role in society were also the centerpiece of the Wayne Lyman Morse US Courthouse in Eugene Oregon by Morphosis Architects. Despite its vulnerability as a terrorist target and other security needs, the courthouse reimagines the public square rather than acting like a fortress; it is a building not only "of the federal government" but also "of the city", comments Eugene planner Nan Laurence.[45] Putting spatial emphasis on the courtrooms to highlight the places where "justice is served", the building "is the first deep look at courthouse design in decades."[46]

Other examples of disruptive symbolic and aesthetic messages are found in critical design, such as Walker's wall phone (see previous chapter p. 132) or the fries voting ballet (see p. 179). Aesthetic disruptions typically build persuasive power and in these examples they evoke persuasive feelings.

Federal Courthouse A building of justice, of the city as well as of the federal government. Photo courtesy of the City of Eugene.

Spatial programs in architecture offer the opportunity for disruptions to the norms of use, and a few cases illustrate this through unexpected mixing of uses; for example, placing a nursery school in a seniors' home, an art gallery in a self-storage facility, or affordable housing above a public library.[47] In these cases, rather than "solidifying" the social patterns associated with a given type of user—for example, typical patterns in a senior care home— a whole range of new, and in some cases unknown, patterns may emerge. The new mix of uses changes the range of social interactions but also loosens the control of any one group over the space.

Pop-up reading room The UNI project deployed on the street. Photo courtesy Howeler + Yoon Architecture.

The use phase also presents opportunities to disrupt the narrative of place, and this is done in a number of cases that involve portable structures and materials. An example is the UNI project by Streetlab. The UNI is a portable reading room that can "temporarily transform almost any urban space into a public reading room and venue for learning." Inspired by a call for lighter, cheaper, quicker solutions (from the Project for Public Spaces), the Streetlab project developed UNI in response to the fact that the commercially dominated offerings in many city neighborhoods don't reflect the broader goal of creating a well-educated society; spaces for learning should be more prominent, accessible and enjoyable.[48]

Other examples that have been mentioned previously include the Nomadic Prayer Space, the mobile urban farm, and the floating swimming pool. There are also examples of a nomadic (floating) museum, a portable theater that adapts to disused offices and shops and even a portable "town hall" in a new town in Utrecht, the Netherlands.[49]

In product and material terms, disruptions sometimes involve resource use. These approaches make it convenient to reduce reliance on dominant systems of natural resource supply and management, and also challenge the efficacy of the dominant system. An example is wind-up or human-powered appliances. Another example, mentioned previously, is the Lunar-resonant street light that shines less brightly, or even turns off, when full moonlight is available.

Another approach to technical disruption concerns the *absence* of artifacts or technical systems. For example, the Dutch design council holds a quarterly "power-free day" during which the staff members turn off all electrical and battery-powered equipment and find themselves adopting alternative work patterns.[50] Andreas Ruby describes another example where architects hired to improve a town square realized that architectural intervention wasn't necessary: "instead of repressing the evident uselessness of an architectural intervention with a symbolic project, they proposed a simple catalog of strikingly obvious maintenance measures."[51] These examples challenge the dominant idea that expansion and growth, and automatic consumption of resources and material goods, are always preferred or better.

End-of-life

Rather than accepting the one-way nature of materials use, where we take the materials, make products or buildings, and then dispose of them as waste, design activism disrupts this linear system by intervening at the product or building end-of-life. We might consider these disruptions of the end of life narrative, or as the shifting of resources at the point of end-of-life. In some cases these interventions include revision of the whole life cycle for better end-of-life outcomes, but some approaches work with what they find—old buildings and products.

One example is the US Environmental Protection Agency's Lifecycle Building Challenge competition, for the "design of building materials, components, information systems, and management practices to create buildings that facilitate and anticipate future changes to and eventual adaptation or dismantling for recovery of all systems, components, and materials."[52] Example entrants include modular designs for deconstruction, reuse and adaptation.

Previously mentioned examples also address this phase of the life cycle. The Grohome and the Katrina Cottage, both of which can be updated as time goes by, address durability and longevity. The "Design for Reuse Primer" for architecture disrupts routine specification procedures that often make it difficult to reuse building materials.

Another example of rethinking disused buildings comes from the city of Chicago where the Archdiocese of Chicago has closed a number of Catholic churches. Working with the Chicago Architecture Foundation, the Archdiocese ran an invited design charrette to develop ideas for adaptively reusing the church structures. Focusing on one particular church, the proposals preserved the church building, reused a school façade, and introduced programs such as a health clinic, housing and a community center.[53]

At the scale of a product, designers are also disrupting the take-make-waste system by reusing waste and working against product obsolescence. One example is Brooklyn artist and furniture designer Jeff Taylor who regularly creates work that adaptively reuses waste or surplus material. Taylor created lamps out of high-density polyethylene pipe used for natural gas and also works with aerospace industry "seconds."[54] Previously mentioned examples, such as fashion decoding and reworking of existing clothes, or sharing clothes over time, also address the end-of-life narrative for design objects.

Designer Miles Park has examined how to reclaim the lives of electronic products which otherwise tend to have short lifespans when they're outdated by technological changes. One strategy is "piggybacking" where an additional unit is attached to an old product to give it extended life. An example here is an exploratory device that allows analog AM/FM radios to receive digital audio broadcasting services, potentially extending the life of millions of household radios as digital radio services are rolled out. The piggybacked unit picks up digital signals and rebroadcasts them as FM signals that the analog radio receives.[55]

Extended life A piggybacked unit allows AM/FM radio to receive digital audio broadcasts. Photo courtesy of designer Miles Park.

Reflecting on design disruptions

We can make a few observations about design activism's use of the capacity for disruption to build power for change. Many of these disruptive examples build exchange power by putting alternative "offers" on the table. The examples present mainly generative activism, as David Hess calls it, rather than "protest" activism.[56] They generate real alternatives to the status quo that people can bargain for or use as a persuasive tool. These disruptions relate to codes of behavior and protocols, narratives and physical configuration.

Many of the above examples also affect the distribution of, and access to, resources. This perhaps marks design activism out from conventional activism as well. Rather than simply bodies-on-the-line as a resource, design activism brings a shifting of physical configurations, alternative access and other resource implications. For example, when we consider who has the ability to create a park or who has the ability to set up a church, the park(ing) space park and the Nomadic Prayer Space offer unconventional answers. Similar shifts result from projects such as fashion hacking, the Katrina cottage, or the UNI portable reading room. Each of these projects shifts capabilities and control to a local group of users, rather than investing centralized authorities with decision-making and control of resources.

Aligned with the idea of generative activism, the examples are diverse in their tone as well as their instigators. Although some are confrontational, many play down the idea of "disruption" and instead emphasize innovation, opportunity, need or transformation. Some of the designers in the above examples may not identify themselves as activists, but rather as innovators. Yet they meet the definition for activism introduced in Chapter 1, namely action on an issue that is neglected or excluded, but socially or environmentally important.

Framing/unveiling

Another view of social movements sees them in terms of their capacity to create and shape meaning—how they *frame* issues.[57] Sociologist David Snow suggests that frames work to focus our attention on certain elements as relevant, "in frame" while taking attention away from elements that are "out of frame."[58] He notes that frames are essentially "articulation mechanisms" by which one story is told instead of another.

Activists frame issues to best reveal the need for change, reasons for joining the cause or newsworthiness. For example, the peace movement made significant progress during the 1980s when it adopted the framing of a "nuclear freeze."[59] Extremists provide another example, when white separatists adopt frames, such as "pride" and "heritage," used by other minorities.[60] Although framing is often thought of as sloganeering, publications, petitions, rallies or other events, there is a precedent for the use of spaces and objects to frame issues visually and spatially, for example, in the way the peace movement deployed nuclear-free "zones."[61]

The process of framing to unveil issues is also explored by sociologist Tim Jordan, who notes that "speaking truth to power" is a process of revealing exploitative power, sometimes through a "manufactured vulnerability" that explicitly tests the fairness or ethics of the status quo. To manufacture vulnerability, activists often place themselves in vulnerable situations, such as living in a tree-house to prevent trees from being cut down.

Jordan comments that such actions "both create media spectacles in which activists uncover the morality of modern life and also attempt to alter that life directly" by physically preventing tree felling, for example.[62] Architect Kim Dovey highlights unveiling as well, commenting:

> It is generally in the interest of those in power to hide conflict, and in the interest of the subject [of power] to expose it. A large part of the struggle over power is the struggle to make its operations visible, to bring it into a domain where its legitimacy can be tested.[63]

Figure 6.3 Framing tasks

Diagnostic framing	Prognostic framing	Motivational framing
Define the problem and who is responsible	Identify better alternatives and anticipate opponents	Call to action supported by rationales and motives

Sociologists Robert Benford and David Snow suggest that there are several framing tasks for any social movement organization, including diagnostic framing (what is the problem?), prognostic framing (who can solve the problem/what should be done?) and motivational framing (why it is important to do something/call to action). These tasks are summarized in Figure 6.3. At least one study indicates that robust diagnostic and prognostic framing is important in gaining desired campaign outcomes.

Another important factor is how well a frame resonates with key audiences—how credible and salient the frames are, for example.[64] Activists invest effort into finding ways to grab media attention, since media coverage can amplify the frame and carry a persuasive message further. The spectacle generated by disruptive activism lends itself to this media attention. Frames don't exist in isolation, however, and typically framing contests occur, often through the media, where one frame is constantly challenged by others.

Framing in design terms

In design terms it may be difficult to distinguish framing from disruption. Indeed, it is possible to view many of the design-related disruptions as what one might call "material" framing.[65] Here the term "material" is broadly inclusive of physical and visual elements. Material framing is the way in which a structure, object or process works to focus attention in one area instead of another, largely through material, visual and spatial experience.

An example occurs when a previously "illegitimate" site is used for housing or a park, as in Chess Park (Chapter 3), which reclaimed a disused alley with a hardscape park. The siting "frames" the limitations of current conceptions, rules and norms around the use of space, especially with respect to certain groups. Rather than framing by telling people, in slogans or speeches, that we need alternatives, design frames these issues by materializing or visualizing an alternative as a real choice.

When alternatives are materialized and visualized, they often help uncover what Henri Lefebvre called "contradictions of space," simultaneous yet conflicting experiences of spatial life.[66] For example, when people see or experience the Nomadic Prayer Space, perhaps in a parking lot, the idea of an "inclusive society" (or inclusive city) is contrasted with this portable tool that formalizes the issues of an excluded group. The disruption of the Nomadic Prayer Space is also its material "frame."

This example also captures other contradictions of space. For example, it challenges our assumption that permanent is always better by acknowledging the value in flexibility. Rather than lobby (or advocate) for permanence, the nomadic space is a tool for people to organize themselves as they choose. Seen in this light the portable, self-assembled prayer space transfers to local communities decisions that once required centralized power and authority to create long-term structures, such as the clergy and the cathedral. If permanent structures do eventually emerge from nomadic practices, they arise from the community's own experience of use.

Physical framing requires strategic choice. A spatial contradiction may exist, but out of the many possible ways to articulate spatial alternatives or to materially emphasize contradictions, design teams and other activists try to choose a frame that is most resonant for the widest audience. Which frames make the strongest alternative "offer" or carry the most persuasive messages? The methods and tactics from Chapter 5 offer ways to think about the framing process. For example, does the frame emerge from the users themselves in a process of organizing? Or do frames arise from the designer's own interpretation of how to best advocate for a group or issue?

Looking back at the examples of design activism's disruptions, we can see that these also frame issues. For example, designers reframe a product's end-of-life by offering "life extensions." Unconventional patterns of use frame new ways of configuring our lives to better address social and environmental concerns. Rating systems and guidelines frame better forms of practice.

Targeting

The final capacity we will consider from social movement activists is the ability to aim—to target calls for change, or to deploy their disruptions and frames with the right audiences. In conventional activism, the "target" serves the role of linking the change imagined by activists to the capacity (embodied in the target) to make the change.[67] In this way conventional activist events often make "demands" (such as to pass legislation or to provide needed facilities) of specific targets (mayor or city council) and to link those demands to larger campaigns as well as to public attention.

Targets might include a politician who can vote a bill into law, other public figures with influence, the public at large (for example, in campaigns to increase household recycling rates), or powerful institutions (such as churches, universities or industries). To some extent, targets such as politicians and institutions reveal themselves in the structure of daily life. Yet good aim also requires creatively assessing the landscape for potential targets and adapting quickly and strategically to targets and even opponents.[68]

Targeting in design terms

Compared to conventional activism, design activism often seems to only weakly define targets. This is partly because in the case of any particular project, such as Chess Park, much of the change imagined by the activists becomes real when a proposed design is fabricated. The built or manufactured form itself is seen as the change, rather than one step toward broader patterns of change. In this case design activism is not organized into campaigns; rather a project is seen as an end in itself—the clients and end users are the targets.

Another challenge for design activism is the way it unfolds over time and through space. Temporal unfolding makes quick and strategic adaptation difficult, because as architect Michael Shamiyeh observes, it takes several years to design and construct an architectural project, but by contrast, "there are hardly any political or economic factors that, after having served as the bases of architectural decisions, have not changed—and radically so—over this same length of time."[69] Design and construction processes are slow, even "static," relative to the dynamic conditions surrounding them.

Time, scale and reach

But the spatial and temporal "unfolding" of design may hold different targeting opportunities. For example, it is possible to consider the wider effects of projects through three spheres of influence with distinctly different spatial relevance. Douglas Schuler characterizes one sphere as containing the material world around us, both natural and constructed. Another sphere is of the mental conceptions we have about the material world around us (our knowledge, ideals, theories and models). The last sphere is of human agency, the socially produced daily experience of the world.[70] Architects may recognize this scheme, although drawn from different sources, as being very similar to Henri Lebevre's notion of space, the basis for Edward Soja's trialectic of space mentioned earlier (Chapter 3).

Taking an example of outdoor street lighting, we can consider design activism and targets in terms of these three spheres (expressed in Figure 6.4). The first sphere (the material world around us) is characterized to a large extent by the

Figure 6.4 Three spheres of spatial influence

The example of street lighting

Spatial practice: cobra head light

The material world around us, spatial norms

Mental conceptions: lighting plan

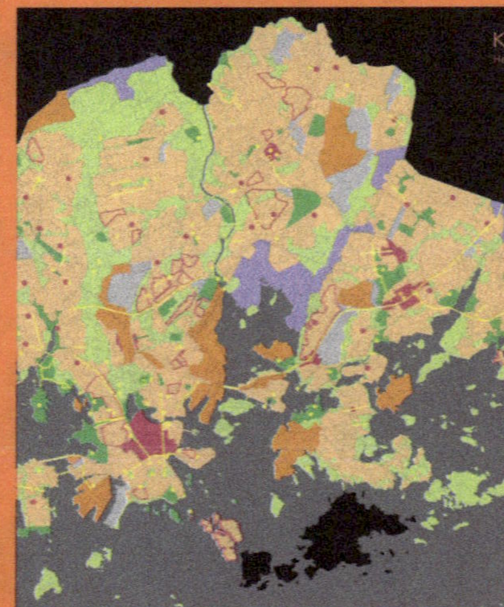

Knowledge, ideals, theories and models about the spatial and material world around us

Agency and interpretation: Chess Park

Imagination and action on possibilities, socially produced spaces

results of spatial practice. Since this practice is increasingly governed by pressures for economic growth, we often see low-cost, standard approaches. In the case of street lighting a standard result is shown as the "cobra head" light familiar on most urban streets. Figure 6.4 shows the second sphere of mental concepts in terms of street lighting as Helsinki's innovative city-wide lighting plan that proposes new ways to think about urban lighting. The third sphere of socially lived experience is shown in the figure as the interpretation of street lighting for Chess Park.

These three spheres suggest different sets of targets as well as different scales at which targets may act. For example, Helsinki's lighting plan disrupts our mental conceptions about the purpose of light in cities. It suggests possible targets such as institutions that implement street lighting, planners, the public (expectation and understanding of lighting), and other stakeholders such as environmentalists. A similar example is the Lunar-resonant street light system (Chapter 3), with lamp brightness tied to availability of moonlight. This proposal also disrupts our conception of street lights.

When new ideas about lighting materialize in experience, they can also affect the other two spheres. For example, Chess Park enters our mental concept of what street lighting can do, and as a mental concept it travels far beyond Glendale, California. This ability to travel shows the role of exhibits and publications in helping individual activist projects to have influence beyond their immediate locations. In this sense targets are unknown, or unfold over time.

We could of course replace these street light examples with others to examine how they exist across these three spheres. Design activism's capacities for disruption, framing and targeting are extended and more complex seen through these spheres of influence.

As you read about examples in this book, some of them begin to change your mental conceptions, which then produce further disruptions if they affect your design practice. In this way lived experiences have spatial reach. If an example is still influential after five years it also has temporal reach, even though the "disruption" created by a new building in lived experience probably expires sooner as people in close proximity get used to it. Reach can also allow an instance of design activism to affect a larger scale than its immediate context. For example, one building, or a small collection of buildings, could successfully challenge building codes so that regulations, and then spatial practices, change across an entire state.

We might argue that once enough cases of socially produced alternatives arise and influence our mental concepts, we start to see new norms. This type of process has unfolded through rating and labeling systems. In effect, the rating system—based on a collection of successful projects in lived space—worked its way into broad-based spatial practice. At this point the bar for normal practice begins to be raised and a new round of activism begins, to raise the bar even further. This pattern may be emerging with portable and pop-up public spaces, such as parks in parking spaces, mobile urban farms or pop-up public reading rooms.

The practical aspects of lived experience also give activism reach. An example is the supply chain—those actors who provide parts, skills, materials and so forth for fabrication. In Chapter 5 we considered how a challenging major building project serves as mobilization, partly of the supply chain. We can also see this in terms of disruption—nearly any design that disrupts routines and norms has related disruptions somewhere within the supply chain, which becomes a target for activism and may wedge open more opportunities for change, when people gain new skills or experiences that make the alternatives easier next time.

What arises from this discussion of targeting is that design activists rarely make demands in the same way that protesters do. Rather, we might see design activism as making suggestions that others put into play in demands, bargaining or persuasion. Thus, for example, the athletic headscarf is a suggestion, and Muslim girls and women can then bring it into bargaining over whether or not headscarves are safe for gym class. The park(ing) park was a suggestion, which groups picked up and used in the process of creating a city's pavement-to-parks program.

In addition, design activism operates across time and space, through three spheres of influence, in ways that make its targeting challenging and complex. Each sphere has a range of targets, since different types of decision-making occur in each sphere. Sometimes targets become apparent later, as design activism unfolds across space and time.

REFLECTIONS

Stepping back from how these activist capacities operate, we can reflect on other ways in which they might be similar to, or different from, conventional activism, in terms of effectiveness, budget and how it all adds up.

Effectiveness: building new norms

The above discussion suggests that activist capacities of disruption and framing have reach and can affect different scales, but it is perhaps not as clear what factors might make these capacities more or less effective. Project-level change is good, but ultimately we need societal or population-level change. We saw that for conventional activism, disruption's effectiveness was measured by how extreme it was, or by how well it illustrated the salience of an issue. What constitutes an extreme disruption in design terms? Are there different factors that might affect a design disruption's effectiveness? Similarly, conventional activist frames are effective to the extent that they diagnose a problem and identify solutions so as to resonate with a wide range of audiences; how does this compare with physical or material framing?

What would "maximum disruption" mean in terms of design activism? In conventional activist terms extreme disruption usually means putting bodies on the line to stop routine activities or amassing huge numbers of protesters. In design terms extreme might refer to the radicality of the idea, an extreme aesthetic or broad participation.

The examples in these pages show a range of radical ideas, such as that a parking space is available for hire as a park, that you could develop a relationship with the sheep that produced the wool for your sweater, or that a farm or swimming pool is mobile. Architectural programs may also be radical in terms of how they mix uses within a given space or landscape. A radical, or at least provocative aesthetic also helps. Cliff Pearson at *Architectural Record* suggests that an important element to any activist story is how to represent it visually, an element that may also give the story reach as far as other media are concerned. A disruption may also be considered more extreme when more people can engage with it. International park(ing) day is an example of this, where it is easy for anyone to get involved.

Persuasive disruption is another feature of conventional activism that we can examine in design terms. How does an instance of design activism convey that the issue holds a great deal of concern for many people? In conventional activism this salience is conveyed through numbers, worthiness, unity and commitment (WUNC, mentioned earlier). For example, large numbers of people conduct a vigil while holding symbols of unity (AIDS red ribbon) and behaving in ways (such as respectful silence) that illustrate worthiness or commitment. Design activism projects may be able to manufacture some events or activities that would allow for this kind of display, such as petition signings, teach-ins or exhibitions.

Material framing suggests that architecture and design may have something new for social movement actors to consider in terms of diagnostic frames (what's the problem?) and prognostic frames (what should we do about it?). Although we might read design activist projects as statements about prognosis—what we should do about an issue—in some ways the design premise of experimentation, prototyping and material investigation may be seen more as part of diagnosing the problem rather than a final statement of what to do about it.

For example, as architects and designers explore portable, pop-up public spaces or local production, they engage in a classic diagnostic process that "problematizes and focuses attention on an issue, helps shape how the issue is perceived, and identifies who or what is culpable, thereby identifying the targets or sources of the outcomes sought."[71] They contribute to figuring out the problem rather than stipulating specific remedies. Thus, despite the appearance of "solving a problem" at the project level, what some design activism may be doing is building more cumulatively toward a diagnosis—which shapes a clearer idea of what to do (prognosis). Although not every experiment results in a useful finding, we might view the approach as implementing design thinking to social movement activism, in the same way that "design thinking" has been rolled out for businesses, and even governments.

Whether design activism is trying to understand what's wrong or to describe solutions, indications are that instances of activism are more effective when they form part of wider campaigns that approach change through design *and* other mechanisms. For most social change, design is necessary but not sufficient.

For all activists, framing becomes a challenge when issues are increasingly interlinked and cut across scales. Similarly, framing is a challenge when we are dealing with pervasive issues such as consumerism and growth, which are in some ways an issue for everybody, and thus an issue for nobody. This is where it is useful to return to the four consumerist challenges (see Chapter 3)—pricing, pace of stimulation, loss of commitment strategies and consumerist social language. In activist terms these are also "frames" that connect projects and events to the broader problems of consumerism and markets. These frames also offer a different way of thinking about strategic points for disruption, alongside the points of disruption through the design life cycle.

Capacities – are they really low budget?

One may also ask, upon reflection, if the capacities of disruption and framing are in design terms really all that low budget.

It is true that materials and structures are typically not as cheap as a group of volunteers lying in blockade on a road. However, one has to compare these design activist capacities for building power with design's more conventional capacities for building power. Many of these conventional capacities are tied to financial gain; for example, consumer companies induce change in the marketplace through large investments in product design and development based on consumer desires, needs and behaviors. Companies also support new designs with expensive marketing campaigns. Typically pursuing change through these mechanisms is beyond the financial reach of most design activism.

Other conventional design capacities are tied to centralized control that stem from design features of a system, such as big oil (referring to countries and companies that produce oil and the technologies that rely on it such as cars and buildings), big computing (companies that produce operating systems) or housing development (large-scale suburban housing developers). Centralization such as this is often maintained through political lobbying that involves investment in political campaigns, access to decision makers in exclusive contexts of wealth (clubs, social networks), and other forms of financially-based lobbying (including advertising). This is not to suggest that universal operating systems or suburban housing developers are necessarily bad, but rather to emphasize that their capacity to build power through design (either to bring about change or maintain the status quo) lies beyond the reach of most design activists.

In architectural terms, cities attempt to change their conditions by investing large sums in "splashy urban trophies," from sports stadiums to cultural centers.[72] These and other grand urban gestures often serve the role of developing what we might call an authorized narrative of a place. The chances that these narratives can reflect broader social concerns are reduced, since these spaces rely increasingly on investment and concessions to large corporate investors. Here again, the point is not that corporate investment in public space is wrong, but rather that most design activists do not have this same capacity to authorize narratives.

Capacities of framing and disruption seem relatively low budget in comparison to the capacities of design through high-stakes research and development, industry lobbying, political campaign or development contributions, high-budget marketing campaigns, and access to decision makers.

CONCLUSION

In this chapter we have reviewed the capacities of disruption, framing and targeting that design activists have for building power to bring about change. Examples and discussion suggested that these capacities might come into play in various ways, such as stages of the life cycle, parts of the supply chain, spheres of spatial influence, and the four consumerist challenges. This terrain is summarized in Table 6.3.

Table 6.3 Points for disruption, framing and targeting

Points	Example
Life cycle stages	Commissioning, fabrication, use, end-of-life
Supply chain	Skills, materials, processes, parts, services, decommissioning
Spheres of spatial influence	1. The norms of our measurable, physical spaces and environments. 2. Ideals, models, theories and other mental conceptions of space. 3. Lived experience where real life intervenes to modify or change norms of spaces and places
Consumerism and growth	1. Pricing. 2. Pace of stimulation. 3. Loss of commitment strategies. 4. Consumerist social language

In light of these capacities we can see the methods and tactics of the last chapter not only as ways of calling for change, but also as ways of building power to try to bring about change. They make use of disruption, framing and targeting to build or amplify exchange power and persuasive power. Even though these concepts from conventional activism help us to make sense of design activism, it is clear that design has some particular dimensions—particularly its unfolding over time and space—that distinguish it from conventional activism.

Seen in the light of power and the capacity to build power, the question of how activism "adds up" becomes political. In struggles to change societal norms, to transform our systems and practices, there is always a strong tendency for dominant market systems to bend changes to profitable ends. Transformation requires much stronger support from outside the market, support from governments and civic organizations who derive their power from citizens, rather than from consumers.

NOTES

1 Lawrence Lessig, *Free Culture: How Big Media Uses Technology and the Law to Lock Down Culture and Control Creativity* (New York: The Penguin Press, 2004), p. 12.
2 Michael Gecan, *Going Public: An Organizer's Guide to Citizen Action* (New York: Anchor Books, 2004), p. 36.
3 Kenneth E. Boulding, *Three Faces of Power* (London: Sage, 1989), pp. 16–17.
4 John Scott, *Power* (Cambridge: Polity Press, 2001), p. 16.

5 Neil Fligstein and Doug McAdam, "Toward a General Theory of Strategic Action Fields", *Sociological Theory*, Vol. 29, no. 1 (2011), pp. 1–26, p. 5.
6 Gecan, *Going Public*, p. xix.
7 David J. Hess, *Alternative Pathways in Science and Industry: Activism, Innovation, and the Environment in an Era of Globalization* (Cambridge, MA: MIT Press, 2007), p. 23.
8 Gecan, *Going Public*, p. 36; and Kim Dovey, *Framing Places: Mediating Power in Built Form* (London: Routledge, 2008), pp. 11–13.
9 Boulding's view aligns with other views on power such as John Allen and John Scott. See John Allen, *Lost Geographies of Power* (Oxford: Blackwell, 2003); and Scott, *Power*. Allen identifies *instrumental* power as aiming to "bend the will of others" (sticks and carrots) and *associational* power as aiming to form "a common will" through communication and association (hugs) with others (p. 123). Akin to Allen's "instrumental power" Scott highlights forms of power that rely on restraints (rewards and punishments), as well as forms of power that rely on social bonds such as trust, obligation and loyalty. While sticks and carrots may be generally aligned with sovereign power, hugs are generally aligned with culturally diffuse power.
10 Dovey, *Framing Places*, pp. 10–12.
11 Dan Lockton, David Harrison and Neville Stanton, "Making the User More Efficient: Design for Sustainable Behaviour", *International Journal of Sustainable Engineering*, Vol. preprint (2008); Dan Lockton with David Harrison and Neville Stanton, *Design With Intent: 101 Patterns for Influencing Behavior Through Design* (Windsor: Equifine, 2010); and T. A. Bhamra, D. Lilley and T. Tang, "Sustainable Use: Changing Consumer Behavior through Product Design", in *Changing the Change* (Turin, Italy: Allemandi Conference Press, 2008).
12 The problem of business interests financing political campaigns is well known, but a timely illustration arrives with research showing that since the 2010 election, the Conservative Party in the UK received more than half of its donations from financiers, hedge funds and private equity firms. Many of these large donations qualify donors for personal meetings with the prime minister. Rajeev Syal, Jill Treanor and Nick Mathiason, "Revealed: How the City Bankrolls the Conservatives", *Guardian* (1 October 2011).
13 Stewart R. Clegg, *Frameworks of Power* (London: Sage, 1989), p. 4.
14 Verta Taylor and Nella Van Dyke, "'Get Up, Stand Up': Tactical Repertoires of Social Movements", in *The Blackwell Companion to Social Movements*, ed. David A. Snow, Sarah A. Soule and Hanspeter Kriesi (Oxford: Blackwell, 2007), p. 268.
15 John Scott, *Power*, pp. 9–12.
16 Robin Murray, Julie Caulier-Grice and Geoff Mulgan, *The Open Book of Social Innovation* (London: The Young Foundation and NESTA, 2010), p. 8.
17 Tim Jordan and Paul A. Taylor, *Hacktivism and Cyberwars: Rebels with a Cause?* (London: Routledge, 2004), pp. 145-9.
18 See, for example, Byron Miller and Deborah G. Martin, "Space and Contentious Politics", *Mobilization: An International Journal*, Vol. 8, no. 2 (2003), pp. 143–56; Edward W. Soja, *Seeking Spatial Justice* (Minneapolis: University of Minnesota Presss, 2010), p. 91; and Trevor Pinch, "Technology and Institutions: Living in a Material World", *Theory and Society*, Vol. 37 (2008), pp. 461–83.
19 Thomas Markus, *Buildings and Power* (London: Routledge, 1993), pp. 13–14.

20 Bruno Latour, *Reassembling the Social: An Introduction to Actor-Network-Theory* (Oxford: Oxford University Press, 2007).
21 Linda Nash, "The Agency of Nature or the Nature of Agency", *Environmental History*, Vol. 10, no. 1 (2005), pp. 67–9.
22 Tali Hatuka and Rachel Kallus, 'The Architecture of Repeated Rituals: Tel Aviv's Rabin Square', *Journal of Architectural Education*, Vol. 61, no. 4 (2008), pp. 85–94.
23 Taylor and Van Dyke, "'Get Up, Stand Up'", p. 263.
24 Although it is probably not accurate to say that these are the only capacities at work in conventional activism, this section is based on the fact that these are accepted elements, based in the literature, and therefore can serve as legitimate points of comparison between design activism and conventional activism.
25 See, for example, Bob Edwards and John D. McCarthy, "Resources and Social Movement Mobilization", in *The Blackwell Companion to Social Movements*, ed. David A. Snow, Sarah A. Soule and Hanspeter Kriesi (Oxford: Blackwell, 2007); and Doug McAdam, Sidney Tarrow and Charles Tilly, *Dynamics of Contention* (Cambridge: Cambridge University Press, 2001).
26 Doug McAdam, "Tactical Innovation and Pace of Insurgency", *American Sociological Review*, Vol. 48, no. 6 (December 1983), pp. 735–54.
27 Doug McAdam and Yang Su, "The War at Home: Antiwar Protests and Congressional Voting, 1965 to 1973", *American Sociological Review*, Vol. 67, no. 5 (2002), pp. 696–721.
28 Frances Piven and Richard Cloward, *Poor People's Movements* (New York: Pantheon, 1977); and William A. Gamson, *The Strategy of Social Protest* (Homewood, IL: The Dorsey Press, 1975).
29 See, for example, Katrin Uba, "Political Protest and Policy Change: The Direct Impacts of Indian Anti-Privatization Mobilizations, 1990–2003", *Mobilization: An International Journal*, Vol. 10, no. 3 (2005), pp. 383–96; and Kenneth T. Andrews, "Social Movements and Policy Implementation: The Mississippi Civil Rights Movement and the War on Poverty, 1965 to 1971", *American Sociological Review*, Vol. 66, no. 1 (2001), pp. 71–95.
30 Colin Barnes, "Disability Activism and the Struggle for Change: Disability, Policy and Politics in the UK", *Education, Citizenship and Social Justice*, Vol. 2, no. 3 (2007), pp. 203–21.
31 Jude Stewart, "Modesty a la Mode: Redesigning the Head Scarf for Devotion and Comfort", *ID* (September/October 2005).
32 Jenny Sullivan, "Food for Thought", *ID* (April 2003).
33 Vincent Canizaro and Kim Tanzer, "Environmental Architecture and Sustainability: A Taxonomy of Tactics", *Journal of Architectural Education*, Vol. 60, no. 4 (2007), pp. 4–14.
34 Dianna Dilworth, "Floating Pool to be Reintroduced to New York Waterfront", *Architectural Record* (October 2006).
35 Mark Anderson, "Delta Primer: A Field Guide to the California Delta by Jane Wolff", *Places*, Vol. 16, no. 2 (2004), pp. 54–61.
36 Beth Broome, "Finding Religion in a Shoebox Sanctuary", *Architectural Record* (July 2006).
37 Michael Herrman, *Hypercontextuality: The Architecture of Displacement and Placelessness* (Rome: Consiglio Nazionale Delle Ricerche, 2008), p. 279.
38 Belinda Lanks, "An Architect in Kabul", *Metropolis*, Vol. 25 (July 2006).
39 Lance Hosey, "The Ethics of Brick", *Metropolis* (June 2005), p. 128.

40 Brian Libby, "Returning to its Roots", *Metropolis* (March 2006).
41 Tim McKeough, "Starting Out Small", *Metropolis* (October 2006).
42 "Finding Public Space in the Margins", *ID* (August 2004).
43 Sam Lubell, "Holocaust Center's Design Conjures up Difficult Memories", *Architectural Record* (June 2004).
44 Melinda Tuhus, "The People's Court", *Metropolis* (November 2004); and Bronwyn Law-Viljoen (ed.), *Light on a Hill: Building the Constitutional Court of South Africa* (Johannesburg: David Drut Publishing, 2006).
45 Nan Laurence, email correspondence "re: Wayne Morse Federal Courthouse" (16 November 2010).
46 Then Chief Justice Michael Hogan, in Clifford Pearson, "Morphosis Creates a US Courthouse that Provides Common Ground for People with Different Points of View', *Architectural Record* (March 2007).
47 Jennifer LeClaire, "The Evolution of Eden", *Metropolis* (October 2002); Karrie Jacobs, "The Other Kansas", *Metropolis* (January 2005); and Liz Nakazawa, "A Living Library", *Metropolis* (October 2002).
48 "The UNI: Portable Reading Room for Public Space", *Streetlab* (New York, 2011). Available at http://www.theuniproject.org/about (accessed 13 September 2011).
49 "Mies-Meets-Granpre mobile, Utrecht", *Architectural Record* (December 2006).
50 Aric Chen, "Lights Out", *Metropolis* (June 2004).
51 Andreas Ruby, "Reprogramming Architecture", in *Organizing for Change: Integrating Architecture Thinking in Other Fields*, ed. Michael Shamiyeh and DOM Research-Laboratory (Basel: Birkhauser, 2007), p. 44.
52 *Lifecycle Building Challenge* (Washington, DC: Environmental Protection Agency, n.d.). Available at: http://www.lifecyclebuilding.org/ (accessed 13 September 2011).
53 John E. Czarnecki, "Chicago Competition Considers New Designs for Church", *Architectural Record* (October 2003).
54 Lauren Nelson, "Pipe Dream", *Metropolis* (October 2004).
55 Miles Barwick Park, "Product Life: Designing for Longer Lifespans", Faculty of Art, Design, and Architecture. (Kingston: Kingston University, 2009).
56 David J. Hess, *Alternative Pathways in Science and Industry*, p. 85.
57 Robert D. Benford and David A. Snow, "Framing Processes and Social Movements: An Overview and Assessment", *Annual Review of Sociology*, Vol. 26 (2000), pp. 611–39.
58 David A. Snow, "Framing Processes, Ideology, and Discursive Fields", in *The Blackwell Companion to Social Movements*, ed. David A. Snow, Sarah A. Soule and Hanspeter Kriesi (Oxford: Blackwell, 2007).
59 Daniel M. Cress and David A. Snow, "The Outcomes of Homeless Mobilization: The Influence of Organization, Disruption, Political Mediation, and Framing", *The American Journal of Sociology*, Vol. 105, no. 4 (2000), pp. 1063–104.
60 Ibid.
61 Byron Miller and Deborah G. Martin, "Space and Contentious Politics", *Mobilization: An International Journal*, Vol. 8, no. 2 (2003), pp. 143–56.
62 Jordan, *Activism!*, pp. 61–3.
63 Dovey, *Framing Places*, p. 13.
64 Robert D. Benford and David A. Snow, "Framing Processes and Social Movements: An Overview and Assessment", *Annual Review of Sociology*, Vol. 26 (2000), pp. 611–39.

65 The notion that framing has physical aspects is not unprecedented. Deborah Martin has discussed a concept which she calls "place framing" and which asserts the *neighborhood* as a potent political place in terms of identity, experience and future hopes for a particular neighborhood. Deborah G. Martin, "'Place-Framing' as Place-making: Constituting a Neighborhood for Organizing and Activism", *Annals of the Association of American Geographers*, Vol. 93, no. 3 (2003), pp. 730–50.

66 Miller and Martin, 'Space and Contentious Politics', p. 147.

67 Rinku Sen, *Stir It Up: Lessons in Community Organizing and Advocacy* (San Francisco, CA: Jossey-Bass, 2003).

68 For example, McCammon, Lee Smith and Terrell discuss the strategic assessment of opportunities and targets in the campaign for women's right to serve on juries in Holly J. McCammon, Carrie Lee Smith and Teresa M. Terrell, "Becoming Full Citizens: The US Women's Jury Rights Campaigns, the Pace of Reform, and Strategic Adaptation", *American Journal of Sociology*, Vol. 113, no. 4 (January 2008), pp. 1104–47.

69 Michael Shamiyeh and DOM Research-Laboratory (eds), *Organizing for Change: Integrating Architecture Thinking in Other Fields* (Basel: Birkhauser, 2007), p. 9.

70 Douglas Schuler, *Liberating Voices: A Pattern Language for Communication Revolution* (Cambridge MA: MIT Press, 2008), pp. 32–3.

71 Cress and Snow, "The Outcomes of Homeless Mobilization', 2000.

72 James S. Russell, 'Where Are We Now? Architecture's Place in an Era of Evolving Values", *Architectural Record* (March 2003).

Chapter 7

Speculating on the steady state scenario

For the sake of argument, let us suppose that activist efforts are successful and that affluent countries develop steady state economies that prioritize real well-being. Economic growth will no longer be a central organizing principle, so how will designers be affected by new organizing principles? In this chapter we briefly and broadly consider this question.

A steady state economy obviously incorporates many current ideas for sustainable design and sustainable cities. For example, a steady state economy will require longer lasting, durable goods, and it will require more compact urban development that doesn't rely, perhaps doesn't even include, privately owned cars. Energy-efficient, low-carbon buildings and products will be the order of the day.

Yet many previous and existing scenarios for sustainable cities and sustainable development have tended to put "economic growth" aside or take it as given. In cases where it is put aside, scenarios emerge based entirely on other principles (ecological restoration or social inclusiveness), many of which aren't feasible when put under pressures of economic growth. In scenarios where economic growth is taken as given, a number of proponents argue that sustainable development, underpinned by sustainable design, is the *new path* to economic growth.

Something interesting happens when instead of starting with the growth driven economy and trying to green it, we start with the steady state economy and then consider the changes that result. For the purpose of this chapter we consider three possible organizing principles of a steady state economy:

1. Human and environmental health.
2. Infrastructure and maintenance.
3. Social networks.

These three areas suggest new types of knowledge, areas of practice, and points of collaboration for architecture and design in a steady state economy.

It is worth recalling that a steady state economy still has an operational market and financial transactions still play a large role in daily life. Accordingly some of the roles of architecture and design will continue along conventional avenues. However the likelihood is that the portion of productive activity occurring in the profit-oriented market will be smaller and balanced against other arenas of production such as social enterprises and distributed peer networks.

ACCEPTING SUSTAINABLE CITY AND SUSTAINABLE DESIGN SCENARIOS

Many existing prescriptions for sustainable development resonate with the ideas for a steady state economy. The sustainable design arena has been active for several decades now, stemming back at least as far as architectural responses to the 1970s energy crisis. Theory and practice for sustainability through architecture and design have grown in sophistication, scope and ambition. To the extent that a steady state economy is efficient, resilient, regenerative and fair, it will have a great deal of similarity with many existing sustainable design proposals and practices.

Many close observers of the sustainable development agenda agree that the unit of concern is the town or city. Most people in the world now live in cities, and these are arguably the central places for shaping ecological and social patterns. Further, there is broad agreement on the general outlines of sustainable cities, as suggested by the many consistencies among the columns in Table 7.1. The table draws on principles, goals, elements and ideas for sustainable cities from respected thinkers in the field. Broadly speaking, these tenets of sustainable cities include carbon neutrality, green space and nature, higher degrees of localism which imply distributed systems, and personal and social well-being.

In addition, these general outlines are echoed in more specific proposals for sustainable design of buildings and products, as shown in Table 7.2, which reflects broadly accepted sustainable design approaches. These approaches tend to consider the life cycle of the designed object or structure, minimizing adverse impacts, and improving natural conditions, at each stage of the cycle.

Our steady state scenario broadly accepts these general outlines and acknowledges the continuing, perhaps rising, importance of technical knowledge about how to efficiently use materials, energy and technology (termed "eco-design" for the purposes of this discussion).

Sustainable cities Density, green space, local food, physical activity.

Table 7.1 Common themes of sustainable towns and cities

Sources	**Resilient Cities** by Timothy Beatley, Peter Newman and Heather Boyer	**One Planet Communities** by Pooran Desai	**Ecological Democracy** by Randolph Hester	**Retrofitting Suburbia** by Ellen Dunham-Jones and June Williamson
Elements, ideas, principles and goals	Seven key elements to sustainable cities: • renewable energy • carbon neutrality • distributed infrastructure and services (as opposed to centralized power, waste and water) • photosynthetic infrastructure • closed loop systems • places of distinction (localism driven infrastructurally) • sustainable transport	Ten principles of one-planet living • zero carbon • zero waste • sustainable transport • local and sustainable materials • local and sustainable food • sustainable water • natural habitats and wildlife • culture and heritage • equity and fair trade • health and happiness (physical, mental, spiritual)	Ideas for ecological democracy Enabling form • Centeredness • Connectedness • Fairness • Sensible status seeking • Sacredness Resilient form • Particularness • Selective diversity • Density and smallness • Limited extent (appropriate size) • Adaptability Impelling form • Everyday future • Naturalness • Inhabiting science (landscape, ecological and native knowledges) • Reciprocal stewardship • Pacing	Goals for retrofitting suburbia • reduce vehicle miles traveled (energy/health) • reduce land consumption by absorbing growth through densification rather than spraw • increase local interconnectivity • enhance green space and permeability of built infrastructure • increase public and civic space • diversify housing type and affordability • establish polycentric regions

Table 7.2 Common themes in sustainable buildings and objects

Sustainable Architectural Design **American Institute of Architects, Committee on the Environment**	**Sustainable Product Design, Okala, Industrial Designers Society of America**
Measure 1: Design and innovation Sustainable design is an inherent aspect of design excellence. Projects should express sustainable design concepts and intentions and take advantage of innovative programming opportunities.	Innovate: Meet real needs, use biomimicry, rethink the product benefit
Measure 2: Regional/community design Sustainable design values the unique cultural and natural character of a given region.	Low-impact materials: Avoid damaging materials (toxins, etc.), reduce material use, use recycled materials
Measure 3: Land use and site ecology Sustainable design protects and benefits ecosystems, watersheds and wildlife habitat in the presence of human development.	Low-impact manufacturing: Minimize energy/waste in production, simplify construction, facilitate quality control
Measure 4: Bioclimatic design Sustainable design conserves resources and maximizes comfort through design adaptations to site-specific and regional climate conditions.	Efficient distribution: Reduce packaging, use recycled/recyclable packaging, use efficient transport, localize
Measure 5: Light and air Sustainable design creates comfortable interior environments that provide daylight, views and fresh air.	Reduce impacts from use: Minimize energy and materials during product use, design for durability and reuse, create maintenance and upgrade options
Measure 6: Water cycle Sustainable design conserves water and protects and improves water quality.	Reduce impacts from end-of-product life: Make biodegradable, recyclable or reusable; facilitate safe methods of collection and disposal
Measure 7: Energy flows and energy future Sustainable design conserves energy and resources and reduces the carbon footprint while improving building performance and comfort. Sustainable design anticipates future energy sources and needs.	Source: Okala Edcodesign Guide, by Philip White, Louise St. Pierre and Steve Belletire, 2010.
Measure 8: Materials and construction Sustainable design includes the informed selection of materials and products to reduce product-cycle environmental impacts, improve performance, and optimize occupant health and comfort.	
Measure 9: Long life, loose fit Sustainable design seeks to enhance and increase ecological, social and economic values over time.	
Measure 10: Collective wisdom and feedback loops Sustainable design strategies and best practices evolve over time through documented performance and shared knowledge of lessons learned.	

HEALTH

In many ways a steady state scenario replaces the current priority of economic growth with a new priority of "health" in the broadest sense. Here health has many dimensions and also links a variety of issues. For example:

- Physical health in the form of chronic diseases such as obesity, high blood pressure and heart disease that require "lifestyle medicine".
- Mental health, and in particular its relationship to social health through mechanisms such as social relationships, the equality of society and meaningful work.
- Nutrition and food linking human health to environmental health.
- Mental and physical health, and their connection to nature/green space.
- Connections between natural resource loss or pollution (chemicals, carbon, heat, noise, light), and human and environmental health.

Some of these ideas are captured in Figure 7.1, which attempts to show their inter-relations.

A fundamental implication for design is that holistic health emerges as a prominent design practice area, alongside and often in partnership with ecodesign. Holistic health design practices require sophisticated and integrated knowledge of human and environmental health, with designers working with health implications as readily as they work with visual or formal implications. In addition, even as concern for health is holistic, health is increasingly achieved through distributed health systems that are integrated across urban life.

Figure 7.1 Whole health

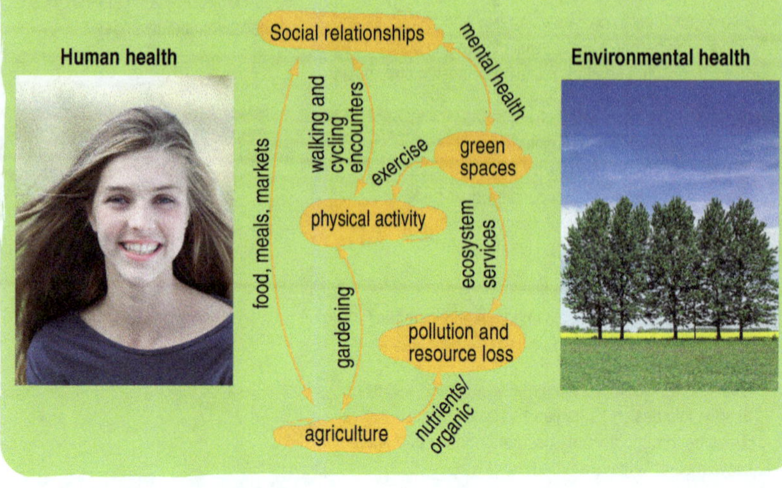

The result is dramatically lower healthcare costs derived from systemically improved health. Consider, for example, a recent study by McKinsey, which found that close to 40 percent of US healthcare costs are attributed to lifestyle-generated medical conditions related to poor diet, social isolation, chemical exposures, stress and physical inactivity.[1] In the US, where obesity is prevalent, studies suggest that taxpayers finance nearly half the costs of obesity-related diseases.[2] Meanwhile, recent research in the UK suggests that stress-related sickness is the main source of absence from work and that at 40 percent, the biggest share of incapacity benefits is attributed to mental ill-health and stress.

Design-related knowledge about health

An important aspect of health is our real-time knowledge. With health as an organizing principle for the broader economy we have much more knowledge about the state of human and environmental health, and beyond that we have much wider participation in developing knowledge about health and acting on it.

In terms of connecting human and environmental health, designer Natalie Jeremijenko comments that we are moving from a time when regulators and industries decide what kind of environmental or health data should be collected and the methods for collecting data, to a time when citizens become involved in "actively generating and interpreting environmental data that is everywhere and available openly."[3] She argues that this "scientific knowledge production" has direct bearing on our lives because we are at risk or benefit from the environmental conditions around us.

Ecology, in its complexity, local specificity and social nature, is suitable for distributed methods of knowledge and action because, as Jeremijenko points out, there is no way to describe what constitutes a healthy environment for everyone, all the time. Jeremijenko sees the value of distributed computation (ubiquitous computing) in terms of this citizen science that can lead to local action. She sees her design-oriented "health clinic" at New York University as authorizing neighborhoods to monitor, interpret and act on their own health data through projects such as the nopark to reduce air pollutants locally.[4]

The issue of monitoring data and interpreting and acting on it in a health context potentially shifts the role of design from objectifying information—artfully presenting a smog of data on ambient urban conditions—to a role in helping create knowledge upon which people act.[5] Design questions ensue, some of which are already being asked today: What makes a health-monitoring system reliable and easy to use? What kind of data can we collect? How can

The "nopark" Authorizing neighborhoods to take their own action for health. Photo courtesy of the Environmental Health Clinic and Lab, New York University.

people access and interpret data in such a way that they are confident to form opinions, challenge existing regimes, and take action to improve health conditions? Finally, what objects and structures do we add to or remove from the environment to improve local health?

Designers also play a role in weaving the status of health into experiences of daily life on a public level. An example is River Glow by The Living, a project to place underwater glowing lights near bridges to give a green light or red light signal regarding the river's water quality. Another way to visualize health concern infrastructure, a topic mentioned previously and discussed again below.

Structures themselves may contain monitors designed to catch potential health problems early. For example, the University of Rochester's Center for Future Health developed the "Smart Medical Home" to monitor elderly inhabitants across a wide range of vital signs, recognizing, for example, that a change in gait can be an early indicator of oncoming neurological disease or stroke.[6] A similar range of "smart" utensils and appliances, some developed at MIT's Media Lab, might report on the safety or nutritional content of food, and the cleanliness of water and air.

River Glow Indicates the water quality at a glance, installed in the East River in New York City. Image courtesy of The Living.

Networks of health

The idea that health is constantly produced across social and physical networks suggests that in a steady state economy we will develop a more integrated picture of the social and material aspects of a neighborhood or place that facilitate holistic health. We will look in an integrated way at places to see how health is produced in combinations of physical activity, social networks, ecological benefits and nutrition.

Currently we have pieces in place. For example, online services such as "walkscore" rank the walkability of neighborhoods, giving one indication of how well the built environment facilitates physical activity, and possibly social interaction. Similarly New York City's active design guidelines (see Chapter 3) begin to show an integrated picture of material and spatial features that promote physical activity. Developing and improving this integrated picture is an obvious area for design research and practice.

As we consider this integrated picture, some interesting ideas emerge in terms of changing the way we look at what we are designing. Whereas before we may have thought about designing a "healthy workplace" (natural lighting and ventilation, safe materials and so forth), in a more holistic paradigm we might focus on designing healthy jobs. The challenge there would be not just the work environment, but the pacing and context for the work, the types and balance of activities, and so forth. Rather than being an invasive or controlling process, this type of design process could be user driven.

Another important aspect of holistic health is its distributed nature. The health system becomes far more than a set of hospitals or health clinics, but rather connects the environment, food systems, physical movement, social systems and green infrastructure.

Currently, important aspects of a holistic health system are compromised because they are seen as isolated. Emily Talen's research suggests that there is very poor spatial logic in the development of parks and other public spaces and their surrounding areas. Zoning around parks she studied doesn't respond to the park as an urban or health asset, and further, "investments for parks and recreation, arts and cultural facilities, housing, economic development, libraries and neighborhood services are not integrated in such a way that investment in one area improves the surrounding context of another."[7] In addition, infrastructure provision is typically divided among a range of professionals, often leading to a piecemeal approach to maintaining and upgrading networks.[8]

In a steady state economy, partly through an organizing principle of health, the opportunities for synergies, linkages and mutually supportive upgrades or

Materialize resource flows P.N.S. General Vara del Rey Square uses a series of devices to materialize resource flows. Design by elii (Uriel Fogué + Eva Gil + Carlos Palacios

One element proposed for the square is the Urban Tree which serves as a meeting point, exercise area, electricity generator, battery-charging station, night-time light and greenery. Design by elii (Uriel Fogué + Eva Gil + Carlos Palacios). Photo Miguel de Guzmán.

Ongoing health Farmers' markets are one element in the ongoing process of health. Photo Corey Templeton.

maintenance are mined across infrastructures and flows. For example, a maintenance visit to an urban agriculture site offers an opportunity to patch up a nearby bicycle lane and install a new piece of exercise equipment in a local park. Similarly, plans to build a new community center are integrated, through a lens of health, with surrounding facilities, amenities and social networks.

A key idea stemming from the discussion of health is that we begin to see as *related* our investments in food supply, physical activity, eating, nature's services (urban cooling from trees, water filtration by soil, etc.) and social connections. They are networks of infrastructure that support whole health. Health isn't something that is solved, but is an ongoing, interconnected social and physical process. This emphasis on infrastructure and ongoing process leads into the second organizing principle.

INFRASTRUCTURE AND MAINTENANCE

Whereas industrialization has been a process of centralizing and hiding infrastructure, a steady state economy is likely to include aggressive redirection of infrastructure toward a more distributed, multi-scale visibility and accessibility.

Distributing and foregrounding infrastructure across the fabric of the built environment presents a range of roles for architecture and design. Infrastructures, such as water treatment, energy supply, food systems, transport structures or recycling, are not in fenced-off pockets of cities and towns, but rather become usable spaces with layers of purpose and meaning. Extending from ecological to social, these are spaces of long-term, often operable amenity.

A central role for design concerns configuring the usable space of infrastructure, helping to imbue it with broader meaning, and humanizing it visually. One aspect is the communication of ecological value—what nature is doing for us, day in and day out. The role of design in communicating ecological value isn't limited to signage ("One million liters of water filtered here annually") but rather focuses on making natural processes and values more accessible, either through hands-on or visual access, or through representation, perhaps also by tying them to health, as described above.

In an earlier discussion of places that offer alternatives to consumer spaces (Chapter 3), we saw some examples—a municipal recycling facility, a water treatment plant—that are beginning to head in this direction. Another example of this work comes from the park design proposed by Elii, for General Vara del Rey Square in Madrid. The park uses a series of visualization devices to materialize solar radiation, energy, rainwater, garbage, and other forms of natural and social capital.[9] Another example is a water intake pump on the Sacramento river that became a public park, offering scarce waterfront public access.[10]

Maintenance

Another implication from the foregrounding of infrastructure and process is the likely shift in emphasis from new build to maintenance, long-term management, renovation and retrofit. Pooran Desai's experience of the Beddington Zero Energy housing development and related projects suggests that property management, sometimes known as facilities management or estates, is an area of opportunity—possibly for architecture and design. Although property management currently has a reputation as the "unglamorous relation of property development" it figures much more prominently in a steady state economy. Desai comments:

> Whereas previously we may have thought about estates management as simply maintaining the buildings and keeping the grounds tidy, if we start seeing places as communities with a positive stance on sustainability, the role of estates management takes on new meaning. The opportunity

extends beyond buildings maintenance, grounds maintenance and waste collection to embrace a host of lifestyle services.[11]

Among these are:

- Transport services such as cycle-share and car-share schemes.
- Local food links and local food delivery.
- Renewable resource infrastructure.
- Community events that build social capital.
- Gardens and composting.
- Outreach and links to the broader community.
- Adaptation, upgrade and "hacking" for the community's own benefit.

Although Desai is mainly talking about multi-family residential communities, it's not a stretch to expand this idea to neighborhood groups, workgroups at industrial parks, or other institutions such as universities. The range of activities echoes ideas from previous sections because it suggests mixing of uses, and lifestyle services involving both social knowledge and spatial manifestation. Randolph Hester notes:

Property management Beddington Zero Energy development and related projects uncovered the role of property management in sustainable living. Courtesy of One Planet Living, Sutton, under creative commons attribution license.

> Given the self-preserving conservatism of everyday life, it may appear to be an oxymoron to suggest that bold futures can be inspired by daily spatial habits. The challenge for the designer is to uncover and give form to common patterns that are especially enabling, resilient or impelling."[12]

The idea of architects, landscape architects, and designers getting involved in what has formerly been known as property maintenance echoes recent work in product design in two areas: service design and design based on social practices. Designers have increasingly turned their attention to services, stemming from the recognition that every product has services connected to it, while all services rely on a range of products. For example, a video screen (such as a television or computer) benefits from internet services, entertaining programs made by television networks, and related services. By designing products as service systems, or creating services that better utilize existing infrastructure, designers often increase efficiency or shift the emphasis from owning a thing, to getting the services that the thing provides. The approach, described well by Oksana Mont, is sometimes known as "product service systems."[13]

Design based on social practices is a parallel proposal recognizing that many products are situated in socially constituted practices, for example, practices of grooming, cooking, driving or gardening. In this sense individuals "are carriers of collectively held practices that may comprise sets of conventions and procedures."[14] Design may be more effective to the extent that it considers practices instead of just objects. Although these areas of service design and practice-oriented design involve new views on designing a "product," in a steady state economy we see designers more engaged with products and spaces *across time*.

In light of the "service" turn in product design, what does it mean for architects or landscape architects to begin engaging with servicing built environments and landscapes once they are built? For discussion purposes let us call this the design of spatial and material services. Broadening the remit of design, expanding it across time, the design of a place is not finished upon "occupancy"; rather, design is a process that continues throughout the life cycle of the structure(s). In this case formal solutions aren't seen as static, but rather works in progress. The architect expects to come back and engage with the people, spaces and materials—to add on to structures, to de-pave areas, to reassign outmoded elements, among other things.

This approach obviously has implications for how buildings are designed at the start, but also for different types of structures. For example, large, heavy buildings present a different case than lightweight, portable structures.

Despite the fact that designing spatial and material services is probably unthinkable (and unpalatable) among most architects currently, there is a range of precedents for this type of approach. One precedent is the move toward seeing building components as services rather than as products. For example, there are cases of cladding, interior carpeting and heating (or cooling), where these components are provided as services. Although currently architects are not necessarily attached to these building products, if the trend continues it could become a role.[15]

A second precedent arises in the growing interest among architects and other designers in systems of urban agriculture and other natural resources (such as water) that change and require adaptation over time.

A third precedent may perhaps be found in examples from adaptable architecture. Stewart Brand profiles the idea of developers building houses in stages providing rooms and additions over time, as residents can afford it.[16] The adaptable growhome, Katrina Cottage (mentioned in Chapter 5), and related modular housing ideas also suggest an ongoing task of configuring, adjusting and reworking structures. Similar experiments are taking place at the office building scale. Studio/Gang Architects adopted this approach with a non-profit theater that updated its facilities over several years.[17] This is somewhat related to interest in portable, collapsible or pop-up structures that by their very nature suggest ongoing evolution and change. They are sometimes more akin to roving installations than finished structures.

Architecture and landscape architecture are in a position to design spatial and material services particularly well because, as Jeremy Till suggests, architects bring to the table a sort of spatial intelligence.[18] An architect or landscape architect, for example, is better positioned than a property maintenance company to help a community or work group manipulate existing spatial constraints in the process of adapting to changing lifestyle conditions.

The idea of designing spatial and material services, however, confronts what Till has identified as architects' discomfort with uncertainty, contingency and indeterminacy. Further, it has implications for education. Just as industrial and other forms of design have seen an emergence in courses and degrees based around service design, is it conceivable that architecture would see a parallel expansion?

SOCIAL INFRASTRUCTURE

An important underlying element running through previous chapters is social infrastructure. In this section we consider the concept of social networks, the expanded concepts of social production and the question of social position.

Social networks

The question of how to make sharing of resources "work," how to coordinate distributed infrastructure systems, or how to collaborate on the ongoing processes of structure and space, all involve more than simply creating the right set of technical features or aesthetic spaces. They also require a degree of social capital and knowledge about how social capital is built into social networks. In this case social networks are not online groups, but rather real-world relationships among people in geographically common areas. In this regard social knowledge becomes central to design in the scenario of a steady state economy.

Previously mentioned work on social networks (Chapter 2) described how behaviors are contagious in social networks—whether you vote, smoke or exercise is profoundly influenced by who you know. This research also suggests that an understanding of social networks may help reduce rivalry over shared places. By viewing users as part of social networks, it is possible to find that:

> two groups that felt they were radically different may have common members, or be connected to the other group through a common tie. In this way, new common ground and shared agendas are identified as platforms for conflict resolution, mutual understanding, trust and potential collaboration.[19]

The research also suggests that the process of measuring and mapping social networks becomes, in itself, a process of building social capital. As people become aware of themselves and their social interactions in a more systematic way, it gives them a better understanding of how their connections are affecting them (contagious behavior) as well as how their own behavior affects others in a network. In a sense it shows very clearly that we are each influencers in our own networks. In addition, awareness of networks might change perceptions of different community members, as networks reveal patterns of relationship and exclusion that would otherwise be invisible.[20]

In a steady state scenario, the process of connecting people—tied to so many other positive outcomes—becomes a more prominent criterion (or metric) for many programs. Steve Broome outlines different types of social ties that loosely constitute "social capital" (in itself a contested term). *Bonding ties* connect people to other, similar people and typically describe relationships with close friends and family. *Bridging ties* are weaker links to people who we don't know very well, such as acquaintances at work or in the neighborhood. Whereas bonding and bridging ties may be thought of as links across a level in

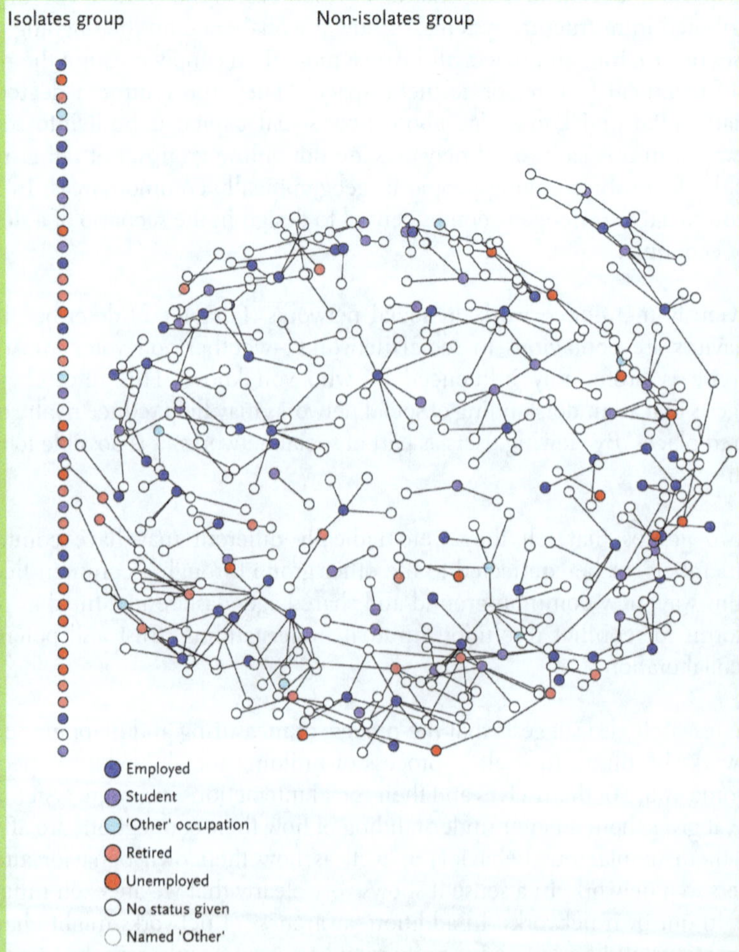

Mapping social networks Each circle represents a person and the color indicates their working status. The line of circles on the left-hand side represents people with no connection to local influence. The linked circles are those people who do have a connection with someone with local influence. The diagram shows that those respondents who are disconnected from local influence are far 'redder' than those with local connections, who are far "bluer". Being retired or unemployed is a risk factor for being cut off from access to local influence. Source: Gaia Marcus, Thomas Neumark and Steve Broome, *Power lines* (London: RSA Conncected Communities, 2011), p. 7.

society, *linking ties* describe relationships we have with people who are above or below us in terms of their capacity to build power. For example, linking ties may occur with people who have more or less income than ourselves, or with people who have more or less responsibility for programs and processes in society.[21]

One implication for design is that "network weaving" becomes a more explicit and prominent skill. To the extent that it becomes part of designing for processes, it may even be a skill that designers are expected to pass on to others through activist methods of organizing and services. Although designers may worry that working with social networks might leave them open to accusations of social engineering, the balance between structure and agency is likely to eliminate that worry. Indeed, community development expert Alison Gilchrist notes that communities as social networks are open, complex systems, meaning that they are unpredictable. In this case she suggests that social metrics in the form of prescribed targets and timescales are typically inappropriate, but "indicators which track changes in capacity, connectivity and cohesion are probably valid."[22]

Contagious Both good and bad behaviors are contagious through social networks.

Another implication for design is the possibility that the design process will more often be turned on its head. Instead of assembling a "participant" group because you need to design something, there will instead be scope to design something for the purposes of building, training, and nurturing groups and social networks. This is already occurring in educational and learning contexts; for example, the Washington State Department of Education is using design as a centerpiece in teaching about sustainability.[23]

Social production

In a steady state economy the production and distribution of wealth is affected by new conceptualizations of prosperity. For example, as discussed in Chapter 4, the production of wealth occurs in social and environmental terms. The distribution of wealth, meanwhile, is accomplished only partly through monetary income.

Work is more evenly shared, through everyone working fewer hours. While hours worked are scaled back—the New Economics Foundation proposes a 21-hour work week—leisure takes on broader meanings and its social and environmental productivity is formally recognized.[24] More of what we do, besides jobs, is seen as productive. The billions of spare, potentially

Production New types of nomadic, mixed and social production.

productive hours per day that we currently have, as suggested by Yochai Benkler (see Chapter 4), are significantly multiplied in the steady state scenario, enabling more people to meet more of their needs through production that occurs outside the marketplace.[25]

Alongside previous suggestions (Chapter 3) that public and collective spaces take on a more prominent role in a steady state economy, it seems likely that these spaces will require social networks, rather than functional programming, as a central organizing principle. The aim would be to enable a broader range of "production" such as paid work, cooperative barter activities, peer sharing and self-provisioning to arise more fluidly across a range of spaces. In this scenario there are far fewer facilities that have idle downtime, such as homes that sit empty all day, cars that sit parked all day, or schools that are empty during evenings and weekends.

Stemming from the notion of more intensively used spaces, scenarios of work are more flexible and, to a certain extent, nomadic. As market activity is contained, while also tied to a broader range of business formats (such as employee ownership or cooperatives), increased social and ecological productivity outside the market are formalized. The result suggests a design arena that supports nomadic production, mixed types of production and other uses that are pinned to social networks as much as to a particular company or institution.

Similar changes also seem likely for homes. In a steady state scenario the extreme pressure for a home to serve as a commodity is lessened. Questions of family types, home sharing and redistribution of some infrastructure (such as tools or appliances) outside the home suggest broadening agendas for residential design. Homes also become a more valued center of production in a steady state scenario.

Social position/distinction

Institutions and practices that helped us mark significant transitions or transformations in life—that distinguished individuals and groups—are changing. As Avner Offer suggested (Chapter 2), to the extent that these transitions involved commitment strategies, such as marriage or family structure, they aren't keeping pace with new contexts of affluence. Similarly, Joseph Campbell has observed that rituals and rights of passage have historically served the purpose of helping people cross difficult or challenging thresholds. He suggests that these rituals and rights supply us with "the symbols that carry the human spirit forward, in counteraction to those other constant human fantasies that tend to tie it back."[26]

In a steady state economy, experience design may become more prominent in different types of ceremonies and symbols that mark rights of passage, accomplishments and passings.[27] These become more central elements of gaining social position or distinction in less consumer driven ways. From a design perspective these passages might entail places, structures, and temporary or process-based elements. Examples are already starting to emerge. The UK, for example, has introduced secular "naming ceremonies" for babies and citizenship ceremonies for those becoming British citizens.

Design may also have a role in playing back social networks to communities, which in itself also gives people a better social narrative of themselves. It helps highlight both distinction and belonging in new, less material ways, and in itself may help people realize their own status within and among networks.

As Steve Broome comments, it is likely that we are all already rich in assets and social connections that are unseen and untapped resources. In a steady state economy these become as much a resource for architects and designers as materials and structures.

CONCLUSION

This chapter presents a highly speculative and partial glimpse of possible design implications of a steady state economy. In this scenario health, infrastructure and social networks serve as new organizing principles, filling some of the gaps left once consumerism and growth no longer serve as dominant organizing principles. These old principles operated in a context of newness and of individualism, but this chapter has speculated that under new principles, connective social and physical infrastructure and ongoing maintenance and adaptation will become more prominent contexts for design.

The steady state scenario, however, doesn't suggest any absence of conflict or utopian vision. Indeed, activism would be alive and well in this scenario, continuing to push people toward higher levels of performance across a range of important issues.

Looking across the three topics of health, infrastructure and social capital, another strong theme is the need to create and manage distributed, decentralized networks (of people, places and things) while also simultaneously integrating our activities across those networks. In this scenario a meta-task for designers, along with other professionals, is to become translators. Steve Broome commented on this need recently in the context of his experience on a large-scale neighborhood renewal program:

I was struck by the isolation of separate thematic expertise, particularly the way community development, housing, planning, the physical or built environment [experts] spoke to each other, or didn't. They all had their own languages, their own approaches, their own views of the world, their own tools, and trying to find translators who could connect up these different domains ... was really difficult.[28]

NOTES

1 McKinsey Global Institute, "Accounting for the Cost of US Health Care: A New Look at Why Americans Spend More" (McKinsey & Company, 2008), pp. 22–23. The study found that 35 medical conditions that are often related to lifestyle, such as diabetes, heart disease, cancer, mental disorders, hypertension and asthma, account for close to 40 percent of US healthcare costs.

2 Eric A. Finkelstein, Christopher J. Ruhm and Katherine M. Kosa, "Economic Causes and Consequences of Obesity", *Annual Review of Public Health*, Vol. 26 (2005), pp. 239–57.

3 Benjamin H. Bratton and Natalie Jeremijenko, "Suspicious Images, Latent Interfaces", in *Situated Technologies Pamphlets* 3, ed. Omar Khan, Trebor Scholz and Mark Shepard (New York: The Architecture League of New York, n.d.), p. 18.

4 Ibid., 28, 33.

5 Ibid., p. 9.

6 Barbara Knecht, "Aging Baby Boomers Want Smart Houses for Their Golden Years", *Architectural Record* (2004), p. 170.

7 Emily Talen, "The Spatial Logic of Parks", *Journal of Urban Design*, Vol. 15, no. 4 (2010), pp. 473–91, 489.

8 Renia Ehrenfeucht and Anastasia Loukaitou-Sideris, 'Planning Urban Sidewalks: Infrastructure, Daily Life and Destinations', *Journal of Urban Design*, Vol. 15, no. 4, 2010, pp. 459–71.

9 Uriel Fogue and Fernando D. Rubio, "General Vara del Rey Square: An Experimental Design for the Construction of Cosmopolitical Neighborhoods', Politics of Design, Manchester Architectural Research Centre, 24–25 June 2010.

10 Rob Turner, "Water Wings", *Metropolis* (April 2004).

11 Pooran Desai, *One Planet Communities: A Real Life Guide to Sustainable Living* (Hoboken: John Wiley & Sons, 2009), p. 152.

12 Randolph Hester, *Design for Ecological Democracy* (Cambridge, MA: MIT Press, 2006), p. 289.

13 Oksana Mont notes that product service systems also have the potential to reduce throughput when companies retain ownership of products and manage them as assets, rather than seeking to sell more of them in "Functional Thinking: The role of Functional Sales and Product Service Systems for a Function-based Society", Lund University (Naturvårdsverket, 2002).

14 Guy Julier, "Design Practice Within a Theory of Practice", *Design Principles and Practices*, Vol. 1, no. 2 (2007), pp. 43–50, 43.

15 See, for example, William McDonough and Michael Braungart, *Cradle to Cradle: Remaking the Way We Make Things* (New York: North Point Press, 2002).

pp. 109–15; and Nathan Skedroff, *Design is the Problem: The Future of Design Must be Sustainable* (Brooklyn: Rosenfeld Media, 2009), pp. 142–9.

16 Stewart Brand, *How Buildings Learn: What Happens After They're Built* (New York: Penguin Books, 1994).

17 Blair Kamin, "Bengt Sjostrom Starlight Theatre", *Architectural Record* (October 2003).

18 Jeremy Till, *Architecture Depends* (London: MIT Press, 2010).

19 Jonathan Rowson, Steve Broome and Alasdair Jones, *Connected Communities: How Social Networks Power and Sustain Big Society* (London: RSA, 2010), p. 10.

20 Ibid., p. 17.

21 Steve Broome lecture, "Scarcity and Consumption", 25 May 2011, University of Westminster, Scarcity and Creativity in the Built Environment (SCIBE) Talks.

22 Alison Gilchrist, *The Well-connected Community: A Networking Approach to Community Development* (Bristol: Policy Press, 2004), p. 35.

23 Gilda Wheeler and Jessica Vavrus, "Washington State K-12 Integrated Environmental and Sustainability Education Learning Standards", State Superintendent of Public Instruction (Washington State, 2009).

24 Anna Coote, Jane Franklin and Andrew Simms, *21 Hours* (London: New Economics Foundation, 2010).

25 Yochai Benkler, *The Wealth of Networks: How Social Production Transforms Markets and Freedom* (London: Yale University Press, 2006).

26 Joseph Campbell, *The Hero with a Thousand Faces* (1949).

27 See, for example, David Kowalewski, *Deep Power: The Political Ecology of Wilderness and Civilization* (Huntington, NY: Nova Science, 2000); Joanna Macy and Molly Young Brown, *Coming Back to Life: Practices to Reconnect Our Lives, Our World* (Gabriola Island, Canada: New Society, 1998); and Stephanie Kaza, *The Attentive Heart: Conversations with Trees* (Berkeley, CA: Shambhala, 1996).

28 Steve Broome lecture, "Scarcity and Consumption".

Chapter 8

Conclusion

Our argument has been that consumerism and economic growth are an overarching problem that requires social change. There are many ways to undertake social change, from individual behavior to corporate policy to democratic lawmaking, but here we have focused on the activism of social movements, which generally entails forms of collective action. The introductory chapter argued that this is an underexplored yet useful way to think about design activism, and the remaining chapters have set out to explore and illustrate usefulness. The resulting picture shows how design might constructively be more political, provides a realistic view of the systemic challenges of consumerism, and, one hopes, leaves room for optimism despite uncertainty. Below we consider four concluding points.

The first point concerns the use of, and connection among, case studies. Practicing designers are accustomed to a trade press (offline and on) that perpetually wows them with the newest aesthetics, radical innovations and seductive styles. Although the case studies presented in this book are in themselves interesting, they are not all new or seductive. The point of the case studies here is to show broader patterns in activist work and broader patterns of response to consumerism.

These patterns can be styled by fashions, but the structure of the patterns isn't changed by fashion or aesthetic (even technical) trends. Take, for example, the activist methods of organizing and mobilization. The underlying pattern of "organizing" doesn't change from one instance to another—from a Fablab making electronic tags for endangered animals, to a reverse engineering fashion workshop, to a community self-build garden project. In organizing, the aim is to enable a group to do something for itself by virtue of getting organized. These broader patterns, such as activist methods, help us make sense of individual cases and give us ways to think about how individual cases add up.

We have looked at design activist case studies in three different ways—three different sets of patterns. The first was in terms of methods such as organizing or mobilization (as already mentioned); the second was in terms of four consumerism and growth challenges. The patterns here concerned pricing and pacing problems, commitments to the future, and a commercially driven social language for status and position. Case studies may respond to these patterns in different ways and with different styles, but the patterns persist. A third way we looked at case studies was in terms of the capacities, namely disruption, framing and targeting, that design has (in common with conventional activism) for building power to bring about change. These capacities form another set of consistent patterns.

This book has argued that these three different ways of seeing design are connected by the theme of values. Society's focus on the value of economic growth and financial wealth squeezes out many social and environmental values—the very values and costs that activism addresses. We might characterize these values as alternate modes of wealth.

Looking at the design cases in terms of how they confront consumer challenges highlighted the issue of social metrics. What shall we measure if not only money or financial wealth? By contrast, seeing the design cases in terms of activist methods highlights ways to call for improvement in terms of these social and environmental values—ways to take action and make concerns known. Finally, looking at the capacities for building power highlights how the methods have influence. All these steps are important: figuring out what the values are (metrics and how we improve them), asking for change, and influencing change.

This brings us back to the question of adding up. Clearly there are challenges in terms of how we develop metrics at the project scale, topped by the challenge of how projects "add up" at the societal level. Not only are we short of some of the measurement tools we need, but we also have to avoid traps such as the rebound effect (or the innovation effect) through which efficiency and innovation increase overall consumption rather than reduce it.

Activist projects, actions and innovations can add up, on one level, in terms of scientific targets informed by the earth's biocapacity. Social and political targets are perhaps harder to conceptualize and agree. Even worse, in a consumerist society our social and political muscles aren't often used. We are out of shape, out of practice. George Packer made this observation about the Iraq War:

> The Iraq war was a kind of stress test applied to the American body politic. And every major system and organ failed the test: the executive and

> legislative branches, the military, the intelligence world, the for-profits, the nonprofits, the media. It turned out that we were not in good shape at all – without even realizing it. Americans just hadn't tried anything this hard in around half a century.[1]

Putting aside whether the Iraq War was, in itself, a good idea or not, we could replace the term "Iraq War" with the term "global warming" or "children's education" or "obesity" and make a similar argument. Packer puts a lot of the problem down to "organized money" which is, in a sense, a different way of framing what we have talked about here as the problems of consumerism and economic growth. He describes organized money becoming a phenomenon following the economic downturn that accompanied the 1973 oil crisis and explains the dramatic rise in corporate lobbying: "by the mid-1970s chief executives had stopped believing that they had an obligation to act as disinterested stewards of the national economy. They became a special interest; the interest they represented was their own." This interest has, to a certain extent, been taken as everyone's interest in an economic system that must spiral upward.

But Chapter 2's overview attempted to show, not least in design terms, that consumerism and growth are not really, in the long term, in anyone's interest, and despite huge uncertainties, Chapters 4 and 7 each speculated about a sustainable, steady state economy. This leads to our second concluding point: that consumerism and consumers in affluent countries are an emerging cause for activism.

Throughout the book we have explored the idea that in view of the problems of consumerism and growth, a much wider swathe of society is "excluded" or "neglected" than activists would typically consider. The book has argued that it is necessary and useful to conceptualize consumers in affluent countries as an excluded or neglected group. This may strike some people as inappropriate, since consumers in affluent countries are clearly much better off than people in most other countries.

Yet it seems clear that over-consumption isn't beneficial to over-consumers and is even more damaging to under-consumers, and further, many over-consumers are trapped in structures of over-consumption. Given the direct connection between over-consumption and so many global, adverse effects, we have to reconsider activism with respect to consumerism.

A post-growth economy helps with this reconsideration. Civil society groups currently protesting the effects of "organized money" have focused on the concentration of wealth among the top 1 percent of the population, using phrases such as "the other 99 percent." By appearing to angle for a bigger share of the financial wealth pie, however, they garnered some critics. Commentators note, for example, how "the other 99 percent" in the US are still in the richest 1 percent with respect to most other countries. This points out the limitations of asking for change in terms of the existing economic system.

The other 99 percent would do better to begin asking not for their share of the current economy, but rather for an entirely different kind of economy—a post-growth, steady state economy. Which leads to our third concluding point, a question. To the extent that activism adds up across movements, does it make sense to propose a meta-movement for a steady state economy? A nascent post-growth movement could serve as a "meta" movement, since it encompasses the issues of a wide variety of other movements. Few activist concerns escape the problems of consumerism and economic growth—escape the ravages of organized money. A post-growth movement offers a meta-narrative across a range of issues—the way it has done throughout this book. The meta-narrative doesn't replace or lessen particular movement issues, but rather could provide ways for activists to build new alliances or cross old boundaries. Without going any further down this provocative path we arrive at our fourth concluding point, another question.

What next for design activism? In educational terms, the timeline in Chapter 1 seems to indicate a strong interest within design education for including social change agendas. There is a fairly rich range of alternative educational formats emerging, only some of which are part of regular university curricula. We might ultimately see specialized design activist training, in the same way that conventional activist training has existed for decades among nonprofit, religious and union groups. Universities may stick with politically neutral "social innovation" as a core piece of a new design curriculum from which activists might spring.

This idea assumes an answer to the question of how much a social change agenda in the design curriculum will incorporate politics, if at all. The idea of political design might suggest a new political strand of design education, in the way that design management might be read as a business strand. The timeline shows some universities in Europe appointing professors of design and politics (even activism). On the other hand, we might simply see the Harvard School of Government, The University of Washington Evans School of Public Policy and other such schools embrace design thinking in their curricula, as business schools have done before them.

There would be some selective cross-over of designers and political thinkers, but anything more? Other disciplines are also interested in spatial politics, such as geography, the sociology of technology and planning. Design disciplines, such as architecture, product design and landscape architecture, arguably bring a much harder edge to the material and spatial concepts in politics, but is their focus ultimately too narrow?

These questions carry over into practice. Although designers might naturally view public policy as boring, fraught with red tape and inspiration-crushing, the number of activist bureaucrats interested in design suggests that it's worth overcoming a natural aversion. A great many government policy and funding activities already exist to address social and environmental issues; how many have been examined through the lens of design—through the conscious influences of space and material—as an agent for change? Areas such as public health, aging, cultural integration, and education are examples where existing policy is starting to get a reinterpretation through a political design lens. Even so, in a context of growth and consumerism, some might view design professionals more as an industry lobby, looking for more work for itself, than as a constructive tool of social change working for the greater good.

Although the concepts of conventional activism are versatile, what can professionals ultimately do with them? For a variety of reasons architecture and design have not developed the robust public service professions found in medicine and law. Some designers are clearly borrowing approaches, such as pro bono services, from these other professions to good effect. But others seem to be investigating innovative approaches particular to design and pertinent to consumerism, materialism and the commons. These approaches investigate the roles of designer and user, models of ownership and access, the interconnection between the social and the material, and the configuration of space through time, among other things.

The range of initiatives and organizations cropping up in Chapter 1's timeline during the noughties suggests a real definitional struggle within design to figure out what design activism is in professional terms. This may become clearer not only through design activities in themselves, but also through interactions between designers and those activists and change agents outside design. What can other social movement actors make of design as an activist practice, described in the terms and methods of conventional activism? And further, do the concepts in these chapters, drawn largely from spatial and material practice, extend to emerging dematerialized forms of design that focus on delivering processes, services or strategies rather than physical stuff?

These chapters have attempted to present some organized thinking over several very broad areas that cut across disciplines as well as across theory and practice. For this reason the book can only be useful in a preliminary way, laying out terms for debate, putting some topics and questions on the agenda, and framing design activism in post-growth terms.

At a recent talk about the book's topic at a local university, one of the design students commented that the idea of a steady state economy, or getting past consumerism, seemed completely unrealistic. And it's true; although we have reached the end of the book, this "unrealistic" story is really only just beginning. The numbers tell us that we need to pick up the pace of the story, and these chapters are offered in the spirit of helping us continue building and contributing to the story in design terms. These are seeds of hope; sometimes things turn out well.

NOTE

1 George Packer, "The Broken Contract: Inequality and American Decline", *Foreign Affairs,* online 11 October, 2011.

Index

For Product Safety Concerns and Information please contact our EU
representative GPSR@taylorandfrancis.com
Taylor & Francis Verlag GmbH, Kaufingerstraße 24, 80331 München, Germany

www.ingramcontent.com/pod-product-compliance
Lightning Source LLC
LaVergne TN
LVHW021123300926
849160LV00010B/839
* 9 7 8 1 8 4 9 7 1 3 5 6 6 *